Roman Britain and Classical Deities

Gender and sexuality in Roman art

Angela Morelli

BAR British Series 482
2009

Published in 2016 by
BAR Publishing, Oxford

BAR British Series 482

Roman Britain and Classical Deities

ISBN 978 1 4073 0427 4

BAR Publishing is the trading name of British Archaeological Reports (Oxford) Ltd. British Archaeological Reports was first incorporated in 1974 to publish the BAR Series, International and British. In 1992 Hadrian Books Ltd became part of the BAR group. This volume was originally published by Archaeopress in conjunction with British Archaeological Reports (Oxford) Ltd / Hadrian Books Ltd, the Series principal publisher, in 2009. This present volume is published by BAR Publishing, 2016.

Printed in England

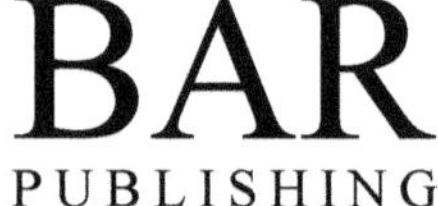

BAR titles are available from:

BAR Publishing
122 Banbury Rd, Oxford, OX2 7BP, UK
EMAIL info@barpublishing.com
PHONE +44 (0)1865 310431
FAX +44 (0)1865 316916
www.barpublishing.com

Contents

Acknowledgements

I would like to thanks Miranda Aldhouse-Green, Janet Huskinson and Ray Howell for their invaluable support and guidance. Thanks to Carole Wolfenden and Mark Muriden for their tireless editing. A big thank you to my excellent friends and colleagues Adrian Chadwick, Eleanor Ghey, Lesley McFadyen and Jullia Roberts who taught me about archaeology. Finally, I would like to thank my family, Antonietta, Steve, Richard and Alys, my good friends, and my colleagues and friends at the University of Wales, Newport, Caerleon campus library for their patience and constant support.

List of illustrations

Introduction

The subject matter of this work examines aspects in the representation of femininities and masculinities in Roman art with particular reference to that of Roman Britain. The body of the study focuses on the visual demonstration of gender for specific deities, personifications and figural images in funerary art.

There are numerous and valuable works written on gender in Roman art. None, however, deal specifically with the art of Roman Britain. For this research I have adopted a theoretical, gender aware approach to the analysis of Romano-British art using the studies of Roman art history and gender studies as a source. As a result, the study often deals with 'classical' Roman examples and then considers those found in Britain from the Roman period. Although this study is predominantly an art historical account, the period depends on archaeology and the evidence produced - the subjects merge; however the bias is towards the history of art.

The first chapter focuses on conceptions of gender in Roman thought and the way this societal construct was worked through the art of the period. I begin with contemporary distribution of gendered items through children's toys and the representation of popular (often clichéd) icons such as Barbie, Lara Croft, Action Man and the Hulk. I am not attempting to contrast modern society and objects with that of the Romans, as this would be unhelpful to the overall study. However, I offer this introduction as an identifiable approach to thinking about gender in visual culture. As for Roman exemplars, I begin by looking at images of children and the particular gender markers associated with them. For women and men I have approached the subjects separately exploring the concepts of the 'Roman ideal' using commentary by ancient authors such as Livy and Cassius Dio. Furthermore, I demonstrate how the endorsed stereotypes were transmitted through art (in this instance sculpture).

The next three chapters deal with paired deities Venus and Mars, Minerva and Hercules and Diana and Apollo. These chapters deal with the deities as the main focus of research, forming compilations of information relevant to each particular god/goddess. Therefore, the time scale is varied and not fixed on one particular period of Roman history. (However, this is not the case for Chapters 5-6, Personifications and Funerary Art as the attention is predominately on the art of Roman Britain). The coupled subjects are connected in some way. Venus and Mars are separately linked with the foundation myths of Rome whilst they are mythological lovers (Chapter 1).They have a specific role within the contrived 'history' of Rome. My interest is in how the deities were presented. How was Venus' femininity portrayed? The 'type' of femininity portrayed depends largely on the artistic inspiration of the piece that presumably reflects the tastes of the patron or a particular title pertaining to the goddess. For example, if a patron wished to advertise his/her Hellenistic tastes then Venus would be a nubile, youthful nude perhaps a copy of the Aphrodite of Cnidus. On the other hand, an example of Venus Genetrix mother of Rome would have a more matronly appearance, courteously draped but paradoxically in diaphanous sheer material. There is a disparity in the portrayal of femininity. Images of Mars appear to have two stylistic categories: a mature figure in full military garb (often highly ornate parade armour) and Hellenic inspired examples depicting a nude youth akin to the Ares Borghese. The former category, I consider in terms of hypermasculinity. This is a theoretical idiom illustrating an exaggerated masculinity, particularly with regard to physical appearance. I consider this as a helpful method in the possible interpretation of Mars. Examples of Mars are contradictory: often he appears to be portrayed as a hypermasculine and martial war god, whilst other representations are the complete opposite, a passive and vulnerable adolescent. The choice of depiction presumably depended on what the artist or patron wanted to represent, or more importantly, on the messages required to be transmitted.

Diana and Apollo are twin deities who share visual attributes that demonstrate their role as hunter deities; these include hunting regalia and associated animals. Additionally, they have unconnected godheads. Diana, for example, is also goddess of the moon, a protector of small children, young animals and of women in childbirth. She is the guardian of woodlands, harbours and roads. Furthermore, she is the patron goddess of Amazons, the mythical female tribe. Perhaps it is no coincidence that her appearance resembles that of a certain type of Amazon with a short tunic facilitating movement, though her upper body is covered unlike these particular Amazon types who were generally depicted with one breast exposed. Diana is linked with Amazons for various reasons: she inhabits an area removed from the 'civilised' world; both hunt and fight like men and are independent of men and she is chaste, rejecting marriage and child bearing (although Amazons welcomed men only for procreation). As a virgin goddess her sexuality is jealously guarded as evidenced by the myth of Actaeon (see Chapter 3). The combined aspects of her godheads and outward appearance form a complex femininity that differs from that of Venus and of Amazons.

Apollo godheads, other than twin hunter god, include his prophetic authority, his connections with medicine as the father of Asclepius and his revered roles as the god of the sun, music and poetry. Apollo commonly appears as a youthful nude figure often with long hair and illustrated with various items associated with his mythology including his bow, a lyre, fawns and laurel leaves. Octavian (later Augustus) had a specific interest in the god and affiliated himself with the deity during the struggle for control (and eventually sole power) over Rome after the death of his adopted father, Julius Caesar.

Apollo embodied characteristics that Octavian found valuable for his political ambition. It is likely that Octavian exploited his self imposed links with Apollo to further his political career by using Apolline symbols. Visual representations of Apollo appear to be analogous with those of Bacchus/Dionysus; both depicted as nude/partially nude youths often with long hair. These subjects are often referred to as having an ambiguous gender or more stereotypically as 'effeminate'. These descriptions are problematic and unhelpful. I propose that this particular category actually celebrates masculinity rather than emulating femininity and draws on youthful characteristics. His masculinity differs from that of Mars or Hercules.

Hercules was a favourite of the goddess Minerva a member of the Capitoline triad - the traditional religious deity group. Minerva appears to share the same visual formula as Athena, Greek goddess of war (Chapter 4). Since there is an extensive time-span between the classical Greek period and that of imperial Rome, it is apparent that there is a long history of this figure type. It is important, however, not to suppose that these personas are identical. It is the artistic/stylistic borrowings that are the issue. Minerva is the chaste goddess of wisdom, of crafts and more apparently of war and assumes the paraphernalia as an indication including a Corinthian helmet, spear and shield. Moreover it is this feature that sways the general interpretation of Minerva's femininity as she carries the weapons of war, objects that are normally associated with masculinity. Overall examples of Minerva, particularly those from Roman Britain depict her in heavy drapery totally covering her body (although occasionally her arms are exposed) it reaches her ankles hiding the overall form of her body. Her helmet covers her head and her hair which is either short or tied back away from the face. Consequently the viewer is not able or perhaps not permitted to see her body or her hair. The visual signs representative of her sex are obscured beneath clothing and headgear. She is supposed to be an 'active' goddess of war, yet her clothing contradicts this. I suggest that her heavy drapery gives the appearance of limited movement restricted by the excess of material rendering her as 'passive'. Hercules, on the other hand, is the epitome of the all-active, hypermasculine 'action hero'. His masculinity draws on his physical super-strength and is confirmed by his exaggerated musculature. The mythology surrounding his character stresses his 'action hero' status, particularly his Twelve Labours. These encompass an array of adventures ultimately concluding with Hercules fighting against a specific adversary, including monsters, an Amazon, fierce animals and chaotic nature, all eventually controlled and conquered. Hercules was a favourite of Mark Antony who claimed decent from the hero's family-line. This connection was ultimately used against Mark Antony, as his enemies seized upon particular aspects of Hercules' legendary deeds to ridicule him. The hero's encounter with Omphale, queen of the Lydian's, is a particular case in point. The protagonists' connection served as metaphors for the relationship between Mark Antony and Cleopatra, specifically when Omphale orders Hercules to swap clothing with her. This role reversal exists in artistic representation and I will discuss this in the relevant chapter (Chapter 4). Later on, Hercules was a particular favourite of Emperors Commodus (180 –192 AD) and Caracalla (211-217 AD). Both, in all probability, were attracted by his gargantuan physical strength and overt masculinity.

The gods and goddesses discussed above were chosen for this study because of their divergence in character, visual variation, and to demonstrate different types of femininities and masculinities.

The final chapter, chapter 5 considers the visual and gendered construction of personifications. These are abstract values, ideals and places in anthropomorphic form. I endeavour to read the visual language employed to exemplify personifications with reference to allocation and application of gender to the individual abstract theme. Although there are several masculine personifications the majority are feminine. One of the main issues to be addressed is to question as to why some abstract themes are deemed to be feminine whilst others are masculine? The study begins with an introduction to the use of personifications for post-colonial propaganda by examining an engraving by sixteenth century artist Jan van der Straet. This narrative composition illustrates the moment America was discovered by Europe. America is symbolised in the form of a seated, naked women. A fully dressed man representing Europe approaches her. He stands near, looking down on her. Not only is he fully clothed, but he also holds items that denote the culture he has left and which he has brought with him to introduce/impose on America. This juxtapositioning clearly indicates imperial objectives, in that the conqueror aims to change America for her own good. This method is recurrent in Roman art, for example Claudius about to slay Britannia, from Sebasteion, Aphrodisias. Britannia is a feminine subject in the guise of an Amazon. The relief has an exceptionally violent composition with Claudius grabbing the hair of the fallen woman as he is about to strike the fatal blow. She is at his mercy with her tunic slipped exposing her breast – she is at risk of attack, both physical and sexual. Britannia is a feminine character who is literally conquered and controlled by the imperial force of Rome, personified by Claudius himself. Other regions and provinces appear in female form, including: Armenia, Africa and Egypt. These are common features of coins, which were useful vehicles for transmitting a particular message – in this case it is one of imperial supremacy. The personification of Rome – Roma - is a feminine character. In visual terms her representation is complicated, drawing on an amalgamation of features specific to other female characters such as Minerva, Diana, Amazons and Venus Genetrix. Victory was also a popular personification signifying the successful might of the Roman war machine. She is a winged figure whose visual representation was presumably based on the Greek goddess of victory Nike. There are numerous examples of Victory from Roman Britain frequently from areas such as Hadrian's Wall and the Antonine Wall. In this chapter (Chapter 5) I have included stereotypical visual formula encompassing the 'barbarian'. These are generally nude, moustached and/or bearded men, fallen in battle or with their hands tied behind their back, but always incapacitated in some way. This is a general attack on the masculinity of the 'barbarian'. He is not in control over his own body and therefore not a real man. Next I consider the personification of the Seasons. These frequently appear on mosaics filling corner sections. Again these are mostly feminised, perhaps equating femininity with nature?

Chapter 1

Conceptions of Gender and Sexuality in Roman culture

This chapter surveys Roman understandings of masculinities and femininities with evidence collated from contemporary texts and visual culture. Each example examines individual pieces in context taking account of specific biases, functions and audiences, spanning from the Republic to the fourth century AD and seeks to determine any developments that may have occurred. The study endeavours to elucidate and analyse gendered stereotypes endorsed by Roman society and to indicate how these were characterised in literature and art. This includes how gender was contrived and transmitted, learning about the stereotype and not a historical survey of the real women and men of Roman society. (The latter is valuable work carried out by scholars such as, Fantham et al 1996; Lefkowitz and Fant 1999; Shelton 1998 and many of their sources are relevant in finding advocated gender roles). Gender is socially constructed and has little to do with biological sex. Gender does not refer to the organic differences attributed to each sex. Fausto-Sterling, discussing separate expectations for boys and girls in education, plainly identifies the distinction between sex and gender.

> If girls couldn't learn math easily as boys, the problem wasn't build into their brains. The difficulty resulted from gender norms – different expectations and opportunities for boys and girls. Having a penis rather than a vagina is a sex difference. Boys performing better than girls on math exam is a gender difference (Fausto-Sterling 2000: 4).

As suggested above, it is social conditioning that generates expectations. Furthermore, gender is not the only issue that is determined in this manner, social conditioning influences perceptions of race, class and sexuality. Thesander considers the difference between sex and gender in terms of the body, 'there is no totally natural or neutral body – even the naked body reflects the culture to which it belongs' (Thesander 1997:19). Butler clarifies the disparity further stating, 'the distinction between sex and gender serves the argument that whatever biological intractability sex appears to have, gender is culturally constructed: hence, gender is neither a casual result of sex nor as seemingly fixed as sex' (Butler 1999: 9-10).[1] This is particularly applicable in Roman thought where gender classification appears to depend principally on actions and attitudes rather than biological sex. Moreover, it is applicable for the elucidation of sexual identity. It is essential not to place contemporary categorisations on the ancient world (Williams 1999; Hallett 1997). Homosexuality, bisexuality and heterosexuality are modern terms that did not apply in the Greco-Roman world. Foucault, discussing Greek sexuality, illuminates this very point. 'As a matter of fact, the notion of homosexuality is plainly inadequate as a means of referring to an experience, forms of valuation, and a system of categorisation so different from ours' (Foucault 1985b: 187). Although the subject is Greek culture, his opinion is duly appropriate for Roman culture and to consider viewpoints on sexuality as the same as our own is suspect and obstructive (Williams 1999; Gilchrist 1999: 56). I am aware that this study cannot cover all areas and layers of Roman society, especially when there is no definite substantiation, and therefore I venture to work with the evidence available. Gilchrist proposes, 'whether gender, social cognition or sexuality are dependent fully on biology or culture is no longer the issue. The interesting questions are how biology and/or cognitive difference are interpreted culturally, how this varies between societies, and how the body and mind may evolve in response to cultural definitions of gender' (Gilchrist 1999: 13).

Contemporary gender construction

Before embarking on the study examining the construction of gender in the Roman period, it is necessary to elucidate contemporary gender construction and then survey Roman perceptions on the subject. As previously noted gender does not refer to the biological sex of an individual. Gender identity is an invention of the culture within which an individual is born. To explore this issue I have chosen contemporary examples. In the western world concepts of femininity and masculinity appear to operate through cultural traditions, and in recent times, through the fruition of the media. Children's toys are blatant examples illustrating this, for example, dolls that follow the same mode as *Barbie* and *Action Man*.[2] Television advertisements (selectively aired during the intervals of children's programmes) bombard television screens with artificial role model type figures; such as pink *Barbie* products for girls or army garbed *Action Man,* and other superheroes such as *Batman* and the *Hulk,* for boys. The dolls indicate unnatural physical stereotypes. The standard female doll is white, tall, and thin with long, blonde hair, and the typical male dolls are white and slender with exaggerated muscle development. Attfield comments that *Barbie* is an idealised, unnatural body based on a stereotypical sexual fantasy.

> Her body proportions were not intended to be realistic – were she to be translated to life size her leg length would make her seven feet tall. Barbie's exaggerated

[1] For a discussion on gender and linguistics see Irigaray 1993: 67-74.

[2] Attfield discusses Barbie and Action Man as gendered objects in detail from the original dolls of 1959 to 1993 including political inferences of their body types and developments over the years (Attfield 1996:80-89).

> bust measurement (twice the size of her waist) has been describes as 'gravity defying', and her tiny feet (the same size as her hands) are too small to hold up her body (Attfield 1996: 83).

This is applicable to a more current character, *Lara Croft*, heroine of the computer game *Tomb Raider* (originally released in 1996). As an active female protagonist, *Lara Croft* has a less traditional role, but her femininity, depicted by her computer-animated body, has the equivalent formulaic elements as *Barbie*. Her tight clothes draw attention to her outsized breasts, which can be seen beneath. Her midriff is showing with her belt and trouser tops highlighting her waist and hips. I suggest that her hyper-femininity distracts from the main purpose of the character - as a heroine. First and foremost she is an objectified body and then a heroine, consequently reducing all serious notions of her as a female protagonist. She will always be viewed as a visual, sexual entity first.

Remaining within the computer graphically illustrated genre, masculine subjects are also susceptible to visual corporeal manipulation, but these appear to be based on the amplification of physical strength rather than overt sexual desirability, for example the *Hulk* (2003) offers a hyper-hyper-masculine body. From an early age, the populace are assigned ideals to emulate, for example the simulated pink fluffy femininity of particular dolls, as opposed to the rugged, military masculinity of toy soldiers or hyper-masculine wrestlers. Aside from the obvious anthropomorphic plastic idols, other toys supply the potential for the division of gender, promoting individual, home-based behaviour for girls versus outside and group activity for boys. The majority of standard girls' toys imitate household appliances and items associated with motherhood in miniature form, including: kitchen items, toy prams, plastic baby dolls that need their nappies changing, plus other various accessories training girls as future homemakers and preparing them for the role of motherhood. Standard toys for boys concentrate largely on simulating occupations, including military toys, miniature tools, medical kits, miniature garages and cars. There is also a strong emphasis on sports, particularly outdoor games such as football, rugby and cricket. The toys I have referred to above are traditional examples. Fortunately there are now numerous gender-neutral items available to the consumer (Gauntlett 2002: 10; Hendershot 1996: 90-102).

The process of dividing and classifying gender begins in childhood and does not end in youth (although there is not enough room to discuss it all here). The market demonstrating modern, Western concepts of masculinity and femininity is endless. Women's magazines inform women how to think, cook, and look to attract prospective partners. Certain girls' magazines introduce and endorse fashion for girls and advice about boys. Yet magazines for boys have nothing to do with girls or potential 'relationships' and focus on action and adventure instead. Men's magazines concentrate on advertising the perfect 'six-pack', physical body, or social status achieved through designer clothes, cars, motorbikes, or property. 'Lads' magazines such as *Loaded* and *FHM* (aimed at younger men) constantly exhibit voyeuristic images of scantily clad or topless women.[3] Ultimately these images define a particular femininity that is analogous with various British tabloid newspapers' habitual representations of topless female 'glamour' models.

Today we are surrounded by visual communication, just as the people of the Roman Empire were through public and private works of sculpture, painting and mosaics. Modern families on television or in poster advertisements, dolls, glamour models, and men with rippling muscles and flashy cars, do not directly reflect society. I suggest that this observation can be applied to people represented in Roman art. In the main, art did not directly reflect real people, but shape an impression, often an idealisation fulfilling and exaggerating ascribed gendered roles. This is particularly true in funerary art (see Chapter 6). As with mainstream contemporary visual communication, Roman art appears to rely on idealisations.

How visual stereotypes were characterised presumably depends on contemporary concepts and definitions of femininities and masculinities. However, this is not straightforward, as there are other important issues to be taken into consideration too incorporating, among others, social status, race and age. Therefore, it may be reasonable to consider that visual culture in the Roman Empire operated in the same way. It may appear that a direct comparison is naïve and unrealistic, as the basic definitions differ. However it nonetheless offers a different way to think about the visual issues of gender in antiquity.

Roman children and the beginnings of gender construction: clothing and jewellery

This particular section examines the way that costume contributed to the specific gender role of children. Social stipulations required that children occupied an inviolable state, protecting them from particular behaviour and actions (see below). Freeborn children wore the *toga*[4] *praetexta* (purple border) as a symbol of their citizen status. This sort of toga specified that the wearer was in an uninfringeable state. For instance the purple border embellished the veils of Vestal Virgin. It was worn by sons conducting a parent's funeral and adorned by magistrates who presided over sacrifices as a duty of service (George 2001: 183-185; Sebesta 1997:532). The purple border signified prohibition, safeguarding the wearer from various actions including the risk of polluting his/her purity by word, gesture or deed, particularly those of a sexual nature. This was specific in the case of children, as confirmed by ancient authors such

[3] See Benwell 2003 for more on masculinity and men's lifestyle magazines.

[4] A full discussion on the toga as national and ceremonial dress can be found in Stone 1994: 13-46, also see Croom 2000:30-73.

as Quintillian (*Education of an Orator* 340), Varrus Flaccus (via Festus 282, 283) and Cicero (*Verrine* 3.23), who focused on the sacredness of *toga praetexta* as protecting children from any form of sexual salaciousness (Sebesta 1997:32-534). Pliny the Elder considered the practice to derive from Etruria (Pliny the Elder *Natural History* 8.198). Furthermore, he observed that the colour purple had always been in vogue in Rome and named Tullus Hostilius as the first of the kings to adorn the purple border, whereas Romulus used it purely to embellish his cloak (Pliny the Elder *Natural History* 9.136). According to Sebesta purple was a colour associated with blood and utilised for apotropaic purposes, 'as blood symbolically represented life, the wide range of red hues, which for the Romans included the hue purpura [purple], has been used in cultures throughout the world to protect those who are seen as particularly helpless and defenceless against evil forces, such as babies, children, pregnant women, and women lying in' (Sebesta 1994:47). Macrobius (*Saturnalia* 1.6.7-14, 15-16) regarded that the adoption of *toga praetexta* mostly derived from the Etruscan period including:

1. The first toga praetexta was worn by Tullus Hostilius because it was the costume of Etruscan magistrates. It continued to be regal costume. When the fourteen-year-old son of Tarquinius Priscus distinguished himself in battle against the Sabines, Tarquin praised the boy in a public assembly and awarded him honorific insignia consisting of the golden *bulla* and *toga praetexta* as marks of his courage.
2. Tarqinius Priscus wished to emphasise the respect due to freeborn boys and ordered that such should wear the golden *bulla* and *toga praetexta,* provided that their fathers had held a curule magistracy or merited the stipend for a horse.
3. The *toga praetexta* was an honour awarded a boy who helped rid Rome of a plague.
4. The first boy born of one of the Sabine women was given the right to wear the *toga praetexta* (taken from Sebesta 1994:51).

Therefore, according to Macrobius, the *toga praetexta* was, in origin, first specified for male children. However, this type of toga was not implemented exclusively for boys. A sculpture group of an anonymous woman and little girl (c.50 BC) clearly depicts the child wearing a toga (Palazzo Dei Conservatori, Capitoline Museum, Rome). Further examples include the image of a girl – representing the daughter of a freedman on a tombstone relief dated to the mid-first century AD at Ince Blundell Hall, and of Domitia daughter of Antonia Minor and Drusus Nero Claudius, on the *Ara Pacis*, (altar of peace) Rome. The south relief of the *Ara Pacis* also depicts the infant, Germanicus (George 2001: 184-185; Kleiner 1992:32-33; Sebesta 1994:46-48, 1997: 532-533). The children are adorned in the *togae praetextae* (over their tunics). Gender distinction is marked by the addition of a *bulla* worn by both Germanicus and Domitius. The *bulla* is a medallion of gold, silver, bronze or leather (which enclosed an amulet) worn by male children, especially by the sons of noble, wealthy and freedmen's families signifying/advertising their freeborn or freed status. Girls may have a necklace with an amuletic symbol. The way hair was fashioned is an additional attribute in the understandings of gender delegation. Boys' hair appears short and wavy whilst girls' hair is often (but not exclusively) more controlled, meticulously combed, braided or tied up (Bartman 2001:5). The child of the Palazzo Dei Conservatori group, according to George, wears a hairstyle that reflects the Hellenic retrospective tastes of the patron, as her hair is believed to mimic Hellenistic models for young girls (George 2001:183).

In adolescence both maiden and youth wore the *tunica recta* (*recta* referring to the cloth ritually woven on a traditional upright loom). According to Sebesta this cloth may have been woven incorporating purple bands and was further indicative of their sexually inviolable status (Sebesta 1997: 533). The transition to adulthood, the rites of passage, was marked by different events. Freeborn boys had ceremonies and various ritual practices dedicated solely for the transition to adulthood. Girls, on the other hand, had no particular ceremony. Their rights of passage allowed only for the link between childhood and marriage, from the guardianship of father to husband. In both instances the *toga praetexta* were given up for adult clothing. The *bulla* and *toga praetexta* were doffed for the toga of manhood the *toga virilis* (adult man, manly) and then dedicated to the domestic *Lares* (Ovid *Fasti* 3.787-8; Croom 2000: 120; George 2001: 184; Sebesta 1997:534). Additionally, when the youth had his first full growth of facial hair, it was shaved and ritually dedicated to the household gods (Suetonius, *Gaius Caligula* 10 and *Nero*, 12.4). The young adult was then eligible to enrol on the census list, join up for military service and from this point on, if he so desired, a man could indulge himself sexually outside marriage provided that it was not with the wife or children of fellow citizens (Sebesta 1997:534). The physical rituals celebrating a youth's transition into adulthood appears to focus on the development of the individual as a citizen. Young women, on the other hand, doffed their *togae praetextae* for the *stola* and *mantle* of the married matron. Their garments of childhood were dedicated to Fortuna Virginalis (maidenly) (Sebesta 1994:47). Moreover, their eventual adult attire was not assumed until they became brides. Before marriage they were required to weave a *tunica recta* and a yellow hairnet proving their ability to weave for her new household and family.[5]

Ideal femininity and sexuality: what makes a woman?

> 'one is not born a woman but rather becomes a woman' De Beauvoir [1949] 1972:295)

The dress of the Roman matron includes the *stola* (long outer garment worn over a tunic), *palla* (rectangular

[5] Sebesta offers a thorough description of the ritual dressing of the bride before and during the wedding Sebesta 1994:48.

outdoor garment used also as a veil) and *vittae* (woollen hair bands). Overall, her attire signified her respectable status as a chaste and modest wife. The long woollen *stola* covered her body, whilst the woollen *palla* was used to veil the head in public, beneath woollen hair bands, which protected her from impurity and alluded to her modesty. It was imperative to cover the head in public as 'the veil symbolises the husband's authority over his wife' (Sebesta 1994:48). *Stolae* and *vittae* remained the basic attire for the matron, changes in costume occurred when there was a shift of status or rank. The *mater familias* (mother of the family) kept the three fundamental garments, *stola, palla* and *vittae,* but was distinguished by a distinctive hairstyle called the *tutulus* where the hair is divided into sections, piled high on the crown and wrapped with woollen vittae (Sebesta 1994:50). Widowhood was marked by the adoption of the *ricinium* (square piece of cloth) instead of the *palla* as a veil, and worn as a sign of grief. According to Seneca a year was the traditional and sufficient period for a woman to mourn a husband (Seneca *Epistle* 63.13).[6] Clothes therefore marked marital status and, more significantly, the reputable status of the matron. Women from the distant, legendary Roman past became useful role models for promotion of virtuous behaviour. Livy's narrations on the Rape of Lucretia and the tragic fate of Verginia offer valuable understandings of the desired qualities, glorifying these specific 'historical' Roman women. Livy was writing about events in the legendary past, consequently it is impossible to determine exactly how much of his own, or contemporary preconceived notions, on ideal feminine virtue were included are ambiguous. However, both accounts are significant.

The sons of Lucius Tarquinius Superbus, King of Rome were at Ardea, at the house of Sextus Tarquinius when the party begin competitively comparing the virtue of their wives. Tarquinius Conlatinus declared that his wife, Lucretia, was the most praiseworthy, and that argument could be resolved simply by travelling home to catch their wives unprepared. The others agreed and found their wives about to attend a luxurious feast and night of enjoyment. Only Lucretia was at home spinning wool with her servants. Lucretia's commendable honour impressed the other men, especially Sextus Tarquinius, who lustfully decided that he must violate her. He travelled back to her house, where he was welcomed, and that night raped her at sword point. Lucretia sent for her father and husband, instructing each to bring a trustworthy friend,

> They found Lucretia sitting in her room, in deep distress. Tears rose in her eyes as they entered, and to her husband's question. 'Is all well with you?' she answered, 'No. *What can be well with a woman who has lost her honour?* ... My body only has been violated. My heart is innocent, and death will be my witness. Give me your solemn promise that the adulterer shall be punished – he is Sextus Tarquinius. He it is who last night came as my guest, and took his pleasure of me. That pleasure will be my death – and his, too, *if you are men.*' ... What is due to him ... is for you to decide. As for me I am innocent of fault, but I will take my punishment. *Never shall Lucretia provide a precedent for unchaste women to escape what they deserve.*' With these words she drew a knife from under her robe, drove it into her heart, and fell down dead (my italics, Livy *Early History of Rome* 1.59, De Sélincourt 83)

The legend, retold by Livy, appears to centre on 'honour', essentially that achieved by sexual fidelity within marriage (even though the matter is rape). For example, Lucretia was at home working wool when the men arrived to check up on them. Whilst at home she was clearly not seeking the attention of other men. The other wives allegedly were, as implied by their attendance at a grand banquet. Whether intentional or not, Livy created a vehicle stressing honour as an aspect of the advocated feminine stereotype. The message is emphasised further by Lucretia, giving life to her character, "what can be well with a woman who has lost her honour?" A legendary woman, through literature, transmits a rhetorical question setting an example to the living. Her resolution to kill herself proves her courage and her conviction as a devoted wife. As she states, 'never shall Lucretia, provide a precedent for unchaste women to escape what they deserve' (Livy, *Early History of Rome* 1.59). This is an excellent example of a significant statement written by a man speaking for a woman, that is that unchaste women will be punished, or at the very least deserve to be admonished. Furthermore, Lucretia questions the masculinity of her avengers daring them to complete their masculine duty and kill the perpetrator of such an abhorrent crime against daughter/wife/kinswoman. The men are unwilling for her to end her life, but she reveals her incorruptible resolve by committing suicide. Lucretia's lifeless body was taken to the forum where crowds gathered. It is at this scene, that Brutus spoke out against the dictatorial monarchy inciting the people to revolt leaving the way clear for a new political system – the Republic.

The emphasis on wool working is notable as a traditional and acceptable occupation for women and girls in the home. Suetonius comments on how Augustus adopted this traditional education for his daughter and granddaughters, whilst being particularly guarded against their interaction with others.

> The education of his daughter and granddaughters included even spinning and weaving; they were forbidden to say or do anything, either publicly or in private that could not decently figure in the imperial daybook. He took severe measures to prevent them forming friendships without his consent, and once wrote to Lucius Vinicius ... 'you were very ill mannered to visit my daughter at Baiae' (Suetonius *Augustus* 64, Graves 1957: 85)

Chastity is the main issue in an alternative legend also recounted by Livy. The fate of Verginia (Livy *Early History of Rome* 3.44-48) like Lucretia is allegedly

[6] See Ellis Hanson for aspects of widowhood including medical writers and the economic aspects of widowhood Ellis Hanson 2000:149-165.

attributed to the downfall of a political system, in this case the despotic *decimvirs*.[7] Once more, the basis of the discord was unwanted attention of a sexual predator threatening the chastity of his victim. Appius Claudius an influential member of the *decimvirs* set his lustful sights on Verginia. According to Livy, Verginia was the daughter of a centurion, drawing attention to her class yet giving credit to her father by stressing his honourable character. As stated,

> Lucius Verginius ... was a man with an excellent record both in military and in civilian life, and *his wife and children had been trained in the same high principles as himself.* (my italics, Livy, *Early History of Rome* 3.44, De Sélincourt 215).

Whether or not Verginius 'trained' his wife and daughter himself is not totally clear, yet this could be inferred. However, it does imply that they have no will/intelligence/self control of their own and have to be 'trained' like animals. Appius took advantage of Verginius' absence, abused his political power, and had Verginia seized claiming she was not the daughter of Verginius, but a descendant of slaves. Verginius was sent for. His claim on his daughter was ignored and unable to alter the situation he stabbed her, asserting it was the only way to make her free. She was better dead than forced to become the slave and mistress of Appius. Furthermore, he had previously betrothed his daughter to Icilius, whom in his angry attempts to resolve the situation demanded,

> I am to marry this girl, and I mean to have a virgin for my bride ... I refuse to let my promised wife pass the night away from her father's house (Livy *Early History of Rome* 3.46, De Sélincourt 217).

Through her betrothed's words, Livy makes it clear that chastity is of more importance than her physical safety or the threat to her liberty. The reaction of the crowd after Verginia's death is noteworthy. Livy offers what appears to be a deliberate gender divide in response to the tragic death.

> Women pressed around – were children, they cried, begotten and born only for this? Was this the re-ward for chastity? – and much more grief at such a time, will wring from women's hearts, *the more pitiful to hear from their very weakness*. As for men – Icilius especially – one thought was upper-most in their minds, one theme, above all, on their lips: the loss of the tribunate and the right of appeal, and tyrannous oppression of the people (my italics, Livy *Early History of Rome* 3.48, De Sélincourt 220).

Apart from the poignant, rhetorical questions, Livy appears to comment on the lack of control women have over their lives and bodies. Their concerns are about the futility of childbirth and parenthood, if they are to be eradicated for the sake of chastity. These are personal/corporeal uncertainties that, as women, apply to them all. Men, on the other hand, react with fear for the public in reaction to despotic political oppression. Their concern is political and not personal, stressing a masculine role that excludes women. Verginius escaped capture and fled to the army inciting them to rebel, whilst Icilius incited the urban populace. As a result, the *decemviri* were overthrown enabling a reassertion of liberty.

The abuse and consequent deaths of Lucretia and Verginia in both cases become legendary catalysts for political upheavals resulting in alternative political systems. As stated by Fantham el al, 'it is significant that each major step in the development of Roman political progress was associated by legend with the defence or vindication of women against abuse by those outside the family' (Fantham et al 1994:227). Dixon takes this issue further by suggesting, 'the purity of a woman's body could thus be a sign for the purity, safety, or political autonomy of the group' (Dixon 2001b: 47).

'Virtue' appears to have been a common umbrella term sought in encouraging correct protocol. This includes behaviour and actions such as: selflessness, loyalty, piety, devotion to husband and family, courage in defence of family (particularly her husband); the covering of the head in public and the adorning of respectable clothing; the rejection of personal vanity; sobriety; effectively managing the household and working wool; and obedience to father and husband, and in particular sexual fidelity within marriage.

Before embarking on a discussion of the selected images, it is necessary to address certain issues. From the above passages it is possible to gather particular aspects that define idealised understandings of femininity. These are supported by standardised images of women. Visual representations depend on particular gendered indicators transmitting information to the viewer, especially in a society where just a select few (who could afford it) were literate (Shelton 1998:100-122).

The standing relief group (as mentioned above, anonymous woman and girl found in Rome, c50 BC in the Palazzo Dei Conservatori, Capitoline) belongs to a corpus of funerary monuments of freed slaves depicted in this manner or alternatively as busts in relief. It is an early example of this type dating to the middle of the first century BC (George 2001: 178). The two figures depicted portray a matron with a girl (presumably her child?) and are thought to have derived from a tomb façade. The matron's pose (slightly facing to the left) suggests the addition of a counterpart masculine figure (now lost). The male figure, if present would probably have represented a husband or father as with comparative sculptures of the period depicting freed slaves (George 2001: 178-189, plate 4, 11.2; Von Heintze 1990:155). She is clearly adorned in the customary *stola* and *palla* covering her head. Furthermore, the *palla* tightly wrapped around her restricts her movement rendering an implication of passivity. A later example of Livia as

[7] For more on early politics in Rome see Crawford 1997: 9-3.

priestess of the deified Augustus AD14-29, from Otricoli, Vatican Museum, also depicts the subject in a *palla* restricting movement, whilst clearly showing the *stola* confirming her status and her veiled head inferring her modesty, and in this instance, piety as a priestess. Her husband, the emperor Augustus was particularly concerned with the moral degeneration in Rome and created certain legislations to impede salacious behaviour and social problems. Taking a retrospective approach he encouraged the high morals he deemed were current in Rome's distant past, 'the good old days'. He introduced severe laws against adultery (*Lex Julia*) making it a criminal offence punishable by exile and confiscation of property (Gardner 1986: 127-131; Lefkowitz and Fant 1999:102; Shelton 1998:54-55). These laws enabled fathers to kill their daughters and their partners in adultery; a husband was permitted to kill his wife's lover. Women found guilty of adultery had half their dowry and a third of their property confiscated and were exiled to an island, (an abject conclusion endured by Augustus' own daughter, Julia). Male offenders shared a similar fate; exile to an island and half of their property was confiscated (Shelton 1986:55). Augustus challenged the decreasing population and paucity of marriages amongst the upper classes by penalising those who refused to marry. As stated by Cassius Dio,

> He imposed heavier penalties upon unmarried men and women, and on the other hand offered rewards for marriage and the procreation of children. And since the freeborn population contained far more males than females, he allowed all those who desired – with exception of senators – to marry freedwoman, and directed that their offspring should be regarded as legitimate (Cassius Dio *Roman History: the reign of Augustus* 54.16.1-2, Scott-Kilvert 1987: 169).

Augustus advertised his own family on the *Ara Pacis* offering a model of family unity as an example to follow. Both women and men are dressed appropriately in their gendered items of clothing including the *toga virilis*, *stola* and *palla* and, as discussed earlier, the children have their own particular status symbolised by the *toga praetextae* and *bullae* (George 2001:184-185; Kleiner 1992:32-33; Sebesta 1994:46-48; 1997: 532-533).

Later sculptures portraying empresses Faustina the Elder, (c.140 AD, found in Rome, Palazzo Dei Conservatori, Capitoline Museum, Rome) and Julia Domna as Ceres, (c.203 AD, Julia Domna as Ceres, c203 from Ostia, Ostia Museum) appear to follow the same formula of adornment. Both sculptures depict imperial empresses. It could therefore be suggested that their semblance presents a paradigm for the female population to emulate. Their heads are covered, drapery (*stolae*) reaches the floor completely covering the body, and they are restrictively wrapped in their out garments (*pallae)*. Hairstyles form a noticeable distinction revealing the different time periods and fashions, yet the basic attire appears to remain the same indicating matronly modesty.

Art works depicting nude women appear to portray only mythological characters including nymphs and goddesses, or those partially nude as a representation of certain Amazon types (see Chapter 3). Reputable Roman women presumably would not be depicted nude. However, this was acceptable if in the guise of a mythical character or goddess such as Venus (see Chapter 2). There are funerary sculptures, however, that have portrait heads and Venus bodies combined to fashion sculptures commemorating the matronly sexuality of the deceased (D'Ambra 1996:219-232; 2000:101-114).

Nude women appear in numerous explicit sex scenes from various media including pottery and wall paintings, for example at the Suburban Baths at Pompeii (Clarke 2002:149-181). However, these images do not depict individuals. Instead they embody objectified, anonymous female and male bodies for voyeuristic purposes. The scenes centre on the acts and not the people. Female-to-female sexual relationships do not appear as popular in art as male-to-male coupling. This may be for a number of reasons. Perhaps examples have not survived, or the lack in imagery might be due to the general status of women, or a reluctance to acknowledge female-to-female relationships. Johns considers the absence is due to a general lack of interest in the love lives of women that do not affect men. As stated, 'in Rome there was again relatively little interest in female love life when not angled towards men, and the general conclusion which presents itself is that the female sub-culture was simply not of sufficient interest to the predominately male artist and writers for them to trouble to chronicle it' (Johns 1982:103). However, it must be noted that composition themes were more likely to be chosen by the patrons and not the artist. Perhaps it was merely that it was not a subject that was particularly in vogue. Nevertheless the lack of evidence renders the subject open for debate.

Men and Youths: Masculinity in Roman visual culture

There are a number of points that pertain to Roman masculinity and sexuality. Moreover there was, as with women, a protocol for virtuous behaviour (*virtus*). *Virtus,* translated means: manliness, manhood, goodness, virtue, excellence, worth, resolution and valour (Morwood 1994: 150). The stem *vir* means man, husband, a true man (Morwood 1994: 150). Therefore, virtue may automatically be associated with masculinity although in contradiction, *virtus* is a feminine noun.

The legend of Horatius Cocles at the bridge, recounted by Livy encapsulates the Roman ideal of masculine *virtus* (Livy *Early History of Rome* 2.10). The Etruscans were moving in to attack Rome so the Romans abandoned their farmsteads and assembled to defend the city. The city walls and the Tiber were adequate protection, except for one vulnerable spot, a wooden bridge. Horatius was on guard at the bridge when the Eyruscans made a sudden attack and captured the Janiculum. Horatius stopped his fellow comrades from throwing away their weapons and retreating. He urged them not to abandon their posts as escape would be impossible and would ultimately lead to the invasion of the city. He ordered them to destroy the bridge whilst he offered to hold off the advance alone. As narrated by Livy,

> Proudly he took his stand at the outer end of the bridge; conspicuous amongst the rout of fugitives, sword and shield ready for action, he prepared himself for close combat, *one man against an army*. The advancing enemy paused in sheer astonishment at such *reckless courage*. Two other men, Spurius Lartius and Titus Herminius, *both aristocrats with a fine military record*, were ashamed to leave Horatius alone, and with their support he won through the first few minutes of desperate danger. Soon, however, he forced them to save themselves and leave him; for little was left of the bridge ... Once more Horatius stood alone; with defiance in his eyes he confronted the Etruscan chivalry, challenging one after another to single combat, and mocking them all as tyrants' slaves, careless of their own liberty, were coming *destroy the liberty of others.* For a while they hung back ... until shame at unequal battle drove them into action, with a fierce cry they hurled their spears at a solitary figure which barred their way. Horatius caught the missiles on his shields and resolute as ever, straddled the bridge and held his ground ... The Etruscans could only stare in bewilderment as Horatius, with a *prayer to Father Tiber to bless him* and his sword, plunged fully armed into the water and swam, through the missiles which fell thick about him, safely to the other side where his friends were waiting for him. It was a noble piece of work – legendary maybe, but destined to be celebrated in story through the years to come (my italics, Livy *Early History of Rome* 210, De Sélincourt 1960:100).

As stated by Livy, Horatius' actions were considered noble. However, there are other features in the passage that reveal the Roman ideal. Horatius demonstrates 'reckless courage' protecting his particular post and ultimately Rome. The way Livy introduces passing supplementary characters Spurius Lartius and Titus Herminius is significant, as he states, 'both [are] aristocrats with a fine military record'. It is no coincidence that these are the only two to offer Horatius support (albeit through shame). Livy appears to recommend their high birth and excellent military record as explanation for their courageous solidarity. Preservation of liberty is additionally essential, whilst Horatius' piety is highlighted by his prayer offered to the river god before he swam to safety. In accordance with Livy, unwavering courage, free birth, an outstanding military career, preservation of liberty and piety are important elements incorporating the Roman masculine ideal and *virtus*. As stated by Livy 'courage, constancy, [are] all the virtues which, in civil or military life, were the true glory of manhood' (Livy *The Early History of Rome* 3.19 De Sélincourt 1960:189).

In the above sections I have discussed how guarded female sexuality was, particularly in marriage. Masculine sexual protocol was as complex, dictating that men should always be the penetrator and never the passive partner. Being passive would entail taking the 'woman's part' which would be fiercely disapproved of and the offender risked the stereotypical title 'effeminate'. Passivity was acceptable for slaves, women and boys, but not freeborn boys. In *Roman Questions,* Plutarch proposed that, 'it [was] not disreputable nor disgraceful to love male slaves in the flower of youth ... but strictly refrained from boys of free birth' (Plutarch *Roman Questions* 101.288; Babbitt 1936: 151). Several ancient authors refer to the particular age at which a youth was desirable as the 'flower of youth' including, Pseudo-Lucian (*Affairs of the Heart* 3) and Virgil (*Eclogues* 7.4). This period is thought to transpire at the start of puberty, generally between the ages of twelve and fourteen when the youth begins to have light downy facial hair, and ends when with the appearance of a full beard perhaps around the youths late teens to early twenties (Williams 1999: 19).

The Warren Cup (mid-1st AD thought to be from Bittir, ancient Bethther, near Jerusalem, British Museum) clearly presents a difference in age between sexual partners (Clarke 1993:275-294; 1998: 61-72; Johns 1982:103). The cup illustrates two couples, one a mature bearded man with his clean shaven youthful lover and the other a young man with a boy. The subjects form a physical, (probably) social and chronological age hierarchy signifying power and control over the passive partner. As Williams indicates, 'this can justly be called the prime directive of masculine sexual behaviour for Romans and it has an obvious relationship to broader structures of hierarchical male power ... penetration is subjugation (in the sense that the act is held simultaneously to be a figure for, and to effect, subjugation), and masculinity is domination' (Williams 1999: 18). However, to maintain dominant masculinity, an over indulgence of pleasure was prohibited, particularly for an expectant young politician. As described by Corbeill, 'overeating, naked dancing, telling jokes – three activities guaranteed to curtail any young Roman's political aspirations' (Corbeill 1997:99). These actions were considered 'effeminate' and rendered the individual open to criticism, and more ominously, attacked their very masculinity. The Warren cup has a noticeable representational hierarchy, and yet, with most erotic scenes the people depicted probably do not represent real individuals – they are simply illustrations of anonymous objectified bodies.[8]

Remaining on the theme of unspecified bodies, there are numerous example of non-Roman adversaries 'barbarian - others' that are essentially non-specific vulnerable bodies that follow the equivalent paradigm as a personification (Ferris 1995: 24-31; 1997:22-28; 2000). Masculine non-Roman 'others' were generally embodied as fallen, injured and naked. Equivalently, Amazons

[8] However, 'good' masculine qualities may also have be portrayed by anonymous objectified bodies, for example those depicting a standing male figure in a toga.

embody the feminine 'other'. They generally appear physically vulnerable and exposed to bodily and sexual assault. Having control over the body, guarding it from physical and sexual violation, was also a requirement of acceptable masculinity. To lose control of the body would render the man vulnerable to passivity, which was considered a natural state for women and slaves (Williams 1999: 125; Alston 1998: 209-210). This specific point is relevant in interpreting the 'barbarian' stereotype. A well-known example is the Dying Gaul (original c. 240-200 BC, Capitoline Museum, Rome). Initially a Hellenistic original, it survives as a Roman copy. It could be argued that this work was perhaps received differently in its original context, maybe with more or less connotations of victory. However, it is the composition of the sculpture that is important to this study. The fallen warrior is incapacitated and naked. His passivity is stressed by the way he looks away from the viewer and at his wounds – he is off guard. Furthermore, he is defenceless against any form of attack, particularly sexual assault. This is reiterated by the positioning of the body, which allows the viewer to see him from all angles – especially his back and buttocks (with the left side slightly raised above the base drawing attention to their form). The sculpture is notably explicit. Yet, it could be argued that he represented a masculine physical form that was worthy as an adversary and not an easy target. As a non-Roman the Dying Gaul may not represent idealised masculinity, but to further the point, the subject has no control over his own body and therefore is unable to demonstrate a Roman prerequisite for masculinity. A number of examples of the fallen 'barbarian' survive from Roman Britain (see Chapter 5, 6). The formula and concept appear to be alike. They are very much a personification of non-Romans and, as a stereotype, have no individuality or personality merely anonymous naked, wounded bodies.

Slaves by the nature of their bondage share the inability to maintain corporeal control. The left panel of the Bridgeness slab fig. 15 (from the Antonine Wall, National Museum of Scotland) depicts a man really on the same level as sacrificial animals. His short tunic and position within the composition suggests his low social position, Keppie suggests that this character is the *victimarius* (the soldier who slaughtered the animals) (Keppie 1984: 27), but the lack of an axe or any other implement suggests otherwise. He appears to be solely attending to the animals, which could also explain occupying the same level as the animals. Overall, the scene there appears to illustrate a class hierarchy. The standing figures appear to be divided by a *vexillum* (a standard or flag of company or group) inscribed advertising the legion represented. To the right of the standard the first two figures were represented wearing togas, one holds a *patera* for the sacrifice. Their clothing and the action of performing the sacrifice indicate high status. To the left of the standard the figures are dressed in tunics and military cloaks demonstrating martial status. Beneath, the flute player plays for the event. Then on the lowest level the animals chosen for sacrifice confront the altar and are joined by the attendant. His lowly status is however, still in opposition to that of the stereotyped, naked fallen captive of the right panel (see Chapter 5).

Conclusion

In this chapter I have endeavoured to demonstrate how socially constructed values contribute to the understandings of gender and Roman art. The *toga praetexta* adorned by both girls and boys secured their purity from any salaciousness or physical harm, thus ensuring that both boys and girls share a neutral state of inviolability. The masculine child however wore a *bulla*, which ultimately acted as a social status symbol and gender marker as only freeborn boys could only wear it. The 'Roman ideal' required that both men and women lead virtuous lives. Women, particularly matrons, were expected to (amongst other things) conduct selfless lives directed towards the successful management of the home (wool working) and to achieve complete sexual fidelity within marriage. Items of clothing and adornments adopted at marriage, including the *stola, palla* and *vittae*, reflect societal customs that ultimately create the gendered facade of a Roman matron. At the onset of adulthood freeborn young men adorned the *toga virilis*. This was the societal mark of manhood and masculinity. Actions were additionally imperative, particularly with regard to sexual protocol. To become a submissive partner denoted a lack of control, and ultimately the loss of masculinity. There were specific rules for children, women and men, to disregard them rendered the offenders open to criticism.

Chapter 2

Venus and Mars: constructions of femininity, masculinity and hypermasculinity

The objective of this chapter is to consider the way Venus, goddess of love and desire and Mars, god of war were presented in Roman art, particularly that of Roman Britain. As Venus represented the epitome of 'beauty' and sexual desire, I examine the way her specific femininity was constructed and consider contemporary concepts of femininity associated with sexual identity. As the god of war, Mars appears to represent a particular construct of masculinity associated solely with warfare, a factor that was of considerable significance to the stability and expansion of Rome. Venus and Mars are primary subjects of choice because of their importance within the foundation myths of Rome, which as a result affects the interpretation of their images. Although Venus was the consort of Vulcan, she had many lovers including Mars. However, the most significant partner in terms of the construction of Roman 'history' was Anchises.

According to the Homeric Hymn, she had a magic belt that allowed her to make anyone fall in love/lust with her. Zeus became tired of his daughter's use of her magic belt, as he also felt tempted by her. Subsequently, he decided to humiliate her and, as mortals were considered inferior to the Olympians, the perfect solution was to have her fall in love with one. Ironically, Zeus did not choose a man at random, but a king, Anchises, King of the Dardanians (*Homeric Hymn to Aphrodite* 45-200) and their son, Aeneas, would later become the founder of what would become Rome. Virgil later reused the legend in his propagandist epic following the exploits of Aeneas in the Aeneid (19 BC). After surviving the sack of Troy Aeneas, urged by benevolent deities, made his way west to Italy. Despite many attempts by the goddess Juno to sabotage his expedition, Aeneas managed to reach Italy where he waged war and founded his city, Lavinium and, with his wife, Lavinia (daughter of a local king, Latinus) ruled a unified populace entitled Latins (Gardner 1993:17).

Suetonius documented the Julian family's claim to be descendants of Aeneas (*Caesar:* 6). Believing themselves directly related to divinity, they represented themselves accordingly. Furthermore they capitalised on the fecund aspect of the goddess of love and mother of numerous offspring as Venus became entitled the 'mother of Rome' or Venus Genetrix (Zanker, 1988:193; De Rose Evans 1992:28). Venus was also associated with other aspects and qualities, including Venus Felix (of good luck, fortunate), Venus Victrix (victory), and Venus Verticordia (the protector of feminine chastity). Octavian established and utilised dynamic imagery of his ancestress associating her with his own life and status. This 'manipulation' was taken to its most extreme during his programme of cultural renewal (Zanker 1988: 33). Furthermore, the alternative foundation myth of Romulus and Remus was also employed to further associations between the Julian family and divinity. It was claimed that Mars seduced Rhea Silvia, daughter of the king of Alba Longa, and consequently became the father of her twin boys, Romulus and Remus. Rhea Silvia belonged to the same Trojan family as Aeneas, therefore linking Romulus and Remus with the Julian dynasty (Zanker, 1988:195). This tangle of different myths ultimately enabled connections to be made between Venus and Mars and the Julian family. Indeed, the continual use of this imagery served to implant further the perceived qualities of these personas within Julian family. In particular, this family sought association with the fertility and opulence of Venus, as well as the guaranteed virtue and bravery of Mars. Therefore, the revival of foundation myths acted as useful propaganda for them.

Before the Battle of Actium, Octavian used such imagery, through art, in a deliberate and sophisticated manner to further his cause. He commissioned coins to be minted illustrating images of his 'ancestors'. One contained an image of a semi-draped Venus, leaning gently on a column and holding soldier's equipment including a helmet and a sceptre, with a shield standing beside the pillar. These items were incorporated to suggest her affiliation with Mars (Zanker 1988: 33, fig 27). Furthermore, he was able to manipulate a wealth of imagery in a wide range of media. Determined to emphasise the apparent endless links between the Julian family and divinity, this elite transported relevant imagery in multifarious, though connected, visual forms from place to place throughout the entire Empire.

On a larger scale, Octavian vowed to build a temple to Mars Ultor (the Avenger) at the Battle of Philippi 42 BC, in expectation of his help in avenging Caesar's assassins Brutus and Cassius. This temple was to have a significant role in the political and imperial future of Rome, therefore illustrating the importance of Mars the Avenger (Augustus *Res Gestae* 21). As documented by Suetonius,

> He [Octavian] therefore decreed that the Senate should meet here whenever declarations of war or claims for triumphs were considered; and this should be both the starting point for military governors when escorted to their provinces, and the repository of all

triumphal tokens when they returned victorious (Suetonius *Augustus 29,* Graves 1957:68).[9]

Therefore, Suetonius described Octavian as creating a physically defined area for performances of masculinity. It was also utilised for ceremonies commemorating the rites of maturity for adolescent boys of elite families. This entailed firstly, the shaving off the youth's first growth of facial hair and then dedicating this to a deity, and, secondly the symbolic change of garments form the purple-striped toga the *toga praetexta* of childhood to the all white adult toga (Suetonius, *Gaius Caligula* 10; *Nero*, 12.4; Montserrat 2000: 170). The specific date as to when work began on the temple is unknown, but it is thought to have been after the Battle of Actium (Kleiner 1992: 99; Zanker 1988:196-197). The Forum of Augustus, within which the temple was a feature, was completed and dedicated in 2 BC. This was located next to the Forum of Caesar that was completed by Augustus and used as a model for his own Forum. Moreover, the Temple of Mars Ultor was based on Caesar's Temple of Venus Genetrix again reinforcing Julian links with the founding deities of Rome.

Within the temple of Mars Ultor was a statuary group representing Mars Ultor, Venus, Cupid and the Divine Julius Caesar. Unfortunately this is not preserved, but a relief from Algiers (Archaeological Museum, Algiers) is thought to represent the same group (Beard et al 1998:332-333; Beard and Henderson 2001: 172; Kleiner 1992:100; Zanker 1988: 196-197). Furthermore, the individuals appear to have bases upon which the figures stand, reinforcing the notion that they are representations of statues. Venus and Mars depicted in their specific roles as Venus Genetrix and Mars Ultor. Venus is predominantly draped, her hair is long, but controlled by being tied back and topped with a diadem. She is majestic and matronly, yet her exposed shoulders, arms and diaphanous drapery force the viewer to acknowledge her as a sexual being. The clinging fabric or 'wet drapery' effect closely covers Venus to the right of the scene. It is generally agreed that this technique was initially utilised as a feature of the east pediment of the Parthenon, Athens (depicting deities assembled to witness the birth of Athena). The female deities were carved in the clinging cloth technique opposing the 'heroic' nudity of the male subjects (Robertson 1991: 140; Boardman 1992: 115-116, figs 80.1, 80.2, 80.3, 80.4; Salomon 1997:203). The female body is clearly visible beneath flowing, sheer drapery – it is clothed but simultaneously offers the suggestion of nudity beneath. This may be a deliberate, erotic effect. The implication of this method depends on the individual representations. To illustrate this I use as examples the East pediment, Parthenon and Venus of the above Algiers relief. Despite the considerable time lapse, the technique was regularly in use into, and during, the Roman period. When the Parthenon sculptures were created (c.438 BC), representations of the female nude were rare unless depicting maenads, supernatural followers of Dionysus/Bacchus or courtesans at the symposium.[10] As pointed out by Henderson, 'preclassical and classical Greek culture made female nakedness, and even 'topless' exposure, a cardinal taboo ... Naked ladies outside their master's chamber could only be transgressive – evil siren, Scylla or Circe, bacchante, or else, typically, the *whore's* body servicing male desire' (Henderson 2002:30, my italics[11]). Consequently, appropriate representations of 'respectable' women and deities were fully clad. The goddesses have the clothing, but at the same time demonstrate nudity, which was unheard of for deities. This approach suggests that the artist intentionally found a way to hint at nudity without obviously showing it, by incorporated the wet, clinging effect, and as a result offered the female body as an object for voyeurism. It is during this period, at the end of the fifth century BC that attitudes towards the female body began to change, until then the youthful male nude was considered the epitome of erotic beauty (Salomon 1996: 71; 1997:203; Osborne 1998:95). Furthermore, as pointed out by Salomon, 'the goddesses on the Parthenon pediment are 'wet' for no logical reason' (Salomon 1997:203). Returning to the Venus of the Algiers relief, her drapery also appears wet, with no justification other than to display her form. I would propose that the Algiers Venus was constructed in this manner with the purpose of illustrating her as a fertile producer of sons. We are shown her body whilst beside her, her son Cupid confirms her fertility, thus advertising her as a role model for women; she represents the epitome of a 'real' woman.

As mentioned previously, alongside Venus is her son Cupid who hands her Mars' sword. His inclusion is both appropriate and useful to the overall theme, as Cupid is her child by Mars[12] (Virgil *Ciris* 134; Plutarch *Amatorius* 20) and together they present a united family of Rome. Furthermore, in the Algiers relief, the child forms a physical link between the adult deities. Venus' drapery slips resting gently on Cupid's head and falls to cover his left arm; Mars' cloak falls behind and beside Cupid's left arm joining the relief figures together and forming a family unit. The draped cloth almost shelters Cupid in a protective manner as if he is 'under her wing.' This reiterates Venus's status as fertile Venus Genetrix, mother of Rome and goddess of Caesar's Forum.

Mars has full military equipment with a shield, helmet cuirass and spear. He appears fit for military action, and it is therefore reasonable to suppose that this represents Mars Ultor (the avenger). His central position and height specifies his importance. Here Mars has a masculinity that was constructed by drawing on the idea of his martial potency. If we set aside the immortality of Mars as the god of war, and imagine this relief as a portrait of a regular general, the result is valuable to interpretation. In

[9] Suetonius included the use of the temple for the purposes mentioned above in his history of Gaius 44, Graves 1957:176.

[10] For more on the symposium see Keuls 1993: 160-171.

[11] Although I agree with Henderson's statement, I do not agree with his use of the expression 'whore', which is unnecessarily derogatory and condemnatory, especially when discussing an ancient society which had different views to our own.

[12] Cicero named Mercury as Cupid's father *Nature of the Gods* 3.23.

the first instance, his beard is noteworthy, as noted by Zanker, 'Romans had been basically clean-shaven for centuries, although there had, of course, always been men who grew beards, especially soldiers' (Zanker 1995:218). Additionally, his beard indicates maturity. At the most basic level this man has the ability to survive warfare and therefore it stands to reason that he must be a good combatant. Clearly this is fitting for a god of war, but it also creates a figure that people could relate to. Furthermore (as we shall see below) many examples of Mars are very similar to that of soldiers, and distinguishing which is which often depends on inscriptions. This excludes official portraiture where beards were, as a rule, avoided. This may have been considered 'un-Roman', possibly reacting against the bearded Greeks of old, although this is also a reason for wearing a beard, reviving Hellenism as with the emperor Hadrian. A trimmed beard and wavy hair became 'fashionable' under Domitian and became widespread under Trajan (Zanker 1995:218).

The inclusion of *Divus Julius* in the group was an essentially sophisticated act of propaganda. According to some scholars, his identification became clear by traces of metal on his forehead (Zanker 1988: 196; Kleiner 1992:100; Beard and Henderson 2001:172). After Caesar's assassination, Augustus placed stars on sculptured representations of his adoptive father. The star, as documented by Suetonius, signified Caesar's apotheosis to join the gods/goddesses. On the first day of the Games dedicated by Augustus in honour of this apotheosis, a comet came into sight, and shone for seven days in succession. This was taken to be his soul elevated to the ranks of divinity, and so the star was added to his divine image (Suetonius *Caesar 88*). The newest addition to the pantheon of Roman deities was deliberately placed next to these important deities emphasising Augustus' correlation with divinity, for what better ruler could Rome have than a man whose family history included people responsible for establishing Rome itself? Caesar's representational construction is also significant. He has a full head of hair, whereas his portraits suggest that he had male pattern baldness (Kleiner 1992: 45, fig 26). His idealistic superhuman musculature is a fabrication promoting and enhancing Caesar's masculinity. Furthermore, the low position of his slipping, sheer drapery draws attention to his pelvic area and his nudity beneath, not only eroticising the representation, but also promoting his masculine virility. Therefore, the combined factors of this sexually charged representation shows an ageless, potent 'father' of the empire who was not only intimately linked with major deities of the pantheon, but a divine figure himself.
Drawing this example concerning the visual language of the Algiers relief to a conclusion, I will now discuss the deities in individual sections beginning with Venus.

Venus of Cnidus

Venus had numerous titles some of which affected the way she was depicted, for example Venus Victrix or Venus Genetrix. Many of the famous Venus types are of recent art historical invention such as the 'Venus of Capua', Venus de Milo or 'Crouching Venus'. Often their titles depend on the area they were found or their particular pose. The majority of archetypal Venus types derive from Hellenistic sculptures of Aphrodite, recorded by ancient writers such as Pliny the Elder (AD 23-79) in his *Natural History* and Roman copies (allowing, of course for variations and development) (Kleiner 1992:4).[13] One of these, the Aphrodite of Cnidus by Praxiteles (c.350BC), has a legendary status (identified from Cnidian coins), (Robertson 1991:140; Beard and Henderson 2001:126 fig 87.c). I have selected this particular example because of the importance given to this sculpture within the history of art. Furthermore, I am aware that the original is Hellenistic Greek in origin and this dissertation focuses on Roman and Romano-British art, but I would suggest that the Aphrodite/Venus of Cnidus (through copies) is as significant and valid a feature of Roman art as Trajan's Column. (Yet it should be noted that the original was from a different society which possibly had different values regarding gender). I have chosen to link the goddesses in this manner not because I believe that they are totally equivalent but because of the continuity of the artistic representational 'type' into the Roman period.

The Aphrodite/Venus sculpture was the first documented and celebrated nude depiction of Aphrodite (Robertson 1991: 140; Smith 1995:79, Boardman 1993: 136-139; Salomon 1996:70, 1997:197; Beard and Henderson, 2001:127). It is likely this was the case because of the tabloid-like rumours that surround the history of the sculpture (Spivey 1997a 310). Pliny noted that the representation was considered too indecent for the people of Cos, who opted for a clothed version by the same sculptor (*Natural History 36:20*). Furthermore, he stated that the sculpture's reputation made Cnidus eminent and his reference to the behaviour of an over amorous admirer made it infamous.

> Superior to any other statue, not only to others made by Praxiteles himself, but throughout the world, is the Venus which many people have sailed to Cnidus to see...The shrine that houses it is completely open so that the statue of the goddess can be seen from all sides, it was made in this way, so it is believed, with the goddess's approval. It is admirable from every angle. There is a story that a man who fell in love with the statue hid in the temple at night and embraced it intimately; a stain bears witness to his lust (Pliny *Natural History 36:20-21,* Healy 1991:346).

Therefore, according to Pliny the shrine that housed the sculpture was as much a part of the visual experience as the sculpture itself. It is interesting to note, as recorded

[13] The subject of Venus within the history of art is a major work itself which unfortunately cannot be undertaken fully here. Fore more on ancient representations of Aphrodite/Venus sculpture see Robertson 1991:40-141; Smith 1995: 79-83; Salomon 1996:69-88, 1997:197-219; Beard and Henderson 2001:113-132.

by Pliny, that the Cnidians believed they had the goddess's approval to publicly exhibit her with an open shrine. This is convenient as it allowed them to be self-justified in the display of her nude representation. Although we are told that the shrine was open, she was however, 'housed'. Her nude body was therefore contained and controlled whilst allowing her objectified form to be the focus for voyeurism. As noted by Spivey, 'this is a major departure. It [the Cnidia] is made conspicuous by the subsequent obsession of Western (male) artists and Western (male) viewers with the female nude, which misleadingly makes Praxiteles the progenitor of what is called the 'male gaze' (Spivey 1997a: 310).

The shrine was additionally documented by the pseudo-Lucian in *Affairs of the Heart* claiming the notoriety of Praxiteles' sculpture. Initially, the characters, Lycinus and Theomnestus deliberate on favoured sexual partners - boys 'at the flower of their beauty' (adolescent period, see below) (Pseudo-Lucian *Affairs of the Heart* 3,; Macleod 1967: 155) or women. Lycinus relates a narrative aiding the debate, where he and his friends Charicles and Callicratidas visit Cnidus and the famous statue of Aphrodite/Venus. Charicles and the narrator were eager to see the famed statue, but Callicratidas was reluctant as the sculpture was of a female subject, and not a youthful male. The Pseudo-Lucian revealed that the temple was not surrounded by smooth paving slabs of stone, but by a fertile garden with luxuriant fruit trees and berry-laden myrtle (which is appropriate as it is the sacred plant of the goddess). This offers an analogous association between food/drink and sex, with fertility and the goddess of love. The Pseudo-Lucian enhances this by stating that every tree was entwined with ivy and rich grapevines hung with thick clusters of grapes, both plants associated and sacred to Dionysus/Bacchus god of wine and promoter of hedonism. As stated, 'for Aphrodite [love/sex] is more delightful when accompanied by Dionysus [wine] and the gifts of each are sweeter if blended together, but, should they be parted from each other, they afford less pleasure' (Pseudo-Lucian *Affairs of the Heart* 12; Macleod 1967:169). The erotic theme continues, as the characters pay particular attention to the objectified female body that can be looked at/on from all directions.

> In the midst thereof sits the goddess – she's a most beautiful statue of Parian marble – arrogantly smiling a little as a grin parts her lips. Draped by no garment, all her beauty is uncovered and revealed, except in so far as she unobtrusively uses one hand to hide her private parts. So great was the power of the craftsman's art that the hard unyielding marble did justice to every limb ... The temple had a door on both sides for the benefit of those who wish to have a good view of the goddess from behind, so that no part of her be left unadmired. It's easy therefore to enter by the other door and survey the beauty of her back.
>
> The Athenian [Callicratidas] who had been so impassive an observer a minute before, upon inspecting those parts of the goddess which recommended a boy, suddenly raised a shout far more frenzied than that of Charicles. "Heracles!" he exclaimed, "what a well- proportioned back! What generous flanks she has! How satisfying an armful to embrace! How delicately moulded the flesh on the buttocks, neither too thin and close to the bone, nor yet revealing too great an expanse of fat! And as for those precious parts sealed in on either side of her hips, how inexpressibly sweetly they smile! How perfect the proportions of the thighs and the shins as they stretch down in a straight line to the feet! So that's what Ganymede looks like as he pours out the nectar in heaven for Zeus and makes it taste sweeter ... while Callicratidas was shouting this under the spell of the goddess, Charicles in the excess of his admiration stood almost petrified, though his emotions showed in the melting tears trickling from his eyes [the narrator goes on to describe the episode described by Pliny about the stain on the marble (Pseudo-Lucian *Affairs of the Heart* 13-14, Macleod 1967: 169-170).

From this text we find the discussant commenting on the ability to view the goddess 'so that no part of her be left unadmired.' The focus is immediately directed to her as the object of sexual appeal and the subject of thoughtful discussion regarding a physical sexual preference for boys or women. In no way do they consider her as a deity. All veneration is replaced with an instant voyeuristic fascination for the proportions of her body, particularly that of her buttocks. Drawing a parallel between the goddess and Ganymede is particularly telling. Ganymede was a Trojan youth renowned for his beauty and became the object of Jupiter's lust. Jupiter turned himself into an eagle and snatched the boy away to be his cupbearer, perpetually within his sights (Homer, *Iliad 20. 231-5*; Virgil, *Aeneid 5. 25;* Ovid, *Metamorphoses 10. 155).* It seems that the passage offers a view of male-to-male homoerotic desire that is unexpectedly obtained from a representation of a female. Yet, it is not the overall image, only the buttocks. As Salomon states, 'the Greek's fixation with the buttocks of a mortal is, of course, not incompatible with homoerotic discourse in general and the Cnidia's buttocks in particular are brought into that discourse by the analogy made to Ganymede' (Salomon 1997:207). The so-called Venus Kallipygos (Museo Archeologico Nazionale in Naples, Italy) or 'beautiful buttocks' is a particularly good example of this obsession (Beard and Henderson 2002:124). The goddess is depicted looking over her shoulder whilst raising her drapery in order to gaze at her own buttocks. The sculptor therefore, offers en example of Venus taking part in her own objectification. She gazes, whilst the audience view her, viewing herself, dual and concurrent voyeurism. Moreover, whilst Venus looks at herself spectators in front can voyeuristically steal a look at her partly exposed pelvic area as she rises her drapery covering this quarter in her right-hand.

Adding to the sexual mythology relating to the Cnidian sculpture is Praxiteles' relationship to the courtesan Phryne who was thought to be the model for the Cnidia and the Aphrodite Anadyomene by Apelles (see above, Athenaios 13.590). Furthermore, it has been suggested that Praxiteles' rendition was the first to demonstrate a female nude in the so-called *pudica* or modest pose (Salomon 1997:197). This shows the goddess being interrupted either before or after bathing; she 'modestly' covers herself, hiding her pelvic area from the intruder's view, (consequently drawing attention to it). Furthermore, this is an empty gesture of modesty as the area behind the hand is visible from different viewpoints, which was the case as recorded by Pliny. The pose gives her a hunched, cowering stance enhancing her vulnerability and passivity. She becomes an objectified subject for gaze, and the viewer, male or female, then has an advantage over her. If we are to take the Vatican Cnidia as an accurate copy, then Praxiteles constructed a femininity that is submissive and vulnerable. According to Robertson the Roman copies are no substitution and follow a traditional pattern and that,

> Praxiteles seems to have tried to start again, to create a statue to illustrate the *feminine principle.* The knees, close together, make an extraordinary narrow point from which the thighs spread rapidly to the ample buttocks and hips, equally emphasised by the shrinking, stooping movement of the upper torso' (Robertson 1991:140, my italics).

Remarkably, this quote is reminiscent of that by Lucian's character the Athenian. Robertson's comments are uncritical and rely on physical description. More importantly, is his concept and use of his expression 'feminine principle'. Out of curiosity, I consulted a thesaurus for words that parallel (and in the same context as) 'principle' the examples were as follows: formula, rule, criterion, standard and law (Knight 1994:443). Hence, according to Robertson, to construct femininity depends on the 'feminine principle', (rule, code, standard and law) that is 'knees, close together, make an extraordinary narrow point from which the thighs spread rapidly to the ample buttocks and hips equally emphasised by the shrinking, stooping movement of the upper torso' (Robertson 1991:140). Is this suggesting that those failing to fit within this category are not sufficiently 'feminine'? Furthermore, as stated above her so-called modest pose renders her submissive and objectified. Is that what it means to be feminine? According to Robertson it does. The Cnidia therefore conjures a range of complex connotations and connections. It is apparent however, that this archetypal Venus example should not be examined uncritically.

A further example is Hadrianic copy of the Cnidia from Hadrian's Villa at Tivoli (Villa Museum). The copy is damaged, the head is missing, lower right arm is missing and the majority of the left with damage to the legs, but her nudity and her stance, (the way her weight rests on her right leg) corroborates her identity. Hadrian was a great admirer of Greece and Greek culture; therefore, it is no surprise to observe his preference for 'retro' classicism (and archaic examples) at his villa. His ideas were generated from his numerous travels. From his visit to Cnidus he made replicas of the fourth century BC Doric Temple of Aphrodite, and more relevant to our discussion, the Aphrodite by Praxiteles that was exhibited at the centre of his temple. This was not the only example of Greek prototypes. He exhibited a range of replicas from the Archaic to Hellenistic periods, with a particular preference for celebrated masterpieces like the Tyrannicides,[14] the Discobolus of Myron,[15] and Praxiteles' resting Satyr[16] (Kleiner 1992:246). What does this tells us about the Cnidia or the emperor Hadrian? First and foremost, it creates the impression that Hadrian considered himself to have an affinity with the creative artists and architects of the past. Cassius Dio makes us aware of Hadrian's ambitions to become involved in architecture. It is Cassius Dio who comments on the dubious reasons Hadrian used for executing the prominent architect Apollodorus of Damascus. According to him, before Hadrian became emperor, he encroached upon a discussion of the emperor Trajan and his architect only to be dismissed as an amateur by Apollodorus who then disparaged Hadrian's own architectural designs (Cassius Dio 69. 4.1-5). It may be that Hadrian chose Aphrodite/Venus within his architectural and sculptural collected works, with the intention of linking himself with the imperial past and the Julio-Claudians, who were allegedly descendants of Venus. As a final point, and returning to the Cnidia, its inclusion in Hadrian's collection demonstrates that the sculpture was still noteworthy and eminent at that time (early second 2 century AD). At this point I will to focus on images of Venus that, akin to the Cnidia, were represented in a bathing context within the composition. This brings us to an alternative Venus template, the Aphrodite Anadyomene.

Venus Anadyomene

The Aphrodite/Venus Anadyomene (emerging from the sea)[17] prototype survives in various forms, large scale and

[14] The Tyrannicides is a group of two sculptures of Harmodios and Aristogeiton, originally by Antenor. The group is so-called because Harmodios and Aristogeiton assassinated the Athenian tyrant Hipparchus 514BC and it originally stood in the Athenian Agora at the end of the sixth century BC, see Boardman 1992:24-25, fig. 3, is the copy from Hadrian's Villa Tivoli. The Tyrannicides have been considered as among examples marking the turning point from Archaic to Classical style (Robertson 1991: 50-53).

[15] See Boardman 1992: 80, fig 60.

[16] See Smith 1995:128, fig 148.

[17] This is, presumably, because of the traditions concerning the genealogy and birth of the goddess.

There are two major myths concerning the genealogy of Aphrodite. According to Hesiod (*Theogony*, 188-200), Kronos, son of Earth (mother) and Heaven (father) indirectly caused the birth of Aphrodite by cutting off his fathers genitals in an act of revenge.

> He harvested his father's genitals
> And threw them off behind. They did not fall
> From his hands in vain...The genitals, cut off
> with adamant
> And thrown from land into the stormy sea,
> Were carried for a long time on the waves.
> White foam surrounded the immortal flesh,
> And in it grew a girl. At first it touched
> On holy Cythera, from there it came from
> To Cyprus, circled by the waves. And there,

small, but all sharing the same motif of arms elevated to the hair. There are numerous examples surviving from Roman Britain, most of which are figurines. It has been suggested that a painting inspired this prototype. The work was by Apelles of Cos, renowned painter of Alexander the Great. His Aphrodite 'rising from the sea' had a canonical status comparable to the Cnidia (Smith 1995: 81). The same woman, Phryne (alleged mistress of Praxiteles) was the model for Apelles' painting and the Cnidia, according to Athenaios,

> [Phryne, Praxiteles' mistress] in the festival of the Eleusians and in the festival of Poseidon took off her robes in view of all the Greeks, unbound her hair and went into the sea. It was with her as a model that Apelles painted his Aphrodite Anadyomene [rising from the sea]. And Praxiteles the sculptor, falling in love with her, made his Cnidian Aphrodite with her as the model (Athenaios 13.590, taken from Pollitt 1990:86).

According to Pliny, some authorities believed the model to be Pancaste, one of Alexander's mistresses whom he had Apelles paint, 'when Alexander realised that Apelles had fallen in love with his subject, he gave Pancaste to the artist (Pliny *Natural History*: 35.86-87, Healy 1991:332). He also refers to the Aphrodite Anadyomene,

> His [Apelles] Aphrodite rising from the Sea, which is called Anadyomene, was dedicated by Augustus in the shrine of his father [Julius] Caesar ... The lower part of it was damaged, and it was impossible to find anyone who could restore it; thus the injury itself contributed to the fame of the artist (Pliny Natural History 35.9, taken from Pollitt 1990: 161).

Furthermore, the painting had decayed by the time of Nero and was replaced with a painting by Dorotheos (Pliny, *Natural History*, 35.79-97). We owe to Pliny our awareness that the painting was still a desirable artefact at the time of Augustus. Furthermore, it shows that it had sufficient importance to be offered to the deified Caesar. On the other hand it is useful for propaganda, as it demonstrates the importance attributed by Augustus to the deified Caesar if an artefact of this significance could be dedicated to him. Perhaps the intention was to encourage the veneration of his adoptive father, which in turn would ultimately benefit himself. Additionally there is the reiteration of goddess as ancestress of the Julian family, conjuring a variety of implications, and possibly including her aesthetic reputation as a Julian trait.

There are a number of opinions relating to what Venus is actually doing with her hair, Smith suggests that she is binding her hair (Smith 1995: 81), Robertson proposes that she is squeezing the water out of her hair (Robertson 1991:180), and Clark curiously states that she is putting on a necklace (Clark 1956:85). Essentially it depends on the individual representation, however as she is rising from the sea, it would seem natural that she would be wringing the water out of her hair. At this point, I will consider examples form Roman Britain as the overall study has particular preference to this period of Roman history.

As mentioned above, there are several examples from Britain (see Lindgren 1980:81-83), bronze figurines all below 10cm in height. They differ slightly, but follow the 'Anadyomene' prototype. All the examples are of a size that allows them to be portable, allowing for mobile/portable shrines. This also allows the nude representation to be handled and touched. The foremost similarity is that all have their arms raised, assisting the viewer to have a full view of the body. The fact that she touches her hair is significant; it draws attention to her femininity and difference as her long, loose (in parts) hair opposes that of orderly, short masculine hair. Furthermore, loose hair suggests undress with its sexual connotations, rather than the controlled, tied hair of regularity and the married state (Bartman 2001:1-25).

Long, loose hair is a specific feature of Venus as opposed to other female deities such as Diana (see Chapter 3) and Minerva (see Chapter 4). Additional features, as we have already encountered, relate to the traditions surrounding her birth from the sea, which generally explains the inclusion of sea/water related objects, (for example water urns) or sea creatures, (such as dolphins). Other traits include fallen drapery, (as she is undressing or dressing), and a specific pose where she bent over putting on or taking off her sandal. A fragment of a commemorative slab from the Antonine Wall, Scotland shows what remains of a triumphal arch supported by spiralled columns and topped with Corinthian capitals (fig. 1). The slab commemorates work carried out on the wall by the Sixth Legion (Keppie 1984: 34-35). What remains may offer us an idea of the overall composition. A cupid supports the centrepiece of a victory wreath that holds the inscription (we can presume that this was the case on the other half of the slab). The occupant of the left panel is open to question, perhaps Mars as there is a link with the goddess. Venus is contained within two columns. Above her is what appears to be a large bird landing on the lintel, possibly the imperial eagle. Here the presentation of Venus is extraordinary. Her identification is confirmed by her pose, as in the examples mentioned above she touches her hair and holds drapery, creating the impression of putting it on or taking it off. It is a bathing context. What is extraordinary about this representation is the way the artisan chose to construct Venus, paying particular attention to the display of her nude body. This

---

The goddess came forth, lovely, much revered,
And grass grew beneath her delicate feet.
Her name is Aphrodite among men
And gods, because she grew up in the foam.
Hesiod *Theogony 178-208*, Wender: 1973: 29

Other myths, name Aphrodite's' father as Zeus and her mother as Dione (daughter of Oceanus and Tethys the sea nymph), placing her purposefully within the Olympian pantheon, (Apollodorus, *Library* 1.1.3; Homer, *Odyssey*, 289-356).

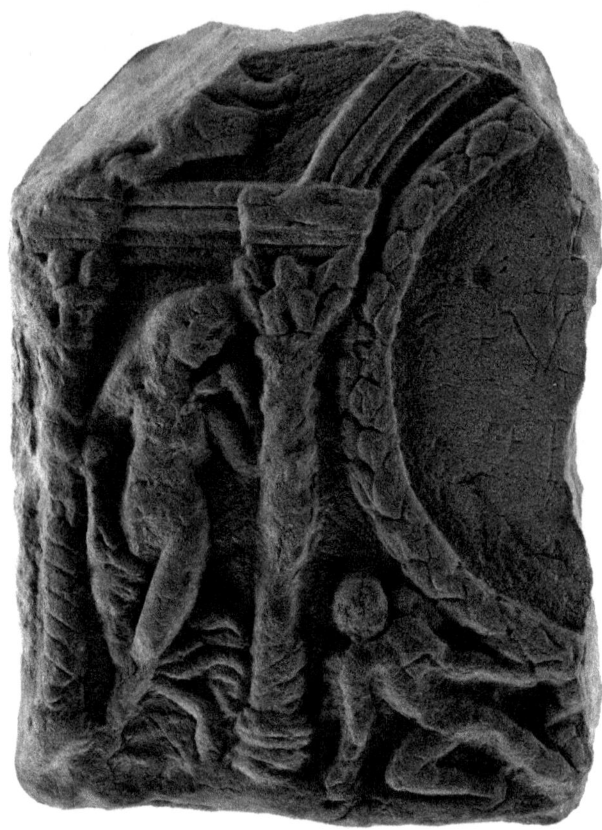

Fig. 1. Venus and Cupid, fragment of a commemorative slab, National Museum of Antiquities Scotland, Edinburgh, Antonine date. © Trustees of the National Museums of Scotland.

was achieved by the precise way she holds the cloth in her right hand as it drops between her thighs, with folds in the fabric indicative of flowing movement to the floor, whether she is drying her legs, or about to put the cloth around her, the outcome is the same. The position of the drapery, like the so-called *pudica* posture, draws attention to the genital region. However, this representation does not attempt to hide the area, in effect it stresses it. Additionally, it draws attention to her sexual availability as, 'nakedness is the most potent visual sign that a body is available for sexual encounter with another body' (McDonald 2001:7). A mosaic pavement, from Low Ham Villa in Somerset illustrates scenes from Virgil's Aeneid,[18] two of which include Venus (figs. 2, 3).

In the central scene, Venus is contained within an octagonal plait-pattern frame flanked by cupids holding torches. The artisan has illustrated Venus contrasting her pale, naked body against a dark coloured cloth, which she holds above her shoulders with the cloth reaching to her ankles. Reminiscent of the Venus Anadyomene, she has her arms raised giving full view of her body. Venus stands between Dido (who is semi-draped) Cupid-Ascanius and Aeneas. Venus is nude apart from a diadem, necklace, armlets and what Toynbee described as a 'fourfold breast and back chain' with a large, oval jewel that separates the area between the breast and belly (then reaching around to the back) (Toynbee 1962:204). The chain carves up her upper body into sections. Although the chain is a piece of decorative jewellery, its appearance is ominous. It is almost like a harness or a yoke with which to control her. Johns describes the Hoxne body-chain (a gold chain from the Hoxne treasure) as 'a kind of gold harness' (Johns 1996:96). Furthermore, it appears to be the only thing worn on her body underscoring her definitive nudity. Beside her, Dido is semi-draped. It appears that the two female bodies are objects to be decorated with jewellery or drapery, which is in direct opposition to Cupid-Ascanius and Aeneas who are fully clothed (fig. 3). There appears to be a deliberate juxtaposition of naked (or semi-draped), light-skinned, female characters alongside clothed, darker skinned males. Possibly this derives from the concept that men controlled the outside domain, whilst women of high status were inside away from the sun and the patriarchal arena.

Crouching Venus

A relief from High Rochester depicts Venus with her two other naked females in attendance at her bath (Museum of Antiquities of the University of Newcastle upon Tyne and of the Society of Antiquaries, Newcastle Upon Tyne). The relief most probably embellished the water tank within which it was discovered in 1852 (Phillips 1977: 75). The central figure is reminiscent of the Crouching 'Venus' by Doedalsas of Bithynia (Hellenistic period), (Phillips 1977: 75, fig 218; Smith 1995: 80-81) for example a statuette from Rhodes (Archaeological Museum, Rhodes, Beard and Henderson 2001: 128, fig 90) the subject crouches in the same manner as in the High Rochester relief and has her hands to her hair. A marble sculpture of crouching Venus, from Rome (2nd AD, now in the British Museum, fig. 4) also shows the goddess in this pose. The general theme is that of the goddess crouching, busily washing or wringing out her hair. She appears to be unconscious of the viewer's presence, which automatically turns the viewer into the voyeur. Her posture, crouched over and distracted, suggests she is not vigilant. She therefore appears defenceless and vulnerable. The sculptor appears to have chosen to show the female form in a vulnerable, weak position, in need of protection. This unquestionably applies to the High Rochester relief, but in this relief more bodies are on display. There is a hierarchical element within this scene. Venus has the centrepiece and her high status accentuated by her position and her size. On either side nude figures attend to the goddess as she bathes. They are not bathing themselves so why are they nude? Granted they are in an environment to get wet, but that does not warrant their total nudity. It has been suggested that these figures are nymphs (Phillips 1977: 75). This would explain their nudity, as they were generally depicted nude. However, I would suggest that they are nude for no other reason that to offer an extra display of the female nude.

[18] For a full account and interpretation of the scenes see Toynbee 1962: 203-205, Scott 2000: 124, Henig 1995: 120.

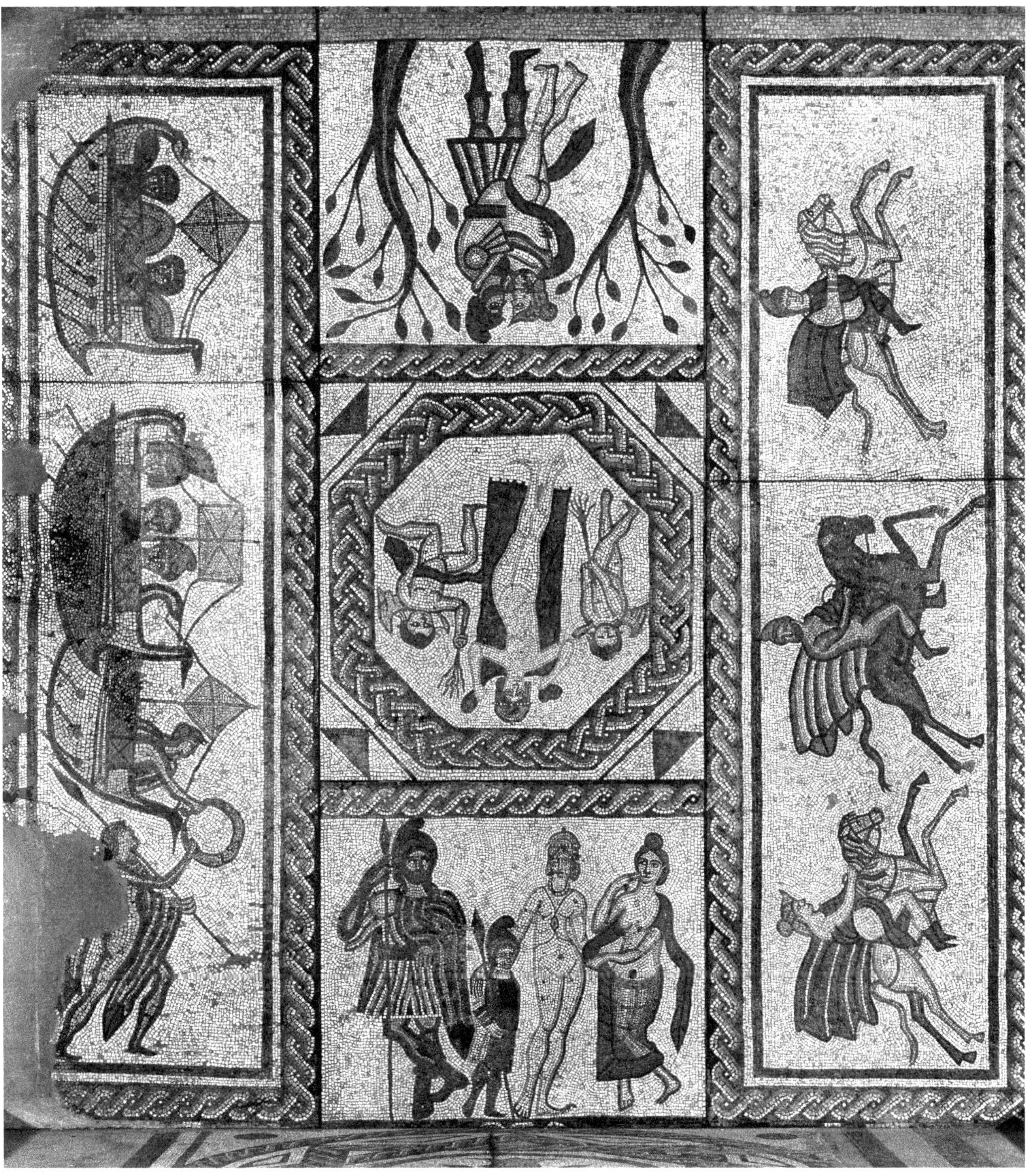

Fig. 2. Scenes from Virgil's Aeneid, Low Ham Villa, Somerset, Fourth century AD, Castle Museum, Taunton. Permission granted by Somerset County Council Heritage Service.

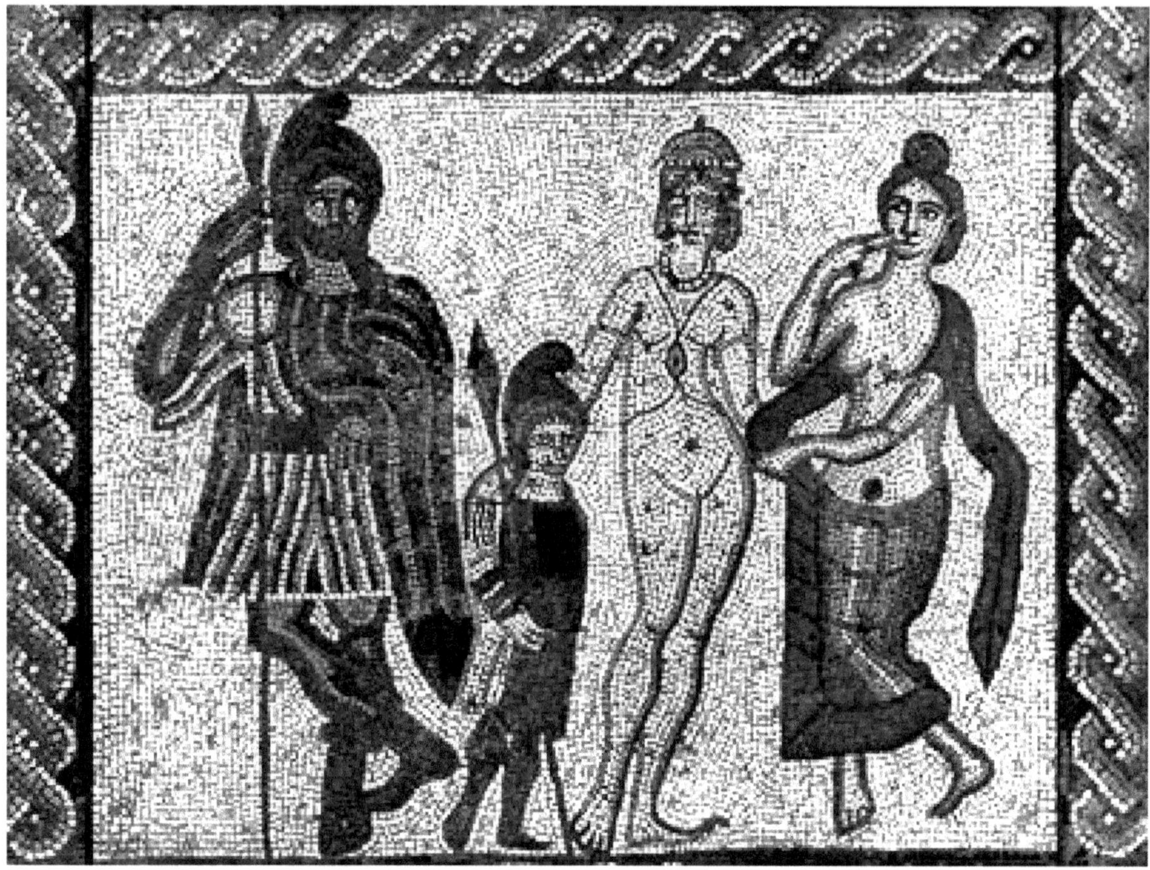

Fig. 3. Detail from the Low Ham Villa, Somerset, Castle Museum, Taunton.
Permission granted by Somerset County Council Heritage Service.

Venus in Sandals

A silver hairpin (12.6cm overall figure 2.5cm) found in the City of London has a small representation of Venus leaning on a pillar while she attends to her sandal. She stands on a Corinthian capital (Lindgren 1980: 85, Johns 1996: 140) fig 5. The choice of figure and pose is notable as it depicts Venus, goddess of love and desire, removing (or putting) on her sandal. However, the fact that it is a functional object must not be disregarded. The thin shaft enters and supports the hair, whilst the wider end (or figured end in this case) protrudes allowing the pin to be removed. I would propose therefore, that the choice of theme was made due to the practical effectiveness of the width and size of the subject and perhaps the suitability of Venus as the goddess of beauty. As this particular Venus type is wide, it is less likely to slip through the hair. Bartman (in her work on 'hair and the artifice of female adornment') draws attention to how hairstyles and ornamentation ultimately contribute to the construction of passive femininity. Hairpins, snoods and hairnets would keep women's hair firmly in place and thus denied any movement, which was feasible for men's hair (Bartman 2001:3). Venus as depicted on this hairpin then becomes an aid to controlled appearance whilst simultaneously advertising the status and wealth of the owner. It may reflect the patron's taste for classical motifs, as this Venus pose type is a known prototype referred to by Beard and Henderson as the 'Venus in bikini' category (for example a Venus from the House of Julia Felix, Pompeii, Beard and Henderson 2001: 115). It is both an effective physical size that displays the association of Venus.

Venus Genetrix and other titles

In the majority of representations of Venus, as the 'mother of Rome' (Venus Genetrix), she is depicted in full-length garments occasionally with her drapery slipping away to reveal a breast. The exposed breast evokes her associations with fertility, nourishment and erotic love (Cohen 1997:79; D'Ambra 2000:110). A statue from Ostia portrays a Roman matron as Venus Genetrix from the second century AD (D'Ambra 2000:107.fig.6.3). The figure is fully draped, but the material is sheer and clings to the body emphasising nudity beneath. This use of drapery (as mentioned above) is as voyeuristic and suggestive as representations of Venus with a breast revealed. In such examples the material works to frame her breast, thus drawing the viewer's attention. This type of representation was utilised by the neo-Attic sculptor, Arkesilaos, on the Venus Genetrix from the temple of Venus in Julius Caesar's forum. This rendition was copied repeatedly,

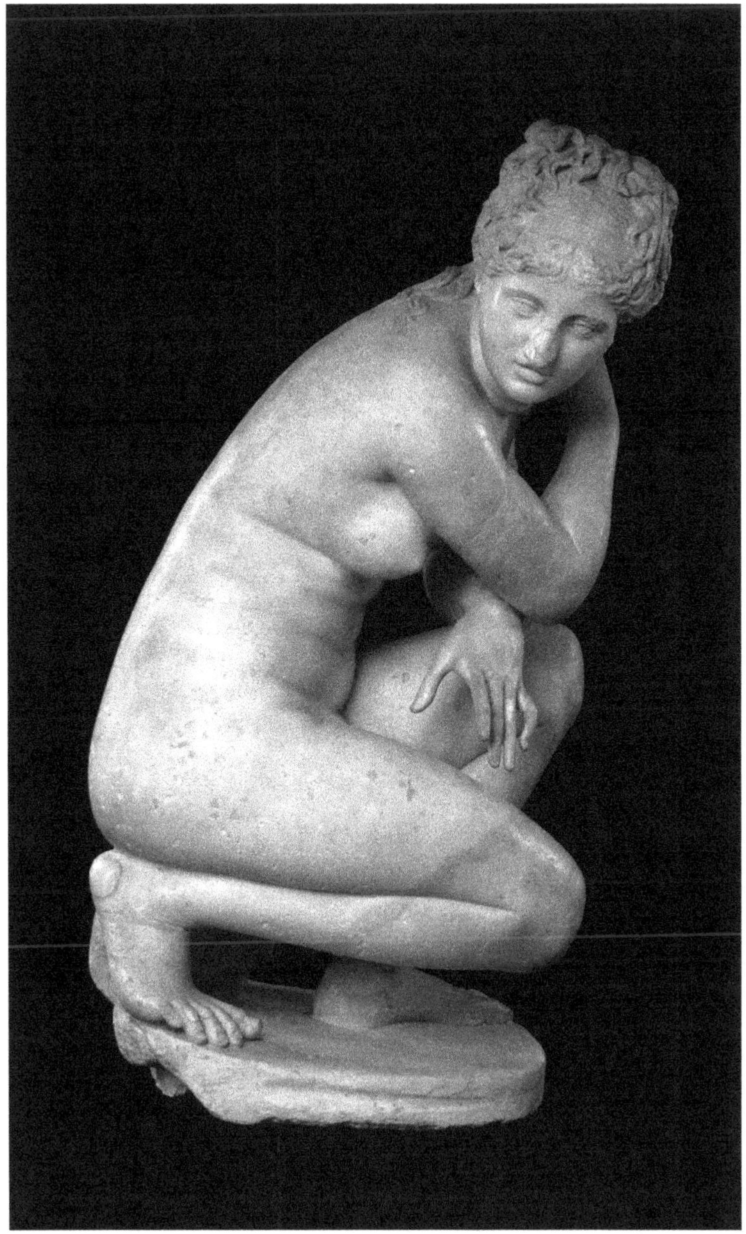

Fig. 4. Marble statue of Venus crouching at her bath. Roman 2nd AD, British Museum, London. © Trustees of the British Museum.

some with a reversed pose or with a slight variation, such as the copies now in the Louvre and Holkham Hall, Norfolk (Haward 1999: 22-23. fig 22 and 23). The Louvre version confronts the viewer offering them a piece of fruit. Nude or semi-nude women handled depicted with fruit (or in this case offering it) have overt sexual meanings. According to Parker and Pollock, women and fruit are juxtaposed, thereby confirming women's association with nature and fecundity, and thus perhaps confirming male dominance as male culture over nature. Furthermore, it signifies sexual availability for the gratification of men's needs and desires (Parker and Pollock 1981:119).

The Verulamium bronze Venus figurine was constructed in the same manner (Toynbee 1964: 83-84; Henig 1995:76). In this particular example the goddess has drapery wrapped around her hips. The material is knotted centrally at the front. However the cloth does not totally cover her pubic area thereby revealing a suggestive outline that runs parallel with the cloth, mirroring, but enlarging the shape and exaggerating the pudendum. Around the back of the figurine, the cloth rests on her lower back revealing the beginnings of her buttocks. Overall, the image is overtly sexual, objectifying her body. Moreover, because of its size (20.5cm), the figurine cannot only be moved, but it can also be handled. Therefore, her femininity was presented as an object that operated through the visual and the tactile. Furthermore, the sculpture appears to be based on a Greek Hellenistic archetype (for example a late Greek Hellenistic, from Rhodes, Vatican Museum in Bieber 1967: 144, fig. 610), perhaps reflecting retrospective tastes (Toynbee 1962: 136-137). The statue at Holkham Hall does not face the

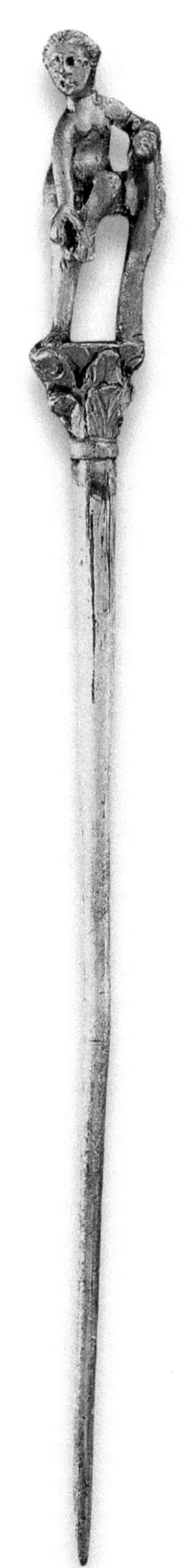

Fig. 5. Silver hairpin showing figure of Venus, British Museum, London. © Trustees of the British Museum.

viewer, but looks away, a gesture that is in itself submissive. In her left arm she holds an upturned jug as if pouring a libation. The movement of the head and the left arm differ, but the stance and raised right arm (holding drapery to her shoulder) are identical. The raised arm draws attention below to her right breast in the same way as slipped drapery attracts attention to the left. Her arm and fallen drapery act as frames, which in turn create boundaries that suggest control of the femininity embodied. The body is 'framed' and located within formal limitations and therefore the representation is itself a performance of regulation (Nead 1992:9).

As Venus Victrix, she presides over the fortunes of the army. A nicolo gem from the Fortress Baths at Caerleon (18.5mm) depicts a semi-draped Venus holding the palm branch of peace and a helmet (Henig 1979: 197; Zienkiewicz 1987:21). In this example, we have a tangle of political connotations. She represents victory for Rome whilst embodying an allegiance to the Julian family (Beard and Henderson 2001:168). Venus became a useful figurehead for individual cults promoting updated Augustan laws encouraging marriage and child rearing. The cult of Venus Verticordia (protector of female virtue) guided women of every status towards marriage and motherhood introducing activities that included the ritual dressing of the cult statue, ablutions and anointment of worshippers and ritual bathing (Fraschetti 2001:44; D'Ambra 2000:102). This is interesting considering the connections Venus has with water. Her birth from the sea consequently lead to the numerous Venus archetypal representations depicting her in connection with water and bathing. The cult of Venus Obsequens (from *obsequor* meaning obedience, compliance) required adulterous wives to make amends for their infidelity (D'Ambra 2000:102). This is the disparity between Aphrodite and Venus, as D'Ambra points out: 'imperial propaganda and cult ritual transformed the seductress Aphrodite of the Greeks into the matronly Venus of the Romans, so the erotic power of statues is domesticated into the sexuality of the marriage bed' (D'Ambra 2000:102). It appears then that it, in some cases, was acceptable for Roman matrons to have themselves depicted as Venus for funerary monuments or honorific statues.

A portrait of a woman as Venus (AD100-120), now in the Museo Capitolino, Rome was found in a funerary context along the Via Appia in Rome (Museo Capitolino, Rome, D'Ambra 2000.fig.6.2). This type of sculpture involved a portrait head sporting a Flavian hairstyle and a Venus body. This example follows a 'Venus of Capua' type (Smith 1995:81.fig 105). The figure has her weight on her right leg with her left propped up on a helmet. Her right arm rests on her hip, whilst in her left hand she holds a section of drapery (D'Ambra 2000:105). The idealised body is nude but for drapery that has fallen to the top of the thighs. Her genitalia are covered to some extent by an arrangement of material supported by her raised leg. The material, whilst giving the impression of covering her, in effect serves to accentuate that particular area. According to Parker and Pollock, the female nude signifies an unconscious male fear of sexual difference, therefore the hidden/omission of her genitalia hides/omits her very femaleness (1981:126). Salomon proposes that nude representations of Aphrodite/Venus self-consciously covering her pubis (such as Praxiteles' prototype the Cnidian Aphrodite, Capitoline Venus or the Medici Aphrodite) show her to be degraded to her very sexuality, thus she/Woman is exposed and vulnerable and therefore contained (Salomon, 1996:72-77.fig.5.1). In addition, the sculpture has a highly ornate hairpiece. I would suggest that this enables the viewer to recognise that the sculpture does not represent 'divine' Venus, but a woman portrayed as Venus. Similarly, a sculpture in the Museo Nazionale Archeologico, Naples, illustrates a Roman matron as Venus (130-140AD). This is a Capitoline Venus type, which represents the goddess, interrupted whilst bathing (Smith 1995: fig 99; D'Ambra 2000.fig.6.1). Again, the portrait head makes it possible to recognise the sculpture for what it is a portrait of a matron as Venus. The sculptures, perhaps, represented the productive sexuality of matrons (D'Ambra 2000:102).

There were many portrayals of Venus, and it is clear that their context, associations and use are a complex subject. The way images of Venus have been utilised for various purposes makes the subject a particularly interesting one. Furthermore it is apparent that there is still work to be done this on subject. At this point, it is appropriate to embark on the second part of this chapter and examine visual communication associated with the god of war, Mars.

Mars

It is thought that Mars may have originally been an agricultural fertility deity (Beard et al 1998: 15). Though a war god his agricultural role did not disappear all together as Cato mentions that Mars was invoked to ward off calamity, disease and infertility (Cato De Agricultura 141), (Beard et al 1998: 15; Lindgren 1980: 100). Mars was part of an archaic triad along with Jupiter and Quirinus. King Numa was believed to have established roles for priests dedicated to the deities thus suggesting a major triad that was in due course displaced by the Capitoline triad, Jupiter, Juno and Minerva (Beard et al 1998:5-6, 43). To begin my study of Mars, I have chosen to start by examining a sculptural example from Rome. This colossal statue, created under the Flavian dynasty, was thought either to have been a companion for the statue of Minerva, which was housed within the Temple of Minerva, in the Forum of Nerva (where the Mars sculpture was discovered) or a replacement for the cult statue from the Temple of Mars Ultor, Forum of Augustus (c.90AD, Museo Capitolino, Rome, Kleiner 1992: 181). His Corinthian helmet has a central plume that protrudes from a sphinx and is flanked by images of Pegasus. This appears to be an intentional retrospective choice of a classical motif as this helmet is reminiscent of that represented on copies of the Athena Parthenos, by Pheidias (Boardman, 1992 fig 97, 102, 103). Furthermore, on the breastplate he wears an apotropaic Medusa head, usually associated with Minerva or again perhaps referring to copies of Athena Parthenos. The common connections are that both deities are patrons of warfare. The cuirass he sports is decorated with griffins and floral-like ornamentation. This is also a feature of his double row of embossed scallop hems. Augustus primarily adopted this array of motifs inspired by Greek models, therefore looking back to a 'golden age' that was, itself, a product of propaganda and visual messages of fertility and opulence (Zanker 1988: 179-183). As Zanker points out, 'grapes, figs, and palmettes all growing out of acanthus branches; ivy and laurel spiralling between heavy volutes; garlands bearing all manner of fruit; all this was meant to characterise the new age as paradise on earth' (Zanker 1988: 181).

This work is comparable with a full-length portrait sculpture of Titus found in Herculaneum (Museo Nazionale, Naples). The overall pose and cuirass motif selection appear to adopt corresponding methods of construction. As mentioned, the sculpture of Titus was found in Herculaneum and therefore pre-dates the eruption of 79 AD. As he was made emperor earlier that year (June) this work may be among the first exhibiting the new leader, if not when he was co-regent (Kleiner 1992:173). Titus was a successful military commander and this sculpture portrays him in victory parade military regalia. The adaptation of Julio-Claudian motifs, the griffins and candelabrum, perhaps reveals dynastic aspirations. The cult statue of Mars similarly celebrates his military prowess as god of war. A bronze figurine from Earith, Huntingdonshire appears to follow this same visual formula as the above sculpture (fig. 6). I am not suggesting that the bronze figurine is in anyway connected with the marble sculptures discussed above, but the similarities are worth noting, particularly the full beard, gorgoneion and the floral-like decoration on the breastplate, and double row of embossed scallop hems. This example, though a fraction of the size of the Flavian Mars, has the same visual signs that place him within the boundaries of masculinity required for a god of war.

Hypermasculinity and Mars

The cult statue, in particular, presents the deity as the epitome of visual hypermasculinity (Neimark 1994: 34–35; Klein 1990: 130), but what does this suggest? The term Hypermasculinity describes a masculinity that is overstated and exaggerated.[19] It is a term that has a variety of implications depending on those who employ it. Klein employs the term when considering bodybuilding subculture and defines the term, 'hypermasculinity: overly muscled bodies, boastfulness, swaggering independence, and worship of power' (Klein 1990: 130). He concludes that bodybuilding acts as a performance reiterating embellished, constructed masculinities. 'Bodybuilding's exaggeration of form can be interpreted as a cultural reaffirmation of cartoon masculinity, the reduction of sex to caricatures (e.g., Rambo or Barbie and Ken dolls)' (Klein 1990:139).

[19] The example of *Lara Crof)* could be described as a visual example of hyperfemininity, with her contrived exaggerated physical form.

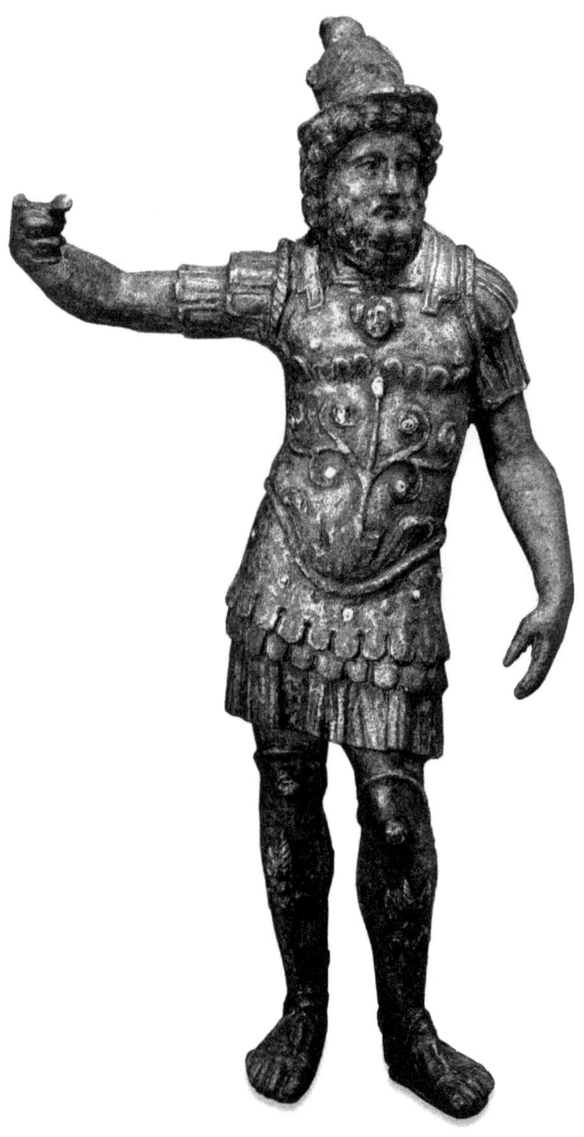

Fig. 6. Bronze Mars figurine from, Earith, Cambridgeshire second half 2nd or early 3rd century AD.
British Museum, London. © Trustees of the British Museum.

Several queer theorists use the term to describe a genre of representation where masculinity is exaggerated in reaction to stereotypical preconceptions that gay men are over feminine. This was an element in gay liberation politics in the early 1970s (De Angelis 2001:133; Burston 1995:96-98). The artwork of Tom of Finland[20] (1920-1991) is a good illustration. Immense muscular, moustachioed, uniformed men could be seen as the precursors of the 'clones' of 1970s pop group The Village People, where each group member has a specific costume relating to traditional working class masculine roles, the construction worker, policeman and cowboy. In Film Studies the term is often associated with masculinity and violence, particularly with reference to action, gangster/mafia films and blaxploitation films (Gabbard 2001:21; White 2001:104; Baker and Vitullo 2001:221-222; Wiegman 1995:173-193). Furthermore, the term is attached to racial stereotypes, for example violent American-Italian men of gangster/mafia films, and hyper-sexual African-American men the 'mythologized black male rapist ...whose hypermasculization begets and nourishes the many cinematic trajectories of 'Shaft' and 'Superspade' (Wiegman 1995:175). Oppliger connects the subject with violence and spectacle in her work on hypermasculinity and American wrestling (Oppliger 2004). Wrestlers appear to embody behavioural role models for aggressive 'manliness' that is inclusive of an anti-feminine focus. As stated,

> 'males who stray from masculine ideals (i.e., adopt feminine characteristics) are severely punished and are marked by such labels such as 'sissy' and 'fag'. To avoid teasing and persecution, boys will often adopt hypermasculine characteristics ...The qualities of self reliance, emotional toughness, and aggressiveness are not only highly valued but are also emphasised as ways to avoid being considered feminine in anyway' (Oppliger 2004:58).

The media reinforces this with visual examples and reiterations of behaviour, which in this example pertains to professional wrestling. The relevance of the case in point is that hypermasculinity is a behaviour that is learnt and performed. For this section of the chapter, I draw on the above theories of hypermasculinity, the anti-feminine focus, violence and spectacle and use the term to think about visual representations of Mars and consider other figures such as Priapus, gladiators and Hercules as comparative subjects. Mars as a god of war embodies these principles. His full armour is a costume of spectacle and his godhead represents the violence of warfare a sphere that excludes women (as soldiers).

Williams employs the term to describe Priapus,[21] Roman god (protector of homes and gardens, and guardian deity of flocks of sheep and herds of goats) depicted with an outsized phallus, 'Priapus' popularity in Rome is suggestive ... he can be seen as something like the patron saint or mascot of Roman machismo and his vigorous exploits with women, boys, and men indiscriminately are clearly a mainstay of his hypermasculine identity' (Williams 1999: 18). His outsized phallus disproportionately imbalances his physical form and plainly accentuates his notorious reputation as an insatiable sexual predator (Shelton 1998: 369). His hyper-phallus unmistakably indicates his hypermasculinity. Hypermasculinity, however, does not continually parallel Roman conceptions of acceptable masculinity. Having an insatiable sexual appetite (as Priapus) infers that the subject has little control over his body and therefore an inability to govern others (Edwards 1997:68).

Male gladiators also appear to fit within the hypermasculine category. Paradoxically though, because they were slaves or criminals and not freeborn or free citizens, they were not considered as 'real' men.

[20] See Ramakers 2000

[21] For more on Priapus see Hooper 1999 and Richlin 1992.

Although some were professionals who fought for money, (particularly in the later Roman period) being part of a gladiatorial school presumably did not usually allow for personal liberty (Junkelmann 2000: 32-33). Exemplary instances of gladiatorial match results painted on walls at Pompeii reveal four combatants to be freedmen, who perhaps had begun their careers as slaves, were freed and then continued to fight in the arena (*CL 4.8055* and *8056*, Shelton 1998:352). Prisoners of war taken as slaves were perhaps the inspiration for various archetypes such as *Thraex* (Thracian) and *Hoplomachus* (based on the Greek Hoplite).[22] These conformed to racial caricatures, perhaps not by the actual gladiator, but rather by the types of costume/armour or equipment defining each particular gladiator type (Shelton 1998: 352). Furthermore, the costumes/armour and characters taken on by individuals were 'larger than life'and as with contemporary American wrestlers, this operated through violence and performance. Their set behaviour and appearance, methods of fighting and the stylised nature of gladiatorial combat itself all served to enhance the gladiatorial spectacle and also served to reiterate this hypermasculine identity. These characters were exotic, dangerous, marginal figures 'other' to their audience/viewers. Moreover, their body shape achieved by intensive training presumably enhanced this. The majority of gladiatorial armour allowed for the body to be on display,[23] particularly muscular the upper body and legs, presenting corporeal vulnerability and subsequently combining eroticism and violence as spectacle, a hypermasculine exposition. Hercules is perhaps the epitome of physical hypermasculinity - his super-human strength and performance being the causative factor. His exploits, particularly the Twelve Labours, necessitated outstanding might to overcome his adversaries, among these were an assortment of mythical beasts, outsized animals and an Amazon (Apollodorus *Library* 5.1-12). His heroic status is excelled by the 'otherness' of his opponents.

A dedication slab from High Rochester, along Hadrian's Wall (east of the north Tyne, University of Newcastle upon Tyne and of the Society of Antiquities of Newcastle upon Tyne) demonstrates could be interpreted as an explicit display of visual hypermasculinity (Phillips 1977:108, fig 297). I have chosen this relief because I believe the presentation of hypermasculine subjects could have acted as visual role models for the soldiers whilst advertising physical valour of their chosen divinities. The Twentieth Legion Valeria Victrix dedicated the slab (*RIB* 1284) and below the inscription (and between two stylised trees), is a striding boar, the emblem of the Twentieth Legion. Mars and Hercules, the god of war and a semi-divine character of superhuman strength, flank the inscription almost in a competition of hypermasculinity. In this particular example, Hercules takes the lead he is altogether a larger figure taller and wider consequently his masculinity becomes exaggerated. Although he lacks the military regalia of Mars he has facial hair and dons his familiar lion skin with its head draped over his shoulder. This pelt enhances the impression of his strength. He wears the skin as a trophy celebrating his ability to kill a lion with his bare hands (referring to the first Labour of Hercules the Nemean Lion, Apollodorus *Library* 2.5.1 and see Chapter 5, Minerva and Hercules). His arm is raised, but his left hand is missing. According Phillips he may have held a bowl containing the apples of the Hesperides referring to his eleventh Labour (Apollodorus *Library* 2.5.11).

In his right hand, he holds a large phallic club affirming his force. Cooper, when considering a photograph by Anthony Azziz and Sammy Cucher, in which a male nude with all traces of genitals and nipples removed, poses holding a baseball bat. According to Cooper, 'in the assertion of male power the baseball bat becomes a surrogate penis' (Cooper 2002:254, fig 234). I would suggest that this interpretation is applicable to the Hercules of the High Rochester relief. The amalgamation of the male nude Hercules, with an oversized club becomes an assertion of male power with the club acting as a phallus, reaffirming his potency and exaggerated masculinity. As Hercules displays his phallic club, Mars asserts his masculinity through his martial veneer and equipment, his spear and sword. Both these weapons cut and penetrate, therefore, Mars holds the power as penetrator. This marked a particular notion of correct masculinity in the sexual politics of Rome. To be a real man necessitated being in control of the physical body and guarding it against sexual violation, if this happened it would render him passive, and therefore not in control. Passivity was considered the natural state for women and slaves. Williams describes this as the 'prime directive of masculine sexual behaviour,' as he states, 'a Roman man who wished to retain his claim to full masculinity must always be thought to play the insertive role in penetrative acts, whether males or females; if he was thought to have sought the receptive role in such acts he forfeited his claim to masculinity and was liable to being mocked as effeminate' (Williams 1999: 125). Therefore, in this relief, Mars as a constructed figure naturally falls within the 'prime directive' of acceptable masculinity. It is interesting to note that he wears the familiar triple plumed helmet of the cult statue of Mars Ultor.

As demonstrated by Williams, though hypermasculinity is a modern theoretical subject, it is useful when considering Roman constructions of masculinity, and I would suggest that they work in the same way. In this particular chapter it is the caricature of a war god. His full beard, body armour and his well-defined musculature illustrate his constructed hypermasculinity. According to Montserrat, 'for the Romans, a man's facial and body hair had immense importance, symbolically placing him at the top of the ascending scale of body hierarchies concocted by the ancient medical writers who followed the lead of Aristotle's pupil Hippocrates' (Montserrat 2000: 154). A statue of Mars from Lanarkshire (Hunterian Museum, University of Glasgow) along the Antonine Wall has a

[22] A full description of these and other gladiator categories can be retrieved from Junkelmann 2000:31-74.

[23] For example the *Murmillo*, *Hoplomachus*, *Thraex* and *Provocator* see Junkelmann 2000:31-74.

particularly well-detailed curled beard (and remnants of curled hair), thus emphasising his maturity and status whilst displaying the Antonine preference for curled beards and hair (Kleiner 1992: 267-315). Furthermore, his apparent martial authority is in conjunction with traditional male values that endorse military leadership (Montserrat 2000:165). Therefore, his armour is an important aspect of the sculpture's interpretation.

A relief from Gloucester (City Museum and Art Gallery, Gloucester) displays a representation of Mars with the remnants of a triple plumed helmet. The inscription on this relief reads,

> *Deo Rom[u]lo | Gulioepius | donauit | Iuuentinus | fecit*
> 'To the god Romulus Gulioepius presented this, Juventinus made it'. (*RIB* 132)

Despite appearances, this relief is not dedicated to Mars, but to Romulus. According to Toynbee, illustrations of Romulus were always in the guise of Mars (Toynbee 1962: 152, fig 63, see Beard and Henderson 2002: 174, fig 122b). This is appropriate as son of the war god, but if there were no inscription, this example could be mistaken for a representation of Mars, although he is beardless. This brings the whole area of identification into question. Perhaps images traditionally interpreted as Mars, may really represent Romulus, or even a particular general? Without an inscription, it is difficult to pin an exact identification. However, it could be argued that identification is unnecessary as this representation may portray military warrior status shaped by social ideals creating a message that does not necessarily reflect a particular character but an essence of the warrior. Other examples from a different contexts may offer more clues, particularly if there are other definite representations of the deity, for instance an altar dedicated to Mars, Victory and the deities of the Emperors from Housesteads, Hadrian's Wall (*RIB* 1596). Further examples from Chesters Museum (Coulston and Phillips 1988, fig. 72) originate from the same area as the Mars altar at Housesteads (*Vercovicium*) and appear to follow the same visual formula. The context within which the sculptures were found is important to the interpretation. It is interesting to note that the majority of hypermasculine representations of Mars originate from a military context. Perhaps these images offered a role model to aspire too. Moreover, it offers a representation of the protecting deity and therefore advertises the strength of the Roman military. It is also interesting that these images were the outcome of a predominately male environment. Do these hypermasculine images, then, portray conceived notions of the acme masculinity? This does appear to be the case, as it is evident that Mars in the images discussed display a masculinity that was considered fitting for a god of war and an avenger of Julius Caesar. At this point, I would like to turn my attention to alternative images of Mars, a more youthful version that are generally depicted nude.

Mars as a Nude

Examples of Mars as a nude found in Roman Britain appear to hinge on the Ares Borghese (Roman copy of Greek original, attributed to Alkamenes, fifth century BC, Louvre, Paris) type as a model. By connecting these deities I am not suggesting the Greek and Roman gods are equivalent, but in a visual sense there may be connections loosely based on reproduced examples. Moreover, the work may offer a Greek construct of masculinity relating to the period from which the original was created. At the outset it is necessary to establish the visual construction of the said prototype, the Ares Borghese. The original Ares sculpture was apparently from a temple dedicated to the god on the Athenian Agora and usually taken as the sculpture by Alkamenes alluded to by Pausanias (*Guide to Greece* 1.8.5) (Robertson 1991:118, Boardman 1992: 228). Though Pausanias mentioned the sculpture, he does not describe it. The example in the Louvre then may be a perfect replica or an adaptation. However, as the focus of this study is Roman art, I shall concentrate on the Roman model and then the examples found in Britain. The sculpture portrays a nude male youth wearing only a close fitting Athenian helmet. The central helmet plume is missing along with the shield and spear that are familiar attributes associated with Mars as a god of war. Yet, this paradigm for illustrating Mars is very different from the examples discussed above. Clearly, his youth and nudity alter the interpretation connected with the cases in point. Becatti, in his wide-ranging study of Greek and Roman art described the sculpture as follows,

> The Louvre Ares, however, shows a new feeling, almost suffused with romanticism, in the curls falling over his temples, the richly engraved helmet, and the dreamy composure of the figure ... these are all features which suited the lover of Aphrodite rather than a god of war' (Becatti 1968:182).

I propose that Becatti misinterprets the sculpture. He assumes the work has a singularly heterosexual interpretation. What Becatti mistakes for romanticism and dreamy pose may have more to do with male-to-male homoerotic gaze (Bartman 2002: 249-271). I have several reasons for asserting this: his nudity, his youth and most importantly the way he looks away from the viewer, all these effects present a submissive pose. This construction of masculinity draws on the concept of the passive sexual partner. He follows a visual formula; his delicate facial hair, which unevenly covers the sides of his face, suggests first growth and demonstrates his youth. The fact that his beard is not totally developed curiously draws attention to his beardlessness. The epitome of physical desirability of an adolescent boy was the period before development of his first full beard and was referred to by ancient writers[24] such as Virgil as that period when the adolescent was blessed with the 'flower of youth' (Virgil, *Eclogues* 7.4) (Williams 1999: 73). As stated by Williams,

[24] See Williams 1999: 296 for a full list of ancient writers.

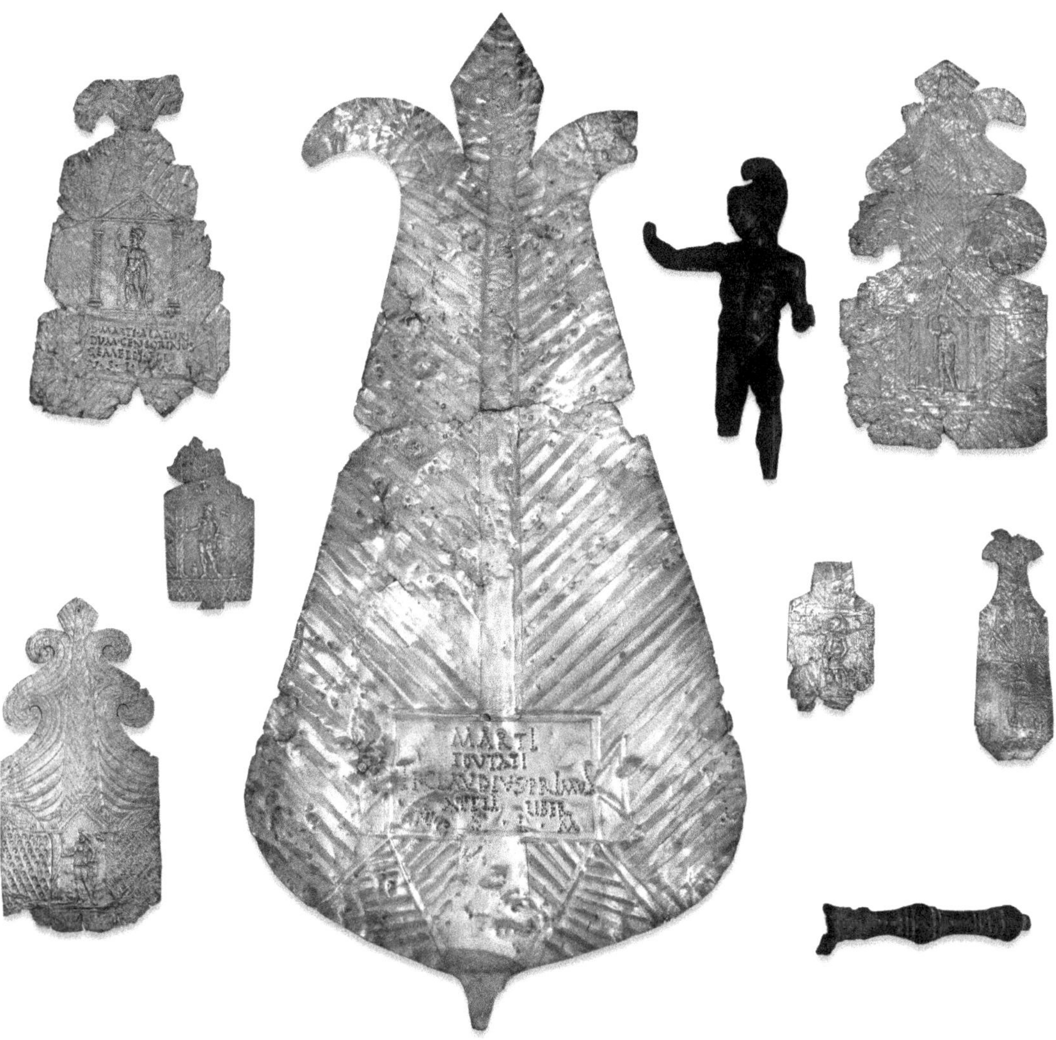

Fig. 7. The Barkway hoard, with figurine of Mars, British Museum, London. © Trustees of the British Museum

> 'for Romans, this period's beginning was marked by the onset of puberty (generally held to occur between the twelfth and fourteenth years and to be marked by the maturation of the genitals ... as well as by the appearance of a light down on the cheeks) and its end marked by ... the arrival of the full manly, beard (which is attested usually to have occurred somewhere around the twentieth year)' (Williams 1999: 19).

Evidently, this sculpture appears to illustrate a youth of this age group. Lucretius in his discussion on 'Sensation and Sex' included adolescent males in his debate,

> When a man is pierced by the shafts of Venus, whether they are launched by a lad with womanly limbs or a woman ... he strives towards the source of the wound and craves to be united with it and to transmit something of his own substance from body to body (Lucretius, *Nature of the Universe* 4.1078, Latham 1960:163).

It is interesting that he refers to boy's limbs as 'womanly', when he was referring, perhaps, to the visibly hairlessness of boys before full maturity. The nakedness of the sculpture also suggests corporeal vulnerability and signals sexual accessibility. Since he looks away from the viewer, the viewer automatically has an advantage over him. He is not in control, and the viewer is. Furthermore, as he does not see us looking at him we automatically become voyeurs. Ultimately, I consider that the Ares Borghese as a Roman sculpture is primarily an object of desire and consequently a contradictory example compared to Mars the Avenger.

Two examples from Britain show Mars as a nude and appear to follow a variation of the Ares Borghese type. One is a bronze figure found among the Barkway hoard (fig. 7) from Hertfordshire, alongside ornate votive plaques some of which have representations of Mars, one has an additional inscription and dedication to Mars (Beard et al 1998: 56, RIB 218).[25] The figure sports a

[25] The plaque in question has an image of Mars depicted within an architectural setting beneath a pediment and columns, the inscription

similar close fitting Athenian military helmet. This example has particularly well-defined musculature given emphasis by a baldric, which passes over his right shoulder and across to the left reaching his waist. Clearly, it is problematic to compare a full size marble statue with a bronze figurine, particularly as dating is a problem[26] and there are notable differences. The movement of the right arm is different in a more open gesture than the Borghese. Davies in her study on gender and body language in Roman art discusses 'open' and 'closed' body language gestures and considers how this can be useful contemporary Roman concepts regarding gender (Davies 1997: 97-107). According to Davies 'open' and 'closed' poses are suggestive of attitude and outlook. As she states, 'poses that stress width and are open suggest dominance and superior status ... they to the interpretation of art and an understanding of give the impression of someone who has no need to be defensive. Closed poses, with limbs held across or close in to the body, suggest the opposite: defensiveness (because the figure is trying to protect itself), lack of confidence, a closed mind, literally shutting off others' (Davies 1997: 101). It is essential to bear in mind that representations of people are just that 'representations', composed fabrications based on what the patron or artist would like the viewer to see in the end product. Therefore, Davies' theory on body language is useful when considering constructed representations of people. The bronze figurines from the British Museum certainly display open poses. The Barkway Mars however, displays aspects of both, hehas an open pose, but he looks away from the viewer in a defensive manner. This presents a grey area in Davies' theory, but I do consider the model valuable, particularly in the case of the Ares Borghese. His 'closed' pose emphasises his youth and vulnerability.

The second example is a bronze Mars figurine from Foss Dyke, Lincolnshire (British Museum, Toynbee 1962, fig.19), and it presents a unique occasion where, not only are the patrons and the artisan named, but it also gives the amount of money used. The inscription tells us that the Colasuni, Bruccius and Caratius dedicated it at their own expense at a hundred sesterces and the coppersmith Celatus gave bronze at the cost of three denarii (*RIB* 274). The figurine has an open pose, his outstretched arm creating width suggestive of dominance and high-ranking status. Furthermore, his upturned head confidently looks ahead. Although the inscription gives us rare and valuable information, it would be remarkable to know why this version of Mars was chosen and not Mars in full military regalia? Perhaps the figurine informs that whoever chose nude Mars preferred to be linked with Hellenic tradition, or to promote themselves as having an understanding of Roman artistic culture.

beneath dedicated the plaque to Mars Alator Dum. 'To the god Mars Alator Dum(...) Censorinus, son of Gemellus, willingly and deservedly fulfilled his vow' (RIB 218). Collingwood and Wright suggest that the *Alator* title is a local name presumably meaning huntsman (Collingwood and Wright 1995:71, RIB 218). However, they are not clear on the meaning of *Dum*

[26] Lindgren dates the bronze figurine at late second to early century third century AD (Lindgren 1980: 108).

Conclusion

It is clear that representations of Venus and Mars have an extensive history in their own right. It is also important to remember the works of art illustrating deities whether sculpture, painting or mosaic, primarily depict constructions of gender that were relevant to the concepts associated with the subject. As demonstrated by the Athenaios and the Pseudo Lucian, the visual and sexual appeal of visual images was sometimes their primary attraction, the religious function being consequential. This, I suggest, was the case for nude portrayals such as the Venus of Cnidus and the Ares Borghese, the nude body first and then the religious significance. Representations of Venus semi-draped, draped in slipping cloth, or wet clothing, are equivalent to the nude and interpreted in the same way. This is also applicable to masculine examples. The subjects become the objectified focal point of voyeurism. Venus was cleverly utilised by the Julian family to promote their own political importance. Later Venus became more domesticated, as her cults were a contrivance controlling women through the endorsement of marriage, motherhood and the atonement for adulterous wives via such cults as those of Venus Verticordia and Venus Obsequens. I think this is apparent when analysing the various Venus 'types' comparing the Roman copies of nude Aphrodite to the tamed sexuality of the domesticated Venus Genetrix types. Images of Mars are contradictory too. On the one hand he was portrayed as the hypermasculine, penetrator and martial war god, whilst on the other hand he was represented as the complete opposite, as a passive and vulnerable adolescent. I think the choice of representation depended on what the artist or patron wanted to portray. The cult statue of Mars, for example, draws on the idea of the god as avenger of the death of Julius Caesar and for this they chose a hypermasculine representation. The Roman adaptation of Ares in the Borghese Gallery then draws on Hellenic inspirations and the connotations this carries with it. It is clear that the subject areas are vast, particularly that of Venus and the importance placed on the goddess as an icon within the history of art.

Venus' femininity appears to depend upon the artistic inspiration and preference of the sculpture type. For example, if this is Hellenistic then this includes young nubile bodies nude or semi-draped, whilst Venus Genetrix types have a different meaning drawing on matronly sexuality and the connotations associated with that. The next chapter centres on the construction of gender for twin deities Diana and Apollo. Diana is generally a youthful subject, yet her femininity is different from that of youthful Venus for a number of reasons that will be discussed in the following chapter. Mars and Apollo are just as dissimilar in their specific masculinity types, particularly when Mars was depicted as a mature, martial figure. However, as evidenced above, this was not the only portrayal for the god of war. Alternative examples reveal him as a youthful nude comparable to Apollo.

Chapter 3

Diana and Apollo: Readings of Gender and Twinship

The aim of this chapter as the title implies, is to consider the visual construction of gender for twin deities, Diana and Apollo. I examine representations of Apollo and Diana and consider individual treatment of each piece and the implications associated with them as subjects, together and in their own right. I am interested in the way the subjects were depicted and how references to their individual personas reflect in their visual construction. A study concerning twinship follows, focusing on its bearing on the subjects and how this was perceived in the classical world.

Diana was the goddess of the hunt, the moon, a protector of those in childbirth, of small children, young animals and she was guardian of woodlands, harbours and roads. A sculpture referred to as Diana of Versailles, a Roman copy of a work attributed to Leochares (Louvre) offers an archetypal visual introduction to the form and identification of the deity. Her appearance resembles that of an Amazon, dressed in a short tunic (but with both breasts covered) with a bow, quiver and arrows. As in the above example, Diana commonly appears with her hunting dogs and/or her prey. Apollo has a number of godheads other than as twin hunter god; among them is his prophetic authority, his connections with medicine as the father of Aesculapius and his celebrated roles as the god of poetry, music and the sun. The Apollo Belvedere is a particularly celebrated illustration of the god (Vatican Museum). I have chosen this work as an opening piece as some believe it to be the counterpart to the Diana of Versailles (Bieber 1967:63). Representations of Apollo generally portray a youthful nude with long hair often presented with a number of items including his bow, a lyre, a fawn and laurel leaves. Fundamentally, the Apollo Belvedere offers a straightforward example of Apollo; he is young with long tresses and nude (with the exception of his cloak, which draws attention to his form), but his strong confident pose is atypical. As we shall see below, more common examples of Apollo appear to be less confident, the youths depicted appear uncertain and looking down or away from the viewer. As this study draws on the history of Roman art as well as that from Roman Britain, it is necessary to start by mentioning the importance placed on Apollo (and as a result also on Diana) by Octavian during his struggle for sole control of the empire. This particularly applies to the period of hostilities towards Mark Antony and Cleopatra (Zanker 1988: 33-77; Kleiner 1992:46-47; Miller 1994: 101; Kampen 1996a: 236.).

Octavian and Mark Antony: Patron deities and propaganda

After the death of Julius Caesar in 44 BC, conflict for control and ultimately sole power continued for another thirteen years. In this turbulent period visual images, especially visual communication through coins, played a significant role in this contest and this was particularly clear between Octavian and Mark Antony (Zanker 1988: 33-77; Kleiner 1992a: 364-365; Miller 1994: 101; Kampen 1996a: 236). Both made use of divine characters to further their cause; Octavian promoted Apollo and Mark Antony identified himself (among others) with Hercules and later Dionysus. The question is, why these particular personas? In the case of Octavian, it is significant to establish why and how Apollo was of use to his cause. Apollo personified contrary features that Octavian found valuable, for Apollo was both an incontrovertible god of retribution, smiting those who strayed further than the proper limits set for mortal ambitions (Homer *Iliad* 1.10, 1.33; Propertius 2.31.12-14), and a gentle god of refinement and culture, a solar god and as a healer god he had an image of restoration. Octavian then promoted the idea that he could heal Rome's ailments. Apollo, as a god of poetry, stood for intellectual dexterity and became the patron deity of poets and politicians at Rome, and for this purpose favoured over traditional Roman deities (Ahl 1994:113). Therefore, through association, Octavian emphasised his own intellectual prowess. Furthermore, because the cult of Apollo was not deeply rooted in Rome, he had little risk of affronting religious traditionalists. As stated by Ahl, 'the temptation to use the god must have been considerable precisely because Apollo was not a major cult deity at Rome and because his major shrines were defunct or dying. The ambitious politician was less likely to offend traditional religious scruples by annexing the Delphic god than by annexing, say, Jupiter or Mars' (Ahl 1994:117). Furthermore, Apollo stood for discipline and morality, aspects that suited Octavian in opposition to the excesses of Mark Antony and his divine patrons, among which were, Hercules and Dionysus. This was utilised by Octavian through visual images to transmit and remind people of his links with Apollo; Apolline imagery includes a snake, a tripod, a lyre and laurel branches (Zanker 1988: 42-53; Kellum 1993:77). However, he faced criticism form his enemies (Antony among them) for his use of Apollo. Suetonius recounted an alleged scandalous incident where at a private banquet known as 'The Feast of the Divine Twelve'; Octavian attended dressed as Apollo himself, the timing of the feast made matters worse as it was during a food shortage (Suetonius *Augustus* 70). An extract from an anonymous satire retold by Suetonius suggests the animosity of his critics,

Apollo's part was lewdly played
By impious Caesar; he
Made merry at a table laid
For gross debauchery
(Suetonius, *Augustus* 70, Graves 1957:89).

Additionally, the alleged taunts of the people following the feast use his adoption of Apollo against him.

Caesar is Apollo, true – but he's Apollo
of the Torments (Suetonius, *Augustus* 70,
Graves 1957:89).

Family ancestry also had an appropriate part in implanting the suggestion of his affiliation with Apollo. In this instance, it is not distant ancestral links, as with Julius Caesar and Venus, but immediate family. It was rumoured that Octavian was the son of Apollo; in the form of a snake, the god impregnated Atia, Octavian's mother (Zanker 1988: 50). As recounted by Suetonius in his particular sensationalist manner,

> Augustus's mother Atia, with certain married women friends, once attended a solemn midnight service at the Temple of Apollo, where she had her litter set down, and presently fell asleep as the others did. Suddenly a serpent glided up, entered her, and then slid away again. On wakening, she purified herself, as if after intimacy with her husband. An irremovable coloured mark in the shape of a serpent, which then appeared on her body, made her ashamed to visit the public baths any more; and the birth of Augustus nine months later suggested a divine paternity. Atia dreamed that her intestines were carried up to heaven and overhung all lands and sea; and Octavius, that the sun rose from between her thighs (Suetonius *Augustus 94*, Graves 1977:101).

Plutarch referred to a similar instance regarding the parentage of Alexander the Great, the god Ammon transformed himself into a snake impregnating Alexander's mother (Plutarch *Alexander* 3; Zanker 1988:50). If these rumours did circulate, then this helpful hearsay placed Octavian in a lucrative position, they promoted the idea that he had multiple divine ancestors (including Venus and Mars) and an exclusive parallel with Alexander the Great. To have such a link also infers shared characteristics, perhaps a suggestion of Octavian as the new Alexander. According to Suetonius, after the deaths of Mark Antony and Cleopatra 'he had the sarcophagus containing Alexander the Great's mummy removed from the Mausoleum at Alexandria and after a long look at its features, showed his veneration by crowning the head with a golden diadem and strewing flowers on the trunk' (Suetonius *Augustus* 18, Graves 1977: 60-61). Dio stated that Octavian actually touched him and as a result, a piece of his nose broke away (Cassius Dio *Reign of Augustus* 16). Furthermore, both shared a common factor, their youth. Alexander's premature death meant that he would be remembered, eternally youthful as Apollo, and Octavian was young in comparison to the more senior Mark Antony. Moreover, to have a god as one's father automatically incurred reverence, not to mention a god of Apollo's particular talents.

According to Kleiner, Octavian started using the image of Apollo and the projected Temple of Divus Julius on his coins of 37 and 36 BC (Kleiner 1992a: 362-363). Mark Antony, on the other hand, continued to promote his political status by exploiting his political marriage to Octavia, Octavian's sister, as evidenced on an aureus of 39BC. The coin depicts profile portrait busts of Mark Antony (obverse) and Octavia on the reverse (Kleiner 1992a: 362-363, fig.2). Further, into the decade (c.32 BC) Mark Antony substituted Octavia's image for that of Cleopatra, yet again Antony used his unions with women to promote his own status (Kleiner 1992a: 364-365, fig 3).

Yet, Octavian was not alone in associating himself with divinity. Mark Antony promoted the idea that his family were descended from Anton, son of Hercules (Zanker, 1988: 42-53; Kellum, 1993:77). Plutarch stated that Mark Antony resembled illustrations of Hercules from portraits and statues (Plutarch *Antony 4.1-2*). Perhaps Mark Antony deliberately endeavoured to resemble Hercules his 'ancestor'. As elaborated by Plutarch,

> His beard was well grown, his forehead broad, his nose aquiline, these features combined to give him a *certain bold and masculine look*, which is found in statues and portraits of Hercules. In fact there was an ancient tradition that the blood of the Heracleidae ran in Antony's family, since they claimed descent from Anton, one of the sons of Hercules, and Antony liked to believe that is own physique lent force to the legend. He also deliberately cultivated it in his choice of dress, for whenever he was going to appear before a large number of people, he wore his tunic belted low over the hips, a large sword at his side, and a heavy cloak. And indeed it was these same 'Herculean' qualities that the fastidious found so offensive – his swaggering air, his ribald talk, his fondness for carousing in public, sitting down by his men as they ate ...which made his own troops delight in his company and almost worship him (my italics, Plutarch *Antony* 4, Scott-Kilvert 1965: 274).

Body shape can be altered through physical training, but on a more accessible level, choice of clothing and how it is worn is deliberate. Mark Antony was using his own hyper-masculinity (and that of Hercules) to further his reputation as a physically powerful individual. Ultimately, this was not a favourable connection as Hercules whilst epitomising masculine physical strength had a long history as a comic character, all brawn and little brain (Green and Handley 1995:50), particularly from Athenian comedy plays dating back to one of the earliest comic writer the Sicilian Epicharmus (550–460 BC) and possibly before. His character became a figure of fun because of his gargantuan appetite and reputation as a drunkard who was far from intelligent. The 'Heracles-and-food routine' (Green and Handley

1995:50) was essentially taken up by Aristophanes in his fifth century BC comic plays *Wasps* (60), *Frogs* (549-78) and *Birds*. By the Hellenistic period, the character is well established and featured in the 'New Comedy' of Menander (c.342 BC-291 BC), particularly in his *Sham-Heracles*. This may explain why Mark Antony had numerous divine patrons. As mentioned above, he also favoured Dionysus god of wine and hedonism. On the word of Cassius Dio, 'painters and sculptor depicted him with Cleopatra, he being Osiris or Dionysus, and she as Selene or Isis', (Cassius Dio *Reign of Augustus* 50.5). Consequently, the oppositions were set up:

Apollo	Dionysus
Sobriety	Hedonism
Stability	Volatility
Rome	Egypt
Octavian	Antony

Mark Antony made it easy for Octavian to use his own propaganda against him (Zanker 1988: 57). As stated by Miller, 'Apolline symbols played a part in his [Octavian's] triumviral propaganda, where they aimed to evoke a sense of order and sanity in his programme as opposed to the Dionysiac excesses of his enemy' (Miller 1994:100). Curiously, sculptures of Apollo and Dionysus appear to follow the same visual principle as illustrated by figures 8 (Cyrene Apollo, British Museum) and 9 (a marble statuette from poonley Wood, near Winchcombe, Gloucestershire, British Museum).

Both are youthful subjects depicted nude with long hair. In his *Dialogues of the Gods*, Lucian formulated a conversation between the deities. Dionysus recounts an encounter with Priapus,[27] where the latter invited him to drink and dine at his home and later when they were inebriated, he attempted to seduce Dionysus. As stated by Lucian,

> Apollo: And [Priapus] made an attempt on you?
> Dionysus: Something like that.
> Apollo: How did you deal with the situation?
> Dionysus: What could I do but laugh?
> Apollo: The best thing to do, no bad temper or violence. He'd some excuse for making an attempt on you. You're so good-looking.
> Dionysus: As far as that goes, he might make an attempt on you too, Apollo. You're so handsome and have such a fine head of hair, that he may assault you, even when he was sober.
> Apollo: Oh no he won't. I have arrows as well as long hair.
> (Lucian *Dialogues of the Gods*: *Dionysus and Apollo*, Macleod 1998:253).

Therefore, according to Lucian both are figures worthy of male sexual desire. It is interesting that he pays particular attention to Apollo's hair as a focus of attraction. Long hair is a particular feature of a bronze figurine of Apollo found in the Thames (bronze figurine, British Museum, Henig 1995, fig. 51). In the Bacchae by Euripides, Pentheus immediately points out Dionysus' desirability.

> Well, friend: your shape is not unhandsome – for the pursuit
> Of women, which is the purpose of your presence here.
> You are no wrestler, I can tell from these long curls
> Cascading most seductively over your cheek.
> Your skin, too, shows a whiteness carefully preserved;
> You keep away from the sun's heat, walk in the shade,
> So hunting Aphrodite with your lovely face.
> (Euripides *Bacchae* 445-494, Vellacott 1972:206).

This passage reveals the subject as desirable for both men and women. Although Pentheus initially suggests the pleasure that women could take from Dionysus' body, by suggesting Dionysus as the pursuer of women. However, his comments about his long flowing hair seductively cascading over cheek betray his own sexual attraction to Dionysus. He pays particular attention to Dionysus' face making a point of drawing attention to the flesh, his cheek and the hue of his skin. The preference for pallid skin presumably alludes to social class (women and men); he does not have to work in the open air and therefore avoid sunburn (Cartledge 1993:63-89). In this play, it is clear that Dionysus aligns himself with wild Bacchante women instead of the civilised world generally associated with men (Green 2003: 99).

Why was long hair so appealing? An easy explanation would be because women, as a rule, had longer hair than men (Bartman 2001:3) and therefore figures such as Apollo and Dionysus resemble women purportedly making them 'androgynous' or 'gender ambivalent' or 'emasculated' (as stated by Osborne on beardless Dionysus, Osborne 1997:523). The performance of gender ascription is more complicated, this reasoning is simplistic and one-dimensional; moreover, it is overtly heterosexual, which in a society such as that of the Romans would not be relevant (Halperin 1990: 17-18; Richlin 1993: 525; Walters 1997:42; Williams 1999:4; Bartman 2002: 249-271). I would argue that these sculptures have little to do with emulating women. Bartman states that, 'some of the hair arrangements found on other sexy boy statues, however, bear little relation to traditional styles worn by either men or women (Bartman 2002: 258). Furthermore, why should we think of Apollo and Dionysus as being androgynous figures? For example, the architecture of Apollo's upper body (fig. 8) with the arms pulled back is all about displaying and enhancing the pectoral muscles of a male body. The *contrapposto* position is a technique to display the body, pushing out the hip and drawing attention to the body shape. It is modern thinking that attaches a 'campness' to the figure, particularly if the subject is male.

[27] For more on Priapus, see Hooper 1999 and Richlin 1992.

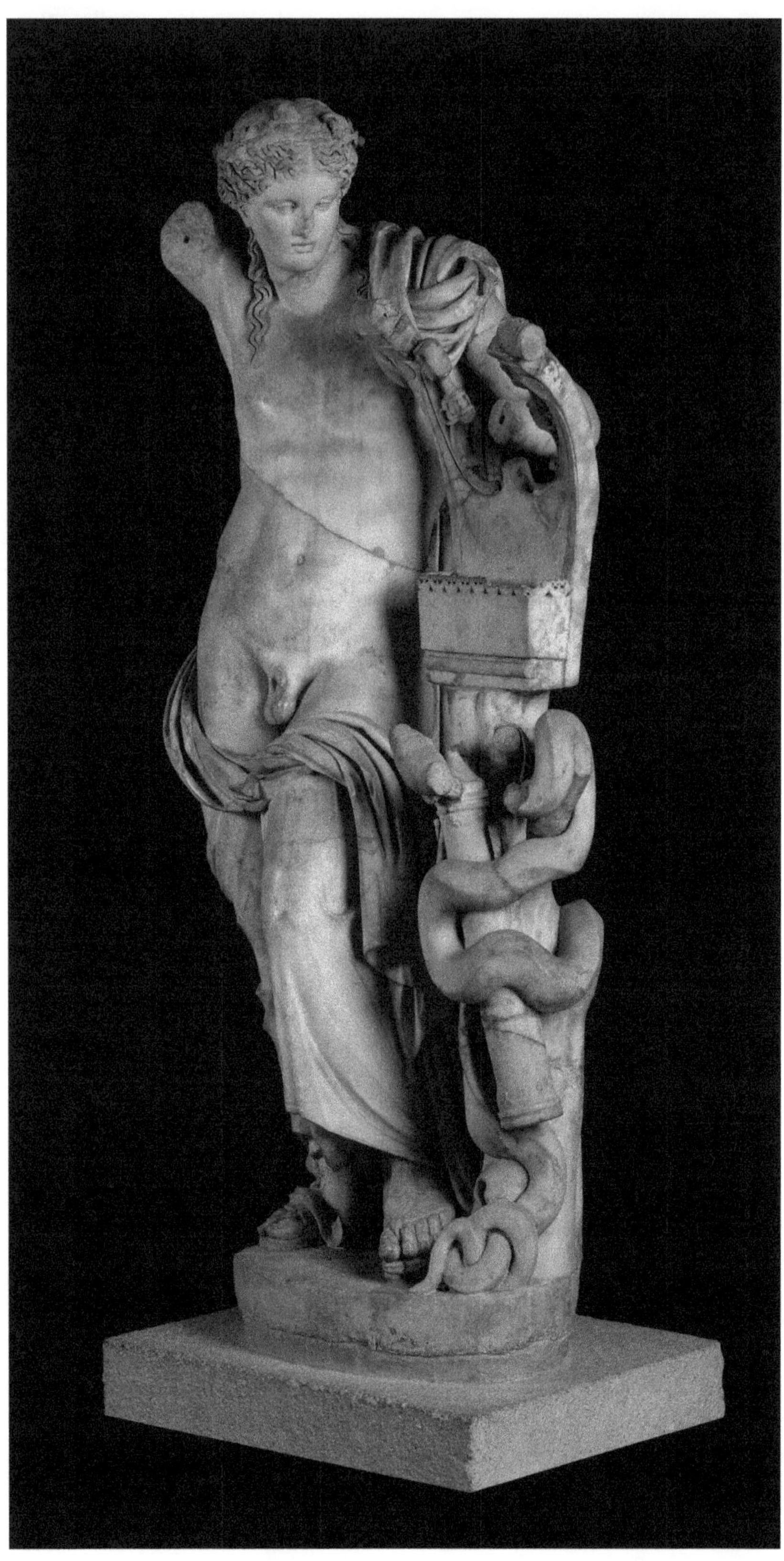

Fig. 8. Marble statue of Apollo, 2nd century 2nd century AD, From Cyrene, Libya, British Museum, London. © Trustees of the British Museum

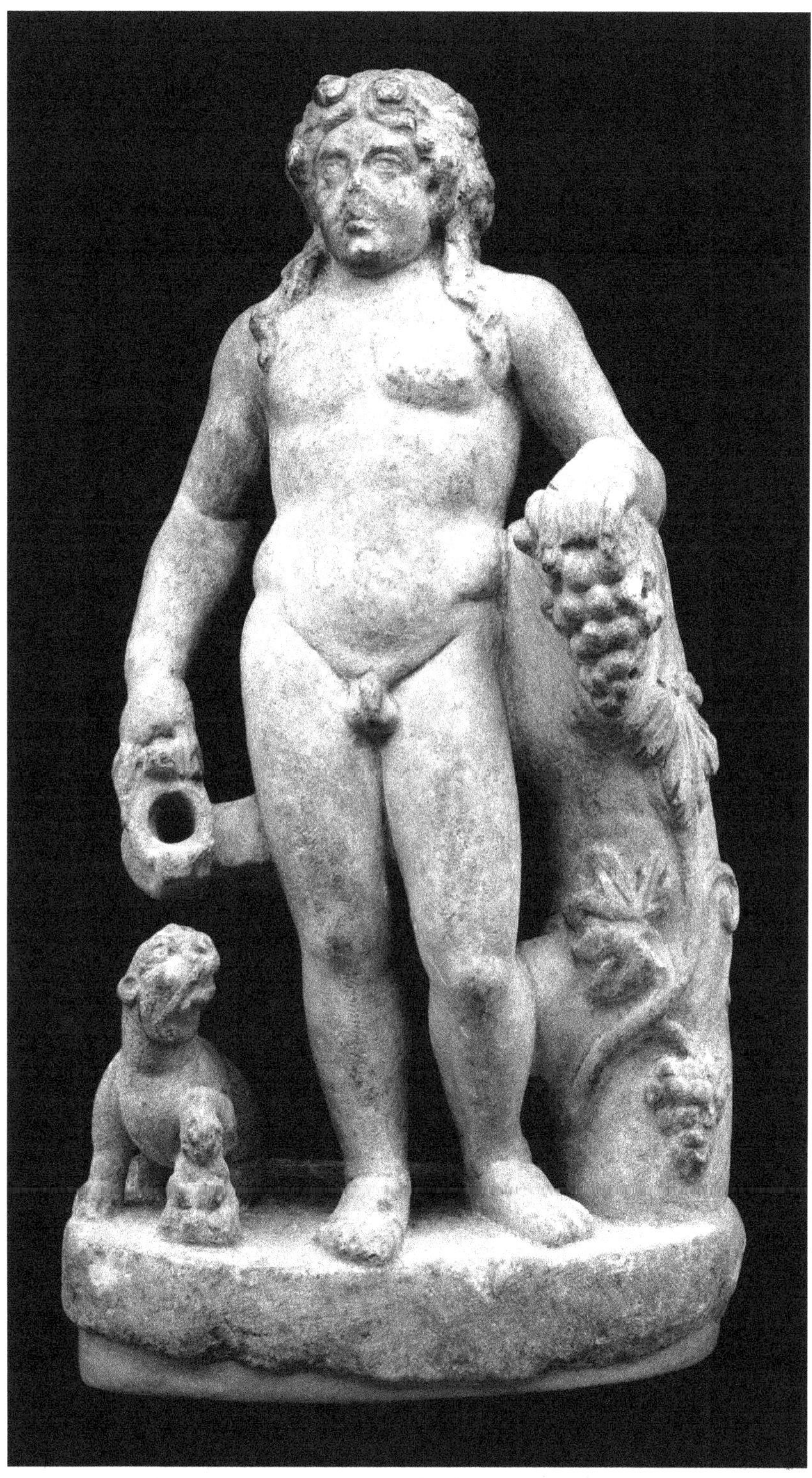

Fig. 9. Marble statuette of Bacchus, Roman Britain From Spoonley Wood, near Winchcombe, Gloucestershire, British Museum, London. © Trustees of the British Museum.

The Cyrene Apollo (fig. 8) reiterates the case in point, it is a semi-nude figure that has drapery deliberated arranged at the top of the thighs drawing attention to the subject's genital area. Moreover, there appears to be a phallic juxtapositioning of Python, entwined around Apollo's quiver and beneath his lyre. His masculinity isprevalent. There is a further similarity: both are from areas outside Rome, Apollo from Greece and Dionysus according to Euripides from Lydia, they are both non-Roman and therefore 'other' to Roman men. Perhaps they represent the epitome of non-citizen desirable passive partners.

On discussing changing views on the celebrity of the Apollo Belvedere over the centuries, Beard and Henderson offered the following informal comments; Apollo has not retained the celebrity he enjoyed in (and just after) the Renaissance. 'A scraped turnip' was the insult thrown at the statue by French art students at the end of the eighteenth century; and since then it has become something of a sport to satirize Apollo's icy heroism, his *vapid effeminacy*, the precious top-knot, and those dreadful sandals. In part, the very conventionality which gives classical art its fame also makes it vulnerable to mockery' (my italics, Beard and Henderson 2001:113).

It seems that the authors, whilst not offering referenced examples of the Apollo Belvedere as a subject of satire, instead put forward their own satirical interpretations. If the authors are being ironic then unfortunately, the statement has the opposite effect. For example, the use of 'vapid effeminacy', these two words together, and the negativity entailed in their coupling means that any deconstruction they are attempting is reversed and ultimately derogatory. For example, 'effeminacy' derives from the Latin *effēminātus* (effeminate) (Morwood 2001: 47) and means, according to the Chambers Dictionary, 'womanish; weak; unmanly;' and effeminacy 'unmanly softness; indulgence in unmanly pleasures' (Schwarz 1994: 536). Ultimately it is a derogatory term. Therefore to say 'vapid effeminacy' is to double the negative and to over emphasis the 'weak', 'vapid womanish'. Above all, use of this word, as a negative term is derogatory to women and when used in the above context it is an attack on the proscribed masculinity of the subject.

I suggest that this specific category of representation the 'androgynous' or 'effeminate' in fact, celebrates masculinity and draws on youthful characteristics of masculinity. In the case of Apollo Belvedere, the subject is definitely masculine. On discussing the pictorial development of Dionysus in Greek art, Osborne remarks on attitudes regarding the use of the male nude, 'exhibiting the body of Dionysus, and exhibiting it in public sculpture, has become acceptable provided that the body is sexually immature' (Osborne 1997: 519). A lack of facial hair indicated sexual immaturity. Furthermore, he claims that this was generally the case for most representations of male nudes. 'Beardlessness is now not a denial of age, as it was in the archaic *kouroi*, but an affirmation of youth, a sign of not having entered into the man's world and in particular of not having become sexually active' (Osborne 1997:523). This, I suggest is applicable to Roman sculpture, especially those that are based on a retrospective Greek paradigm. However, I am aware that the male-to-male sexual activity of the pederastic system, as it was in Greece, may have not have been the case for the period I am addressing (Dover 1979; Foucault 1986; Winkler 1990:18, 113; Halperin 1990; Brisson 2002:66). Nevertheless, the use of youthful subjects is relevant to this discussion.

Nude Apollo appears to represent the epitome of masculine youth and 'beauty'. Warner suggests that male nudes including representations of athletes, gods and heroes had no primary erotic connotations (Warner 1985:131). Beard and Henderson suggest that heroic nudity 'gave nakedness a role as a costume of power ... [and is] not supposed to turn us on' (Beard and Henderson 2001: 112). However, as the discussion on the Cnidian Venus has shown, representations of the nude proved to have overt sexual overtones, so why should this only apply to feminine representations. I would argue that representations of male youthful nudity were largely associated with homoerotic desire (Foucault 1985:61; Williams 1999). The dynamic used to objectify the nude (male or female) works through voyeurism, and voyeurism works through desire. Apollo and other youthful subjects were objectified in this way. For that reason, constructions of Apollo operate through youth and homoeroticism (Salomon 1996:71). As stated by Bartman, sculptures depicting youthful masculine nudes 'in their Roman context possessed meanings that were not only aesthetic or historical but also social and sexual' (Bartman 2002:249). At the same time, the female gaze/desire should not be ignored however difficult it may be to quote written evidence as ancient sources discussing the behaviour of women were typically written by men (Lefkowitz and Fant 1992). Yet, work by women (however fragmented) does survive and a relevant example would be the work of Sulpicia (Rome, first century BC) who fluently conveys her desire for Cerinthus (Lefkowitz and Fant 1992:8-9).

It is also important that we do not employ modern conceptions of sexual identities for the ancient world (Foucault 1985:43; Halperin 1990: 17-18; Richlin 1993: 525; Williams 1999:4; Walters 1997:42). By examining Latin writings of the Roman elite,[28] Walters in his essay, 'Invading the Roman Body: Manliness and Impenetrability in Roman Thought', scrutinized a recurring theme regarding sexual protocol and the concepts of 'manhood' (Walters 1997:29-43). He stated that Roman sexual codes of behaviour classified men as active penetrators who were impenetrable and able to guard the limits of their bodies from invasive attacks of any nature. However, this was only applicable to men of high social status. 'Real' men did not include men of a low status, slaves or non-Roman citizens who consequently lacked the 'manly' qualities of bodily inviolability. This was applicable to adolescents of all social ranks as they occupied a liminal state between

[28] These include, Seneca, (Ep.122.7),

childhood and adulthood. Williams proposes that Roman conjecture on masculine identity depended on a binary opposition of men as the penetrators in opposition to all others who were the penetrated and passive 'other'. The 'other' also applied to women, slaves and boys (Williams 1999:7-8). Seneca in his *Controversies* recounts that a freedman was censored for having had a passive sexual encounter with his owner and his lawyer defended him by stating, 'losing one's virtue [sexual passivity] is a crime in the free-born, a necessity in a slave, duty for the freedman' (Seneca, *Controversies*, 4, taken from Brisson 2002:65). Octavian himself, according to Suetonius, endured attacks on masculinity by his enemies,

> As a young man Augustus was accused of various improprieties. For instance, Sextus Pompey jeered at his effeminacy; Mark Antony alleged that Julius Caesar made him submit to *unnatural* relations as a price for adoption; Antony's brother Lucius added that, after sacrificeing his virtue to Caesar, Augustus had sold his favours to Aulus Hirtius, the Goveneror-General of Spain, for 3,000 gold pieces and that he often used to soften the hair on his legs by singing them with red-hot walnut shells
> (my italics, Suetonius *Augustus* 68, Graves 1957:89).

In this particular translation, Suetonius described sexual passivity as 'improprieties' and the subject sacrificing his 'virtue' or selling his 'favours' all of which confirm the sexual and social status of the passive partner, in this case Octavian. Richlin suggests that it was usual for Roman men to desire both women and adolescent boys and that erotic poetry intermittently lists the advantages of boys over women (Richlin, 1993: 524). So it may be reasonable to suggest that images of nude adolescent males carried erotic overtones. Representations of Apollo perhaps had a dual interpretation. Aside from the obvious sacred associations of Apollo, there is an objectified adolescent body. His youth makes him 'other' to adult Roman conceptions of masculine identity (the penetrator) and therefore sexually desirable.

It is at this point that we witness the manipulation of visual images, as Apollo became the inspiration for portraits of Octavian/Augustus, he was eternally youthful but modified to suite the sitter (Kleiner 1992: 62). Instead of Apollo's long flowing hair, Octavian/Augustus has short controlled hair, deliberately opposing the longhaired philosopher type of the Greek east (Zanker 1995:198-266, Bartman 2001:3). According to Ovid in *Metamorphoses,* Apollo's long hair is a result of his encounter with Daphne. His passion for her remained unrequited. Daphne requested help from her father the water god, Peneus, asking him to allow her to maintain the fruits of her virginity (*Metamorphoses* 1.486-487). Peneus granted her request quite literally and she transformed into vegetation, a laurel tree that does not bear fruit, thus keeping her virginity (Ahl 1994: 123). Once the transition had taken place, Apollo declared that he would never cut his own hair again, but would adorn his hair in her evergreen leaves and that they will embellish his portals and Augustan triumphs (*Metamorphoses* 1.560-563) (Ahl 1994:124). Evidently, this was written in a later period than I am addressing presently, but as an Apolline symbol the laurel had been exploited earlier within Roman visual communication. The laurel was a particularly potent emblem in Roman imagery. In 29BC, Octavian was granted numerous honours by the Senate, including the right to wear a victory (laurel) wreath at all times (Cassius Dio *Reign of Augustus* 20; Appian *The Civil Wars* 5.130) (Zanker 1988: 41). According to Pausanias, the laurel wreath became a sign of victory originating from the Pythian games where winning athletes donned them as victory crowns (Pausanias *Guide to Greece* 10:7.2). This custom has two links with Apollo. Firstly, the Pythian games commemorated Python (the snake) killed by Diana and Apollo[29] and secondly the laurel signifies Apollo's failed rape of Daphne. Octavian appears illustrated on the obverse of a denarius wearing the triumphant laurel wreath (ca 29BC, Niggeler Collectionno, Rome, Zanker 1988: 42, fig. 3.2). His achievement is reiterated further on the reverse of the coin offering a representation of 'columna rostrata' on which stands a statue Octavian. A 'columna rostrata' is a column that has the prows of vanquished ships attached to it. The statue amplifies the point as it makes the column and the success distinctive to Octavian.

After the final battle against Sextus Pompey, Octavian attributed his victory to Apollo and Diana, as there was in the surrounding location a sanctuary of Diana near Naulochoi where the crucial conquest took place (Zanker 1988: 50). He vowed to build a temple to the deities on the Palatine, but this was not finished until the battle of Actium (Kleiner 1992: 82). As stated by Zanker, 'it is fascinating to observe how deliberately Octavian pursued this relationship to Apollo over the next twenty years or so, ...[and] how his sense of mission and his entire program for healing Rome's wound bore the stamp of Apollo' (Zanker 1988: 50). Later when Mark Antony and Cleopatra were defeated at Actium Octavian again proclaimed Apollo and Diana assisted him in his triumph (Zanker 1988:50; Kleiner 1992: 59). When the temple was eventually built, it was located next to Octavian's house on the Palatine and became the location of the hallowed Sibylline Books (Suetonius *Augustus* 30; Virgil *Aeneid* 6.72. Zanker 1988: 51; Kellum 1993: 76).

The temple was based on a Tuscan style; Kellum suggests that the temples archaising manner was hinted by Vitruvius who considered the temple appeared to be of a diastyle[30] (Kellum 1993:76). This choice of architecture, with a retrospective Italic air, is in itself an illuminating gesture. It indicates a conscious celebration of tradition and pride in heritage, rather than a borrowing of cultural trends, such as that of the eastern empire, namely Egypt.

[29] *Homeric Hymn to Apollo* 14, 300-306.

[30] Diastyle as quoted by Vitruvius 'the construction will be diastyle when we can insert the thickness of three columns in an intercolumniation, as in the case of the temple of Apollo and Diana. This arrangement involves the danger that architraves may break on account of the great width of the intervals' Vitruvius (*On Architecture* 3.3.4, Rowland 1999:29).

However, the temple had a series of 'Augustan neo-Attic terracotta reliefs (Kleiner 1992:83). It is inappropriate to the theme of this chapter to explore the temple as subject in detail (see Kellum 1993); however, I will examine a figural relief terracotta plaque that (amongst others) once adorned the temple. A terracotta relief from Antiquario Palatino, Rome (Kellum 1993: 77, fig 28) depicts Apollo and Hercules literally struggling to gain possession of the Delphic tripod (embodying the gift of prophecy itself). Apollodorus narrated that Hercules headed for Delphi to seek purification after he murdered his houseguest, Iphitus. The Pythia refused him a prophecy and Hercules snatched the tripod in order to set up his own oracle. An outraged Apollo fought back until their father intervened in the struggle, hurling a thunderbolt between them (Apollodorus *Library* 2.6.1). The plaque has carvings of an archaic (600 - 480 B.C.) Greek period manner (Boardman 1991; Kellum 1993: 77), rejecting the Hellenistic decadent style associated with Mark Antony and the Egyptian east. The plaque is an implicit allegory illustrating Octavian and Mark Antony's struggle for power over Rome (Kellum 1993; Kleiner 1992:83). As stated by Kleiner, 'Apollo is depicted as the defender of the tripod, Octavian as protector of Rome' (Kleiner 1992:83). Lotus flowers depicted the lower border presumably indicate an Egyptian element, perhaps alluding to Mark Antony's partner Cleopatra. Interestingly the flowers occupy the lower section, literally under the feet of the Roman protagonists. Moreover, for Hercules, this particular episode precedes by his sale into slavery (as recompense for the murder of his guest) and acquisition by the Lydian queen Omphale. As I discuss in Chapter 4, the exotic Omphale became a convenient metaphor for Cleopatra.

In later life, Augustus issued a series of coins (15 BC) on of which depicts Apollo Actius and Diana Sicilia commemorating and recalling his past victories at Actium and Naulochoi (Zanker 1988: 225, figs 179, c-d). Others include Tiberius and Drusus handing over palms of victory to Augustus, on the reverse a bull an emblem of Mars Ultor and Quinarius; Augustus and Victoria sitting on a globe. All are political images. Therefore, there has been a long tradition of propaganda through visual images, imperial imagery reinforcing their long history and geographical reach.

Diana as Amazon

Diana, as their patron deity, shared a special relationship with the Amazons and their all female society (Pomeroy 1975:5-6; Warner 1985:279; Fantham et al 1995:129-135; Cohen 2000:99). Just as Diana resides in the space outside the city, Amazons dwell in the area beyond the known 'civilised' world (Cartledge 1993: 79-80). Furthermore, they equally reject men and marriage; Diana is an 'untamed virginal goddess of wild nature' (Cohen 2000: 99) whilst the all female Amazons welcome men simply for procreation purposes (Herodotus 4.113-119). According to Herodotus, 'the Scythians call Amazons *Oeorpata*, the equivalent of *mankillers*, *oer* being the Scythian word for 'man' and pata for 'kill'' (Herodotus *Histories* 4.113; De Sélincourt 1972: 306-307). Killing is not uncommon to Artemis/Diana; her victims include: Tityus,[31] Actaeon,[32] Orion,[33] Callisto,[34] the children of Niobe[35] to name a few. As indicated above, representations of Diana bear a resemblance to those of Amazons, carrying weapons and clad in similar short clothing, although in most cases Amazons appear with one breast revealed (or with cloth slipped revealing or partially revealing both breasts).[36] There are a number of theories why Amazons appeared this way. As clarified by Fantham et al, 'the *unfeminine* Amazons were said to [cut off and] cauterise their right breasts (the word *a-mazon* means 'without breast') in order to remove any impediment to effective fighting ... or they allegedly fed their female infants on horse's milk to prevent the enlargement of their breasts (my italics, Fantham et al 1994: 131). A Roman copy of a fifth century BC wounded Amazon the so-called 'Lansdowne', 'Berlin' or 'Sciarra' type, perhaps best illustrates this (Metropolitan Museum of Art, New York). This sculpture type survives amid other Amazon types in various Roman copies (including the so called Capitoline and Mattei types both in the Vatican Museum, Pollitt 1990: 226; Boardman 1992: 213-215). According to Pliny, in the fifth century BC the most celebrated artists held a competition amongst themselves, given that they all had fashioned sculptures of Amazons, and when these were dedicated at the Temple of Artemis at Ephesus, the sculptors themselves selected the best. Polykleitos was overall victor with Pheidias second, after that Kresilas, fourth Kydon and fifth Phradmon (Pliny *Natural History* 34.53).[37] Credited for founding Ephesus, Amazons made appropriate subjects (Pindar quoted by Pausanias 7.2.4), simultaneously enhancing the links between them and their patron deity. Whether or not the anecdote is of any truth would be impossible to say, however the figures tend to be associated with the sculptures from Ephesus (Ridgway 1974: 1-17; Pollitt 1990: 226; Robertson 1991: 110-111; Boardman 1992:214; Cohen 1997:75-77). The sculptures appear to define a stereotypical defeated 'Amazon/barbarian/other'; they are constructed as supplicants. Each is injured, with wounds alongside the exposed right breast (the Lansdowne left, and the Capitoline types right) and on the left thigh (the Mattei type) (Cohen 1997:76). According to Cohen, 'each [Amazon] deals differently with her physical and psychological pain in both pose and mood' (Cohen 1997:76-77). I consider this an unconvincing account of the sculptures and, moreover it is melodramatic. Their faces are expressionless as they are idealised, as the

---

[31] Apollodorus *Library* 1.4.1, Pindar *Pythian Odes* 4.90
[32] Apollodorus *Library* 3.4, Ovid *Metamorphoses* 3, *Tristia* 2.103-5.
[33] This was an accidental killing according to Apollodorus *Library* 1.4.3-4.
[34] Ovid *Metamorphoses* 11.
[35] Hyginus *Fabulae* 9 and 10, Ovid *Metamorphoses* 6.146-312.
[36] This type of adornment is not exclusive as there are other examples of Amazons clad in Eastern, Persian-like ornate trouser costume, or with Phrygian hats, particularly on Greek vases see Carpenter 1998 figs. 198, 251 and Boardman 1993a, fig. 233, Fantham et al 1994: 131, figs 4.1, 4.2, 4.4, 4.4. Cohen 2000: 75, fig. 6.
[37] For more on this competition and 'wounded Amazon' sculpture see Robertson 1991: 110-111 and Boardman 1992:214).

sculptural convention of that period (Boardman 1992) and therefore not betraying or portraying a 'mood'. Their poses differ slightly, presumably to create individualised illustrations of the subject, whilst subtly drawing attention to the wounded areas (none actually look directly at their injuries), which is a principal point of their representation; they are defeated 'barbarians'. Furthermore, they are defeated women, who dared to live beyond the limits expected for women of the Greco-Roman world (Pomeroy 1975:5-6; Warner 1985:279; Fantham et al 1995:134; Cohen 1997: 77; Cohen 2000:99). The sculptures construct a femininity that deliberately exhibits passivity, both physical and sexual. They are no longer a threat; this is removed because they have physical injuries, and so have diminished strength; their partially exposed upper bodies prove less of a sexual threat because they appear overcome and violated. As Cohen states, 'their bare breasts, above all, represent a potent visual convention employed by Classical artists to denote female victims of physical violence' (Cohen 1997: 77). It degrades them and removes the threat. Ovid in his erotic poetry, aligns violence with sex (Fredrick 1997: 172-193), particularly in his *Art of Love*,

> It's all right to use force – force of *that* sort goes down well with the girls: what in fact they love they'd often rather have stolen. Rough seduction delights them, the audacity of near-rape is a compliment – so that who *could* have been forced, yet somehow got way unscathed, may feign delight, but in fact feels sadly let down (Ovid, *Art of Love*, 1. 673-679, Green: 1982: 187).

Evidently, the proposal of rape (near or not) is not an offensive prospect to him, as he is advising his audience to be the active, penetrative protagonist and not the passive, penetrated raped. So this advocates the hierarchical category of alleged 'correct' masculinity, penetrate but not be penetrated (Williams 1999: 125).

There is a possibility that the above reading of passivity could be inverted. The fact that the sculptures have revealed breasts may present the opposite effect and be conceptually threatening, perhaps highlighting the Amazon's overt sexuality and little need of men in their society. Moreover, 'respectable' women appeared fully covered (see Chapter 5) (Cohen 1997:77; Zanker 1988: 165-166; Davies 1997: 105; Sebesta: 1997: 536-537). I suggest that the construction of the Lansdowne type deliberately conveyed particular sexual connotations. The Amazon is depicted with her arm raised and her hand resting on her head. According to Clarke, the right arm crooked over the head, is a gesture that has a long history in Greco-Roman art employed for sculptures such as the Apollo Lykeios attributed to Praxiteles (a Roman copy is exhibited in the Louvre, Paris, Bieber 1961, fig 17),) and the Barberini Faun[38] (Clarke 1998: 68; Bartman 2002: 253). It also has a sexual subtext, 'the arm over the head signals an 'opening up' to love ... since the gesture occurs in conjunction with the motif of baring the body (either with clothing falling away by itself or with cupids pulling it aside) ...this gesture indicated a women's sexual availability' (Clarke 1998: 68-70). Moreover, the raised arm draws attention to the upper body. As with the Apollo Lykeios it also draws attention to the head and the hair. The work therefore, is open to interpretations, with a number of readings: threatening or non-threatening. Nevertheless, the overall communication appears to be that of passivity and supplication; they are wounded, exposed and they unconfidently look away from the viewer.

It may seem that the chosen sub-heading 'Diana as Amazon' has little to do with the above discussion. However, I would argue that the interpretation of Diana is close to that of Amazons; the only difference being that Diana is chaste. Her virginity proves empowerment and autonomy. As previously mentioned, they share numerous common features, particularly that they are uncontrolled and self-governing. I propose that this reflects in the way they were constructed and represented. By this, I do not mean that their autonomy was celebrated, but rather the opposite. By illustrating them as active, hunting or the hunted, with short or revealing clothing and with weapons, they were atypical of propagated images of femininity. Their very femininity was under attack (Lefkowitz and Fant 1992: 163-166). This was because they did not conform to the endorsed social norm. This is apparent in the ways that artists and sculptors dealt with these subjects. The powerful, threatening sexuality of the Amazons met with violent defeat and humiliation. However, this would be inappropriate for a goddess. Diana's virginity meant that thinking of her, as a sexually active adult woman was impious and forbidden. A potential sexual encounter with her was a transgressive act, as illustrated in the myth of Actaeon (see below). She is uncontrolled, but as she is chaste, she poses no threat to a patriarchal society, or as a potentially undesirable influence on female viewers. Amazons, on the other hand, ultimately advocate sexual promiscuity with little respect for paternal rights or patriarchal hegemony (Lefkowitz and Fant 1992: 56, 89, 122, 195). Amazons (as Diana) have no male guardians, which was the common practice for both Greek and Roman women, who passed from one man to another through families on marriage (Gardner 1986: 31-67; Lefkowitz and Fant 1992: 62-65, 100-115).

Hunter Goddess: The Goldsmith's Hall altar

The Goldsmith's Hall altar (fig. 10) is among sculptural works discussed in a paper by Merrifield entitled, 'The London Hunter-God and his Significance in the History of Londinium' (Merrifield 1996:105-113). Merrifield believes that the relief depicts a masculine hunter god rather than an illustration of the goddess Diana, as interpreted by Toynbee (Toynbee 1962: 152). According to Merrifield, Toynbee herself was mistaken in her initial identification, which was from a poor photograph and on seeing the sculpture first hand became convinced of the figure's masculinity. Furthermore, Merrifield remarks that it was Hugh Chapman who indicated the figure has a

[38] See Smith 1995 : 135, fig 168.

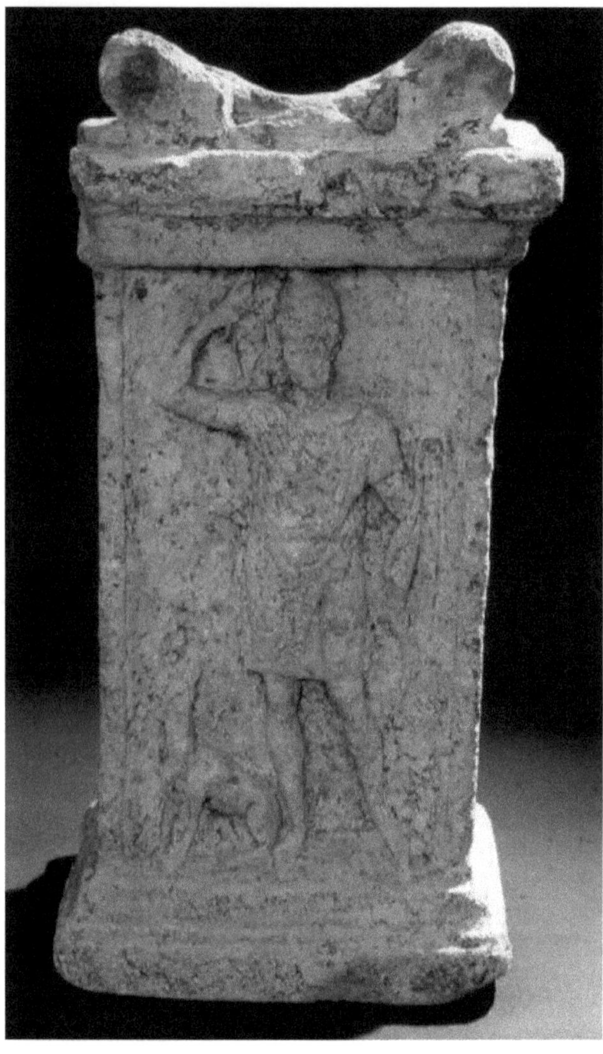

Fig. 10. Diana from the Goldsmith's Hall, Foster Lane, City of London. Permission granted by Worshipful Company of Goldsmiths.

pointed Phrygian hat rather than a high topknot. Moreover, the hilt projecting from her side is as large as that of a sword and not a hunting knife (Merrifield 1996: 106). Merrifield uses the altar as a comparison for a representation of a hunter (god?) with a hound and stag found beneath Southwark Cathedral, to support his argument regarding the popularity of Hunter-god representations (Museum of London, Merrifield 1996:105 fig. 12.1). Furthermore, he links these two with an alternative example of a figure wearing a Phrygian pointed hat from Bevis Marks in the City of London (Merrifield 1996, fig 12.5). He declares that the 'apparent identity of these two figures at once call into question another early find from Londinium,' this being the Bevis Marks sculpture (Merrifield 1996:106, fig 12.5). Yet, his evidence for the 'apparent identity' and visual connections of the sculptures discussed is insubstantial. He offers no reasons or references for the identification of the Goldsmith's Hall altar figure other than the two given above. Moreover, there are no comparisons offered to prove that the figure is definitely not Diana; instead, this unfounded identification becomes an archetype to question the identity of an alternative sculpture. I propose that the relief is an example of Diana the huntress. The images do have some similarities, for example, they wear Phrygian hats and swords (?), but comparisons with examples of Diana are closer and overturn the argument. Traditional illustrations of Diana also have short tunics, and hounds and stags often accompany her. As a comparative sculpture, a Roman copy of a Hellenistic original (Gallery of the Candelabra, Vatican Museum) is particularly close to the altar relief figure in question. The figures share the same pose, with weight resting on the right foot in the *contrapposto* (counterpoise) position, with the right arm raised reaching for an arrow and the left holding her bow. Additionally, the dog appears to be of the same variety and the same posture. However, a few details prevent the images from making an identical match, for example the topknot that is clearly visible on the Vatican sculpture is not on the Goldsmith's hall relief nor is her footwear. However, for comparative purposes, the Vatican sculpture is overall a closer case in point.

Additionally, it is constructive to examine a comparative work from Britain. An altar from Corbridge shows a representation of Diana accompanying her brother, to whom the altar is dedicated 'To Apollo Maponus, Calpurnius ..., tribune, dedicated this' (RIB 1121, Museum of Antiquities of the University of Newcastle upon Tyne and of the Society of Antiquities, Phillips 1977, fig. 20). Diana holds the same position with her bow in her left hand with her right arm raised to reach for an arrow. Additionally, it follows that the inscription secures her identity, but on the other hand it raises issues as to why she is not mentioned by name. Illustrations of Diana shaped from alternative media can also follow a similar mode, for example, a cornelian gem from the Roman baths at Caerleon (Roman Legionary Museum, Caerleon, Zienkiewicz, 1987: 15).[39] This gem dating from around the mid third century AD depicts Diana the huntress. Diana appears in mid-hunt and about to take an arrow from her quiver; her hound springs up in pursuit of prey. Although the positions are different, the characteristics are equivalent to the examples given.

Bendis, a Thracian goddess (fig. 11), was also venerated by the Dacians had a similar appearance to Artemis/Diana with whom she was often associated (Tsiafakis 2000:386). As depicted on a relief from Athens (c. 400-375 BC, British Museum), Bendis' pointed cap distinguishes her from Artemis/Diana whilst acting as a stereotypical marker emphasising her non-Greco-Roman origin. I have included Bendis in this discussion, not because I believe that these deities and their portrayals are the same or that there is any direct link between them, instead I want to demonstrate that there were feminine examples, other than Amazons, that were similar to

[39] The owner constantly venerates Diana by wearing her image on a finger ring. The gem acts as a mobile shrine. Because the gems were found in the Roman Baths' drains, it seems that the rings were worn habitually. On the other hand, the gem may have been deliberately deposited as an offering.

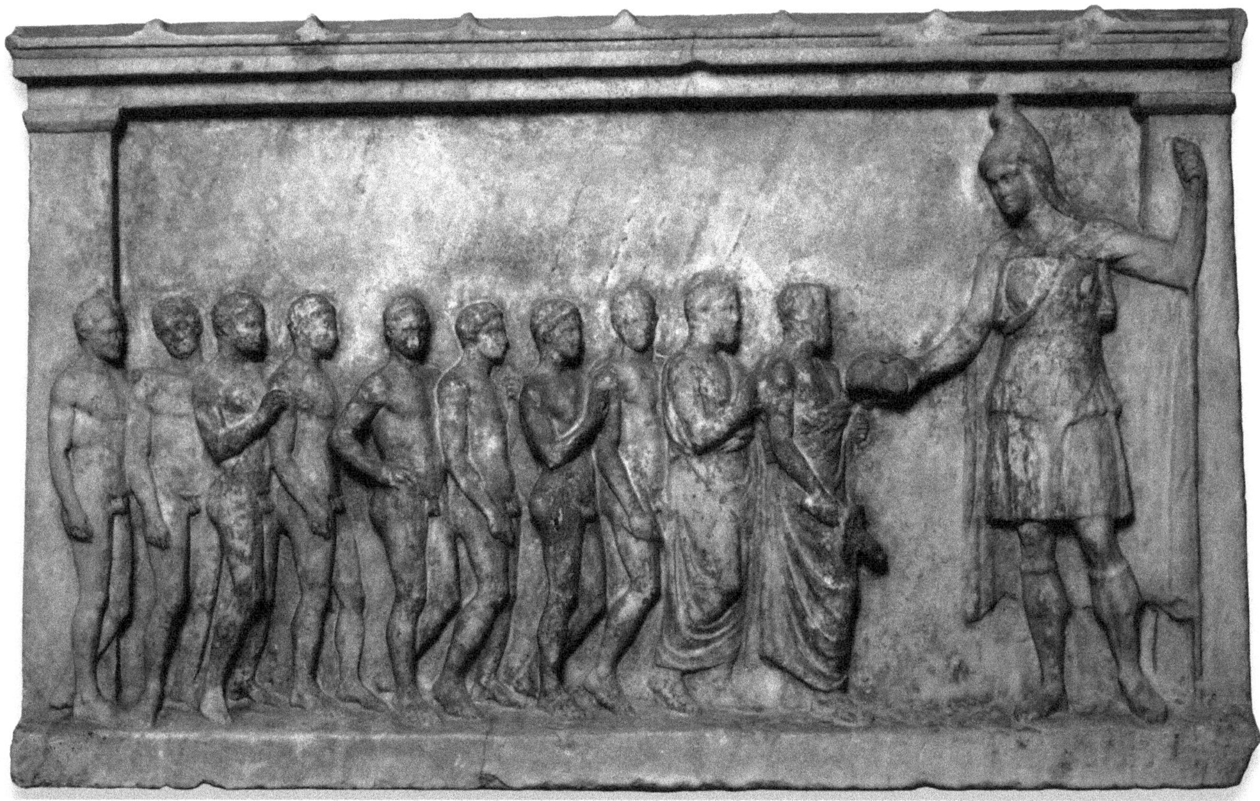

Fig. 11. Relief dedicated to the Thracian goddess Bendis, Greek, thought to be from the Piraeus, Athens c. 400-375 BC, British Museum, London. © Trustees of the British Museum

Diana. Therefore, why should the Goldsmith's Hall subject be male? As mentioned above, Diana often associated with Amazons, who were commonly dressed in Phrygian hats indicating their so-called 'barbarian' status. Perhaps this was a way of depicting Diana with reference to her difference, her wild existence away from civilisation and predominantly her chastity.

Diana: Action Heroine

In his study on the action film genre, 'Gender and the Action Heroine: Hardbodies and the *Point of No Return*' Brown considers how the genre initially revolved around a 1980s construct of the masculine body as spectacle and evolved in the early 1990s to feature action heroines as the main protagonists (Brown 1996:52-70). Stating such films as, *Silence of the Lambs* (1990); *V.I. Warshawski* (1991); *Ace: Iron Eagle III* (1991) and *Terminator 2: Judgement Day* (1991), Brown discusses how they revolve around women who are more than capable of defending themselves and of defeating their adversaries and introduces the central characters as 'hardbody heroines' (Brown 1996:52). Critics of this new influx of heroines suggested that the protagonists were merely men in women's clothing (Brown 1996:53,54). The traditional female role as passive/victim of violence becomes active/inflictor of violence. As stated by Brown, 'the image of heroines wielding guns and muscles conflated with binary gender codes of the action cinema to render these women as symbolically male' (Brown 1996:53). I am aware that binary coding is too simplistic in the study of gender as each case is individual and has its own narration, although borrowings from opposite codes do occur, it is this movement or 'borrowing dynamic' that creates identity. I introduced this section with film theory because I think it offers an interesting parallel with Diana and the construction of her femininity. Like Connor (*Terminator 2: Judgement Day,* 1991) Diana has roles conventionally associated with men. She may not have the obvious 'hardbody' muscular form, yet her shoulders, arms and legs are displayed in a more muscular fashion than goddesses such as Venus or nymphs, or even Apollo and Dionysus whose deliberately constructed soft forms signal sexuality. Diana has square set shoulders like Connor. In addition, with these square set athletic features, the Diana sculpture is literally a 'hard body' as it is marble. Furthermore, it is noticeable that in this particular film still, Connor has her hair tied up and hidden beneath a baseball cap. Like Diana, her (long) hair is controlled and out of sight, suppressing any preconceptions, loose, long hair may invoke such as that of a state of undress and its connotations. Undoubtedly the most significant aspect is the use of lethal weaponry, meaning that they perform violence, which is traditionally masculine territory. Connor has a gun in her hands. There is a direct connection between the body and the weapon. Her extended arms also extend into the weapon itself. Similarly, Diana is reaching for and touching her quiver of arrows. Their choice of weapon acts as a physical extension of their bodies. As we are aware, Diana is a female subject, yet in the majority of her exploits, she matches her brother in weapons and action. Appropriate examples are, the elimination of the giant Tityus, who attempted to rape her mother Latona (also called Leto in Greek versions) (Apollodorus *Library* 1.4.1), and the slaughter of Niobe's children in retribution for her impious comments against Latona (Apollodorus Library 3.5.6; Homer *Iliad* 24.612). Diana is equal to Apollo in action. It is also notable that these acts of violence came about in defence of their mother. Latona summoned her children to her because Niobe mocked her for only having two children as opposed to her own numerous progeny. Intriguingly or perhaps predictably, Apollo sets out to kill the boys and Diana the girls (Homer *Iliad* 24.612*)*. Moreover, emphasis on the gender divide occurs by the locations of the children, the boys are out hunting and the girls are indoors spinning (Apollodorus *Library* 3.5.6.). Diana, like Connor performs as an action heroine. The question is, why is this acceptable for Diana and not for other feminine subjects? I suggest that the answers depend on the disparity between Diana and the majority of feminine characters and deities, that is, her existence in the wild as a hunter and her virginity. She was conveniently located in areas removed from reality and therefore posed no threat as a direct influence. She was able to hunt and fight because of this and her chaste life, an aspect that was certainly not encouraged in women, particularly under Augustus when he brought about legislation on marriage and morals. The Leges Iuliae imposed criminal lawsuits for adultery and raised major penalties for those who deliberately remained unmarried, but rewarded parents of several children (Zanker 1988: 157).

Other examples from Britain

Further examples from Roman Britain include the remnants of sculpture that originated from the temple site at Chedworth, and recognised by Henig as Diana Venatrix (huntress) (Henig 1993:10). Although most of the limbs and head are missing, the short tunic with a belt resembles other illustrations of Diana. Other obvious subjects wearing short tunics are Amazons; whilst the sculpture is damaged there are no clear signs of feminine form making identification uncertain.

Fragments found at Ashcroft, Cirencester (Corinium Museum, Cirencester) are thought to have once been a sculpture of the goddess. A sculpted head and neck were found along with this particular base, other bits of statuary and an inscription (*RIB 105*) (Henig 1993:11). Henig accepts that in all probability the two are associated (Henig 1993:11). I am inclined to support this observation for two reasons; firstly, both were carved from the same material, oolitic limestone (as were most sculptures in the Cotswold area) and secondly from a comparative visual perspective, the way the hair was carved. If her hair were long or carved in a more intricate fashion then classification would be especially questionable. However, the hair, tied back from her face is common to representations of Diana. The addition of hound paws on the base offer more evidence for a credible connection and identification.

A relief of Diana found within kilometres of Chesterholm (Vindolanda) shows Diana within an architectural niche (Housesteads Museum, Hexham, Coulston and Phillips 1988:4). A stag - suggesting the hunt accompanies her. Diana has her customary pose, reaching for an arrow in her quiver, her bow in her hand. Coulston and Philips propose that this relief originated from the same shrine as an altar to a rural deity from Chesterholm (Coulston and Phillips 1988:304).[40] Diana's pose, as with other illustrations, is active, reaching for her arrows she occupies an area usually associated with masculinity; she is the penetrator, and she penetrates with arrows.

Occasionally narrative compositions can implicate Diana without actually representing her, for example those of the hunter Actaeon. The Four Seasons mosaic From Dyer Street, Cirencester, has a well-preserved example of the transition and attack of Actaeon (Corinium Museum, Cirencester, Hutchinson 1986: 400; Scott, 2000: 132-133). This came about because of a voyeuristic episode in which he found and spied on Diana whilst she bathed. 'Actaeon's fate is not only a result of the fact that he saw what he should not have seen, but that Diana beheld him in the act of viewing' (Platt 2002:87). Outraged by his impious behaviour, viewing a chaste goddess naked, Diana changed him into a stag. His dogs failed to recognise him and attacked him as they would other prey (Apollodorus *Library* 3.4; Ovid *Metamorphoses* 3, *Tristia 2.103-5*) (Cohen 2000a: 123; Platt 2002:87-112,). According to Platt, there are examples of the myth where Diana is nude, for example, a 4th style painted porticos of Pompeii II.2.2-5, House of Octavius Quartio or Loreius Tiburtinus. Though the onlooker views her naked form she does not look at us, our indiscretion remains unnoticed. 'Thus the viewer is given a privileged and by implication, less transgressive view into the goddess' space, while the transgressive viewer within the myth is reduced to peering into the scene from an inferior position within the painting' (Platt 2002: 97, fig 32,33). Moreover, she indicates that it is only in the Imperial period that nude depictions of Diana occur when illustrating this particular myth (Platt 2002:96). It is curious that a virgin goddess was illustrated nude, yet we are reminded of her sexual status by the fate of Actaeon. Within this particular joint composition, the figures are dependent on each other. Perhaps nude images of Diana were not acceptable without Actaeon to reap the retribution for voyeuristic irreverence.

It is an interesting coincidence that both are hunters; presumably this allows Actaeon to occupy the same space as Diana as she resides in the area outside civilisation, in the wild, where he could hunt. The Dyer Street composition catches Actaeon in metamorphosis with stag's antlers sprouting from his head. According to Cohen this is a Greek artistic tradition where, 'in anticipation of the hunter's horrible end, Greek art focuses on the final instant during which the viewer can

[40] The altar depicts a rural scene within a freeze depicting trees and fawns the above level shows a tree with a stag running beneath it (Coulston and Phillips 1988:116).

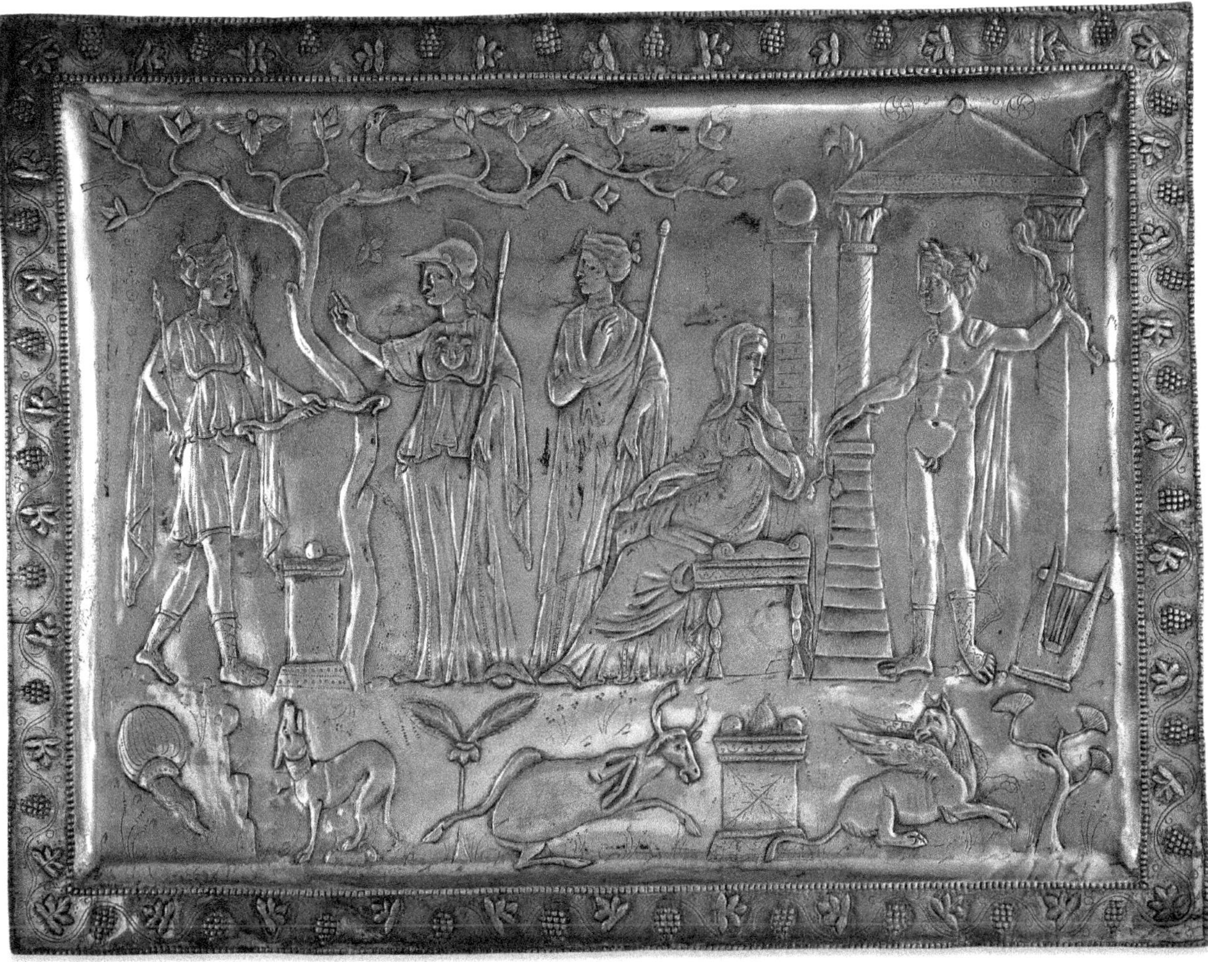

Fig. 12. Corbridge Lanx, 4th century AD, British Museum, London. © Trustees of the British Museum

still perceive the doomed Actaeon's humanity' (Cohen 2000a: 115). On the word of Plutarch, stag's horns were nailed up in all other shrines of Diana except that on the Aventine (where horns of cattle were used) (Plutarch *Moralia: Roman Questions* 264:4). Additionally, by including the antlers, it not only alludes to his transition into an animal, but it also doubles the reference to his masculinity. The way both dogs attack the one leg – the positioning of the lighter coloured dog draws attention to his upper thigh and genitalia. He is a man developing the physical characteristics of a stag, a very masculine creature, and like other horned animals, considered as the essence of virility (Osborne 2002:119). The moment chosen as composition is one of a male nude with the virility of a stag; it is lewd and appropriate considering his impious misdemeanour.

A plasma gemstone from Gloucester (Gloucester City Museum, Henig 1974, fig 254) illustrates Diana adorned in an animal skin, her appearance altered by it and is different from the standard illustration of Diana. Henig suggests that this image follows a pattern after a fourth century statue perhaps by Kephisodotos the Younger, Son of Praxiteles (Henig 1974:39). Furthermore, Diana adorned in animal skins has a long tradition as evidenced on the reverse of the Boston krater attributed to the Pan Painter (fifth century BC), where she wears a fawn skin (Cohen 2000a: 116, fig 4.5). The addition of the animal skins enhances her link with wildness and ultimately her 'otherness'.

The Corbridge lanx (fig. 12) offers an interesting rendition of Diana and Apollo together (Toynbee 1962:172.fig.121; Henig 1996: 163-164). The scene depicted has various narratives within one composite image. It covers two levels, with mythological figures as the major scene and a collection of beasts, trees, and other objects below. Diana and Apollo face each other; between them is Minerva, an image identified as Asteria-Ortygia a Delian goddess (as stated by Toynbee 1962: 172) and their mother Latona who sits on a cushioned stool. The way Latona appears within the composition is significant, her seated position, her stance and her headgear all have particular importance. Her lower, seated position is an interesting contrast to the upright poses of the other figures. Of the five figures, she is the only non-deity and occupies her own middle level. Though sitting with her body towards Diana, Latona turns around to look over her shoulder at her son, the only masculine figure of the piece therefore showing a preference and inevitably giving Apollo a higher status. Although Latona looks towards Apollo, he does not return her gaze, but looks over her head at Diana and towards Minerva and Asteria-Ortygia. Latona's status as a 'mortal' is emphasised by her older age (as parent of the twin deities) in contrast to the eternal youth of the deities. Furthermore, her covered head stresses her matronly status and respectability (Croom 2000:87).

The twinship of Diana and Apollo appears emphasised by their symmetrical juxtaposition; they almost mirror each other. They face one another in poses that suggest movement which contrasts with the fixed figures of Minerva and Asteria-Ortygia whom appear restricted by their long constrictive drapery (see chapter 5). Before Diana is an altar showing her divinity and below it, her hound looks up at her. Apollo, framed by an impression of a temple, holds his bow with his lyre at his feet below his sacred griffin. There is a clear division of environment between Diana and Apollo. Diana, Minerva, Asteria-Ortygia and Latona appear under a tree; the women are associated with wild nature and Apollo with buildings and temples. Anthropologist Levi-Straus through his analysis of myth and belief systems (Levi-Straus 1987:83) offered the precept of nature/women and culture/men. The symbolic scale provides a structure of differentiation concerning the roles set up and represented within society, defining and evaluating its activities. According to Warner, this symbolic scale is particularly relevant to representations of the female nude where the body is nature in contrast to male culture (Warner 1985:312). As stated by Parker and Pollock, 'as female nude, woman is body, is nature opposed to male culture, which, in turn, is represented by the very act of transforming nature, that is, the female model or motif, into the ordered forms and colour of a cultural artefact, a *work* of art' (Parker and Pollock 1981: 69, 119). However, in Greco-Roman art the male nude was more associated with culture, as discussed in Chapter 2 on Venus, the male nude originally took precedence over representations of the female. Apollo's representation on the lanx, located below a temple, places him firmly within culture, indicated by the temple itself denoting religion and architecture, and ultimately civilisation. Furthermore, it is a perfect example of the ways in which images of Apollo operate through an explicitly visual nature. The ways in which his 'youthfulness' and 'nudity' become framed by a 'border' or architecture is like a depiction within a depiction (Nead 1992:9)

Diana and Minerva face each other, although the tree trunk divides them. Together they share a particular femininity, illustrated by the way they have their hair up or covered and have weapons and armour normally associated with men; perhaps they were invested with these because they chose not to fulfil roles normally associated with women by choosing to remain chaste. The goddesses' visual constructions diverge with idealistic feminine portrayals of passivity and sexual availability and as such, they appear desexualised, neither female nor male but operating within an ambiguous position. It seems that because they rejected marriage and motherhood they were not envisaged as women in their own right, but were made more masculine or were portrayed as having had a very particular masculine-femininity (Halberstam 1998). Furthermore, they oppose concepts of prescribed female conduct. Their femininity was constructed in a very different manner from sexually active and mother deities such as Venus (see Chapter 2).

Twinship in Context

In conclusion, to this chapter, I consider Diana and Apollo in terms of their twinship. There has long been an interest in twinship over a wide variety of cultures (Douglas 1966:49: 188,208; Schwartz 1996; Argenti 2001:32-5, 40). However, the majority of literature deals principally with identical twins. In book seven of *History of Animals*, Aristotle indicates that among animals, if twins are of different sexes then they have equally as good a chance of surviving as same-sex twins. However, this, in his opinion does not apply to humans and states that if this is the case then very few male-female twins survive (Aristotle *History of Animals* 7.4). Hippocrates asserted that if a pregnant woman lost the fullness of either of her breasts then a child would die; if this occurred on the right side then the male child would be lost and the left for the female (Hippocrates, *Aphorisms* 5.38).[41] According to Plutarch, when twins are born, if one dies at birth the surviving child is named Vopiscus (Plutarch *Coriolanus* 11). It appears then, that there was perhaps a certain amount of symbolism and meaning associated with the birth of twins.

Aristotle claimed that on some occasions it was possible for paternity to differ for each twin. He asserted that if two conceptions occurred within a short interval the mother carried them as twins, and he gave the legend of Iphicles and Hercules as an example (Apollodorus *Library* 2.4-5l; Plautus *Amphitryo* 1096-1143). He illustrated this idea further by offering an example of an adulterous woman who had twins one of whom resembled her husband and the other her lover (Aristotle *History of Animals* 7.4). Of the cited same-sex twins within classical mythology (Livy 1.3 –1.6, Plutarch *Romulus*), Castor and Pollux (the Dioscuri) are perhaps second only to Romulus and Remus in notoriety.[42] Sons of Leda, Castor and Pollux have different fathers Castor the son of Tyndareus, and Pollux of Jupiter, whom turned himself into a swan in order to seduce Leda (Apollodorus 3.10.7; Euripides *Helen* 254, 1497, 1680).

This is one aspect that sets Diana and Apollo's twinship apart from the twins cited above in so far as they have the same, immortal father; of those cited above, Castor and Iphicles have mortal fathers, which consequently affects their fate and vice-versa. Iphicles died in battle against the Lacedaimonians (Apollodorus *Library* 2.7.3) and Castor fell in battle, though he eventually shared immortality amongst the stars with his brother, but only after his brother requested it from Jupiter (Apollodorus

[41] See Cartledge for Pythagorean principles (*Metaphysics* 586a table) showing the Greek binary cultural classifications placing women on the left along with darkness, crooked and unlimited – men on the right with light, straight and limited (Cartledge 1993: 13-16).

[42] However, Apollodorus recounted, that Leda had a multiple birth of four children, pairing Castor with Clytemnestra and Pollux with Helen (Apollodorus *Library* 3.10.7).

Library 3.11.2, Lucian *Dialogue of the Gods* 26). Romulus and Remus on the other hand shared the same paternity (Mars), yet Remus fell at the hands of his own brother (Livy 1.3 –1.6; Plutarch *Romulus* 2). It illustrates that although they are same-sex twins, they are not two halves of one being, but they are individuals and very different.

A further interesting point is of the pairs discussed above, Diana has instant maturity and was able to act as midwife for her mother, immediately helping her deliver her twin brother, Apollo (Apollodorus *Library* 1.4.1). Presumably, Diana helping her mother in childbirth essentially clarifies her role as goddess of childbirth. In Apollodorus' version of their births, Diana has no infancy and is automatically capable of the care and protection of her mother and twin, perhaps hinting at women's traditional role as midwives. Her compliance to protect and help pregnant women when she chose to remain chaste contributes to her complexity as an individual character. Apollo, on the other hand, had a brief infancy; the goddess Themis[43] fed him with nectar and ambrosia that rapidly aided him in his growth and maturity. After days, he was able to call for his bow and quiver (Homeric Hymn to Apollo 300-306). The advantage of this twinship of instant and delayed instant maturity is that the subjects are able to act more or less straight away. Their first dual mission entails a vengeance attack and slaughter of Python, whom sent by Hera, had persistently chased their mother in all directions over the earth (Apollodorus *Library* 1.4.1).

Hyginus, on relating the ill-fated tale of Niobe, expresses how she took pride in her own numerous children. She ranked her own children above Latona's whom she slighted because Diana dressed in man's clothing and Apollo was woman-like with long hair (Hyginus *Fabulae*.9). My interpretation of this statement is that Niobe is not describing them in terms of gender ambiguity, but she is individually attacking and ridiculing them and their mother. Hyginus' Niobe suggests that to contravene the delegated gender roles degrades them and allows them to be ridiculed. It would be suspect to assume that because they are twins their gender ascription acts on a compensatory basis, for example Diana having masculine weapons because Apollo is supposedly 'feminine', or that she is as masculine as he is feminine. This is not the case, gender ambivalence does not apply; Diana is definitely female and Apollo male. The difference with these mythological characters is the different types of femininity and masculinity they possess. Diana's femininity draws on her aspects as a huntress, virgin, goddess of childbirth, patroness of Amazons and this reflects in her visual appearance. Apollo, though some maintain is androgynous, has a particular masculinity that does not rely on feminine aspects, which in fact has little to do with women and more to do with youthful masculine beauty and homoeroticism. As the above passage suggests, gender ascription, whilst not embedded naturally in people it is learnt within the environment, which we live (Butler 1999). However, it also illustrates and reiterates that gendered roles are not inherent, but learnt.

The subjects of the following chapter are Minerva goddess of war and Hercules semi-divine hero. Diana and Minerva share common aspects: they are both chaste goddesses who occupy realms (godheads) that are generally associated with men and masculinity. Although Hercules commonly appears nude or semi-nude his body shape and physicality are in opposition to illustrations of Apollo. As previously mentioned, Apollo represents (amongst other things) masculine youth, whereas the majority of Hercules images depict a mature bearded figure (unless depicting him in childhood). These are discussed in the following chapter.

[43] Themis coincidently was able to foretell the future (Ovid *Metamorphoses* 1.260-415). Apollodorus names Themis as responsible for delivering the oracles at Delphi, before Apollo himself acquired the prophetic authority (Apollodorus *Library* 1.4.1).

Chapter 4

Minerva as active goddess of war (?) and Hercules, 'action hero' of the Greco-Roman World

This chapter focuses on the Minerva goddess of war and Hercules, the semi-divine hero. The aim is to examine their gender construction through the visual communication of Roman art and Roman British art. I have chosen Minerva and Hercules because of their specific roles and connections. Minerva was an important Roman deity, (one of the Capitoline triad) and she had a particular importance in Roman Britain especially in *Aquae Sulis*, modern Bath, Avon. She was a particular favourite of the emperor Domitian[44] and along with Vulcan she was a protector patron of Hercules, with the intention of benefiting him throughout his life, (Hesiod *Theogony* 318-319; Apollodorus *Library* 2.4.11; Diodorus of Sicily 4.14.1-3). Occasionally they appear within the same iconographical compositions (see below). Minerva was a virgin goddess of war, wisdom and handicrafts and I consider how these aspects influenced the way her femininity was presented. Hercules, on the hand was not a full deity, but a semi-divine hero and my interest is in how the artisans and patrons chose to present Hercules' masculinity. To do this it is necessary to consider the subjects individually.

Minerva

Minerva was a significant member of the Roman Pantheon, belonging to the Capitoline triad along with Jupiter Optimus Maximus and Juno Regina, with a temple dedicated to them on the Capitoline hill at Rome. Visual representations of Minerva appear to imitate the visual paradigm connected with Greek goddess Athena patroness of Athens. As the goddess of war, holds the weapons of war a spear and shield and she sports a Corinthian helmet (crested and peaked, occasionally with a face mask). On her aegis, is the head of Medusa,[45] given to her by Perseus after his quest to kill the gorgons (Apollodorus, *Library 2.4.3*; Ovid: *Metamorphoses 4.780*). Often representations of her sacred bird the owl and/or a winged Victory accompany her. Additionally Pliny named the olive as her sacred tree (Pliny *Natural History* 12.3).[46] A study of the visual construction of Minerva would not be complete without reference made to Greek prototypes, the majority of which survive as Roman copies. As a prime example, I have chosen the lost cult statue by Pheidias depicting Athena Parthenos (virgin) from the Parthenon, Athens, (previously referred to in Chapter 2 – Venus and Mars) because of the its value as a possible archetype and not because I believe the goddesses were equivalent or that Greek and Roman dress were the same, particularly considering the disparity in time scale. Evidently, Greek and Roman dress differed, but the basic components for the make up of Minerva's artistic construction and femininity appear to resemble. For example, her weapons of war, helmet and shield, but most important is the long draper practically covering her whole body. Pausanias commented on the Athena Parthenos statue describing it as follows:

> The statue is made of ivory and gold. She has a sphinx in the middle of her helmet, and griffins worked on either side of it ... the statue of Athena stands upright in an ankle length tunic with the head of medusa carved in ivory on her breast. She has a Victory about eight feet high, and a spear in her hand and a shield at her feet, and a snake beside the shield ... the plinth of the statue is carved with the birth of Pandora (Pausanias *Attica* 1.24.5-7. Levi 1979:69-70).

Unsurprisingly, such a valuable combination of material did not survive antiquity. Roman artisans took up this format and copies give us an idea of what she may have looked like, for example the Varvakeion Athena of the second century AD (Boardman 1992:110. fig.97). In addition, Pliny recorded the description of the statue, and gave us information relating to the compositions on her shield and sandals,

> On its [the shield] convex side Pheidias engraved the battle of the Amazons; and on the concave side, battles between gods and giants. And I shall cite her sandals, on which depicted battles between Lapiths and Centaurs. (Pliny, *Natural History* 36.18-19, Healy 1991: 346).

[44] For the emperor Domitian and Minerva see Chapter 6 - Funerary Art, and D'Ambra 1993: 5, Kleiner 1992:192.

[45] Minerva was the sworn enemy of Medusa and was according to myth responsible for the gorgon's appearance. Originally, Medusa was human and, according to Ovid, she had been an attractive woman with particularly striking hair until Poseidon raped her within the sacred temple of Minerva. Enraged by this blasphemous action, the goddess took her revenge, yet it was, ironically, not Poseidon she punished, but Medusa. Minerva attacked Medusa's most admirable asset, her hair, transforming her locks into live snakes (Ovid, *Metamorphoses*, 4.780). According to Apollodorus, the goddess turned Medusa into a gorgon with huge teeth, protruding tongue and glaring eyes; both her newly acquired gaze and inimical facial expression were sufficiently powerful to turn people into stone (Apollodorus: *Library*, 2. 4.3).

[46] Pliny's choice of the olive as her sacred tree, presumably originates from the myth of the battles between Athena and Poseidon for Athens. Poseidon took possession of Athens by violently thrusting his trident into the Acropolis at Athens that caused sea water to gush out and created a well. Athena on the other hand took a less violent approach and planted an olive tree. Eventually Zeus intervened and the possession of Athens decided by the remaining gods/goddesses, Athena won as she had given a more useful gift (Herodotus *Histories* 8.55, Apollodorus *Library* 3.14.1, Pausanias *Guide to Greece* 1.24.5).

Overall, it consisted of various compositions located on separate areas of the statue, such as the shield (with a central gorgoneion), sandals, and base. The images are mainly propagandist narratives illustrating the military and political power of the Greeks. For instance, the shield illustrated the battle between Greeks and Amazons on its exterior and the battle between gods and giants on its interior. The Greeks and gods attack and overthrow the 'other', thereby creating a polarity between Greeks (or more precisely Athenians) against non-male, warrior women Amazons and the gods themselves in conflict with non-human giants (Cartledge, 1993).[47] Accordingly, representations of the goddess had a history of involving the presentation of propagandist themes. A possible variant on the Athena Parthenos was found at the villa of Hadrian at Tivoli (Villa Albani, Rome, Boardman 1992, fig 201). The figures are akin for the most part with specific attention paid to the aegis and her long heavy robes. Her ankle-length, full drapery is a point of interest; what does it imply? At a basic level, her whole body is covered (although in some illustrations her arms are on view); even a helmet covers her head. As a result, we cannot see her body or her hair, which is short and concealed beneath the helmet. This implies that we are not permitted to gaze at her body or her hair.

Apparent visual signs indicating her sex are concealed beneath clothing and headgear. Her physical form and sexuality are suppressed; we are not to think of her as a sexual being. Her clothing acts as a visible sign analogous to that of a Roman *matrona* or married women. On marriage a women donned the *stola* a long, strapped garment that reached the feet, guarding the lower legs and feet from the gaze of others (Ovid *Art of Love* 1.31; Zanker 1988: 165-166; Davies 1997: 105; Sebesta: 1997: 536-537). Sebesta comments that, 'to see a woman's ankles and feet uncovered was essentially equivalent to seeing her 'naked', a right reserved only to her husband' (Sebesta: 1997: 537). Moreover, Zanker states that, 'in the context of social legislation [Augustan] the *stola* became a symbol of female virtue and modesty ... wearing a *stola* was not only an honour but a "protection from unwanted attentions"' (Zanker 1988: 165). The *stola* then visually indicated matrons' sexual inviolability (Sebesta 1997:535). I propose that this is why Minerva has long garments, as a chaste, virgin goddess her drapery, as the *stola* indicates her sexual inviolability.

A further archetypal example described by Pliny as 'Marsyas Wondering at the Flute in the Company of Athena by Myron (Pliny *Natural History* 34.57).[48] A Roman copy now in the Liebighaus Museum, Frankfurt (Robertson 1981: 117, fig 159) draws attention to the goddess' short hair as her thick, individually carved curls extend beyond her helmet. This type of animated curled hair is usually a feature of portrait sculptures conceivably evoking the personas of Hellenistic rulers such as Alexander (Zanker 1988: 10; Bartman 2001:3). The goddess has the same features; hair implies movement and therefore an active role that was usually associated with men and representations of masculinity. Minerva therefore transgressed conceptions of conventional femininity by having a masculine trait. Conclusively then, archetypal Athena/Minerva[49] 'types' are useful to the present study, I am not suggesting that all the images of Athena/Minerva are direct copies of these prototypes, but these examples are important to discuss in the understanding of visual representation and communication of the goddess. Moreover, I am aware of the time lapse, but I think that this is important. It is clear that in some cases a retrospective aspect was preferred for a number of reasons depending on the patron or creator. Furthermore, although the images I have discussed are copies of Greek masterpieces, however faithful, they are still Roman works of art and within the study area.

Images of Minerva from Roman Britain

The most prominent site in Britain relating to Minerva has to be the Temple of Sulis-Minerva in Bath, Avon. The iconic bronze head of Minerva was found within the baths complex vicinity (Roman Baths Museum, Bath, Cunliffe and Fulford 1982:9, fig 25). Identification depends on the crown of centrally parted hair, which most probably formed the base for a Corinthian helmet. Sulis was a British water deity and healing goddess who presided over the sacred spring at Bath. Philologically, her name is associated with the sun, which may be an allusion to the heat of the natural spring water (Green, 1992: 201). The baths complex with its naturally hot spring water was celebrated as a healing sanctuary. The connection between Sulis and Minerva, it would seem, occurred because of their association with healing. As Minerva *Medica* the goddess was patron of those practicing medicine. Furthermore, Minerva's association with Athena links her to Asclepius, the believed founder of medicine. According to Diodorus of Sicily, the goddess had given Asclepius two phials of Medusa's blood. One filled with blood from the left side, with which he could raise the dead, the other from the right, with this he could annihilate enemies instantly (Diodorus of Sicily *Library of History: 5.746*). A relief from Carrawburgh, Hadrian's Wall illustrates Minerva and Asclepius (Chesters Museum, Coulston and Phillips 1988: 31, fig. 85). The representation of Minerva survives in full, but only the calves, feet and customary snake entwined staff of Asclepius survive. The figures stand within a niche. Minerva wears her customary crested helmet, full drapery and aegis with the gorgoneion. Her shield rests behind her legs with just a semi-circular edge showing. I think it is interesting how much attention there is to the carving of her drapery, as with the image discussed above her body shape is masked

[47] For more on the Greeks and polarity with 'others' see Cartledge 1993.

[48] For an example of the group, see Boardman 1992: 61, fig. 61. According to Smith the original group may have had topical contemporary references claiming Athenian cultural superiority over rustic, flute playing Thebes, Athena embodying Athena and Marsyas Thebes (Smith: 1995:106).

[49] The goddesses are joined in this manner, not because I believe that they are direct equivalents, but that the image type has a long history into the Roman period.

by weighty adornment. Such weighty clothing gives the impression of inactivity, as it would obstruct movement. This is evident on a relief from Bath (Roman Baths Museum, Cunliffe and Fulford 1982, fig. 25) again the goddess is weighed down with bulky, long drapery. This is a contradictory attribute for a goddess of war, whose very title suggests action.

A freestanding sculpture of the goddess from Cambridgeshire has a slight indication of movement as she rests her weight on one leg (Woburn Abbey, Befordshire, Huskinson 1994, fig 10a). Nevertheless, the principle is the same fully covered and hampered. The way this example has a *palla* [50] (type of mantle) draped and wrapped around her body is evocative of statuary representing women with robes securely bound around them, generally covering the arms and particularly the hands.[51] Croom, in her study on Roman clothing, comments on how the *palla* in all probability was once intended as a protective garment against bad weather, however it quickly became an essential covering for a 'modest' women and ultimately no respectable woman would appear in public without her head and body covered (Croom 2000:87). Furthermore, she comments on the impractical quality of the garment, for as with the toga, the *palla* needed at least one hand to keep it in position. As she states, 'the *palla* was therefore no more suitable for working in than the developed forms of toga, and while that was no problem for the rich who had slaves to carry objects for them, it would have been cumbersome for the majority of the population' (Croom 2000: 87). To be respectable therefore requires a restriction in movement, passivity and inaction. Additionally, Davies in her study on gender and body language in Roman art observed that such garments imprisoned the arms and forced the wearer to perform an array of barrier gestures creating the impression of uncertainty and a lack of confidence. As Davies points out, 'even the boldest and least repressed Roman women appear in public statues as if behaving defensively (defensively being seen as a sign of modesty)' (Davies 1997: 102). Therefore, as a goddess of war you would not expect illustrations of Minerva to appear defensive or repressed, yet I propose that her visual construction was treated in the same way. Furthermore, it is worth mentioning that Minerva was also a goddess of wisdom; inferring education, was this to be repressed also? There appears to be a general theme promoting inactivity whilst giving the impression that women had a lack of control over their bodies and indeed their whole being and should therefore be controlled.

Minerva features on a silver skillet handle from Northumberland, part of the Capheaton Treasure (fig. 13) (Toynbee 1964:304-305; Lindgren 1980:100; Henig 1984:43-46). The handle has elaborate decoration demonstrating a water theme with a temple perhaps

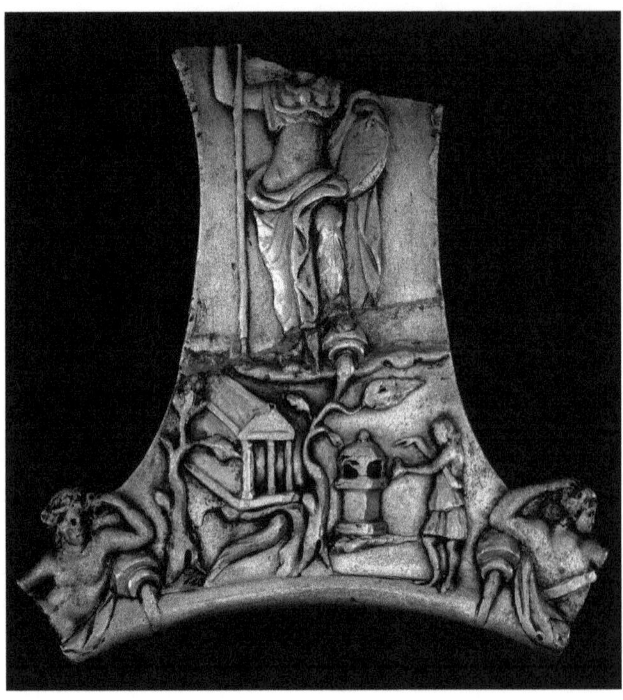

Fig. 13. Silver handle showing Minerva, 2nd or 3rd century AD, from Capheaton, Northumberland, British Museum, London. © Trustees of the British Museum

indicating an illustration of a sacred spring complex. It would be agreeable to imagine this was a portrayal of the Temple of Sulis-Minerva, but as we have no way of knowing, it is unfortunately a fanciful notion. However, what we can assume is that this silver handle was a part ornamental object that was certainly a status symbol of wealth and knowledge of classical subjects (Toynbee 1964:304-305; Lindgren 1980:100; Henig 1984:43-46). The presentation of Minerva in this piece is extraordinary. The colour of the fallen drapery draws attention to Minerva's hips and midriff part of it falls away revealing her leg, although Minerva is clothed in her familiar long drapery, the way the arrangement of the cloth is reminiscent of a Venus, principally the Venus of Arles (Louvre, Paris) or Venus of Capua (Museo Nazionale, Naples) types.[52] The Venus of Capua in particular has her leg raised resting on the helmet of Mars, on the skillet handle, Minerva also has her leg raised, but her foot rests on an overflowing urn. As discussed in the previous chapter on Venus (Chapter 2. Venus and Mars), nude figures precariously draped in fact draw attention to the particular area that is covered/uncovered. On the skillet handle, by the different use of colour, the contrast of silver and gold colours exaggerates the position of the drapery. Furthermore, the way Minerva's stands with her weight on one leg emphasizes her hips and her waist thus accentuating her body shape. This is contradictory to the examples discussed above, where Minerva has her femininity and sexuality suppressed, and I would argue that this example is quite the opposite, her femininity and sexuality is on display. As mentioned above, Minerva

[50] A *palla* , worn by women , was a large rectangle of material that enveloped the body from shoulder to knee or lower calf (Croom 2000:87).

[51] See Davies, 1997:103 fig 9 and Croom 2000: 87-88 fig.41.

[52] For more on these and other Venus types see Smith 1995: 79-83.

was a chaste goddess; therefore, this construction was a curious choice. Her pose draws on that of Venus rather than Minerva, yet she is fully clothed creating a dual but conflicting image. Ultimately, the example portrays a paradoxical example of Minerva; she is a virgin Venus in clothing.

A relief found at Aldsworth in Gloucestershire has two carved figures Henig identified as Minerva and Mercury (Henig 2000:362-383). The relief was found in a field in Aldsworth overlooking a flat plain of a Romano-British settlement (Henig 2000 362). The two deities stand side by side within an architectural style recess. Although the right corner including the head of the goddess is missing, Henig's identification is probable. Mercury has his familiar attributes, namely the wings in his hair, a purse, a caduceus and a cockerel.[53] Minerva follows the usual visual formula. Her heavy tunic reaches the floor and her mantle falls across her body, in her right hand, she holds a spear and in her left, she grasps what appears to be a shield. According to Henig, this is the first example of the deities together from the Cotswolds region (Henig 2000:363). Minerva holds her weapons of war, her spear and shield, equipment (as stated previously in Chapter 3 - Diana and Apollo) that was associated with masculinity. Mercury holds a caduceus symbolising his identity as herald of the gods/goddesses and a purse signifying his role as a prosperity god. Portrayals of Mercury are generally youthful and nude.

The Farnese Hermes (Roman copy original of a late fourth century original, Vatican Museum, Rome (Smith: 1995: 64, fig 69) and the Hermes and Dionysus as a child (Roman Copy after Praxiteles, Archaeological Museum Olympia) may be among prototypes for illustrations of Mercury, as the two were ultimately associated. The treatment of the carved curled hair is a feature that appears on Mercury sculptures from Roman Britain, for example that of the Mercury from Uley[54] (fig. 17-19), Cirencester (Corinium Museum, Lindgren 1980, plate 27) and Cambridge, University Museum of Archaeology and Anthropology, Lindgren 1980, plate 13). Moreover, they tend to have the same stance, with weight resting on one leg, emphasising the body shape. Youth and nudity places them within the same visual category as Apollo (fig. 8) or a youthful Mars, for example Ares Borghese.

As discussed previously, images of the aforementioned deities project passivity attributable to a number of characteristics, including youth and body language, particularly relating to the position of the head and the lack of eye contact with the viewer.[55] I propose that the Aldsworth Mercury is no different, and as the work follows a similar paradigm, it carries the same implications. Furthermore, the visual dynamics between Minerva and Mercury in this relief are complex. I propose that in this example, Mercury appears more vulnerable and passive in comparison to the goddess. Minerva has war paraphernalia associated with masculinity. Although the right hand corner is missing, their shoulders are at the same level; therefore, it is reasonable to assume they were the same size; if anything Minerva's heavy drapery takes up more body space. This contributes to Mercury's submissiveness, as generally masculine subjects had a higher position within the composition, their bigger bodies thus stressing their higher status. Furthermore and possibly the most apparent difference is Mercury's nakedness; Minerva's body is covered whereas his is exposed and vulnerable. The portrayals of masculinity and femininity are not straightforward; they are a complicated combination of gendered signs illustrating a feminine-masculine goddess and a god whose masculinity projects submissiveness and passivity that was associated with women and adolescent boys. At this point, I will turn my attention to Hercules, a persona that frequently appeared within the same composition as Minerva.

Action hero: the exploits and labours of Hercules

In 1970 Arnold Schwarzenegger appeared in *Hercules in New York*, it may seem a little curious to add this case in point to this study, but I consider film as a visual medium akin to art. Both are examples of created material culture offering narratives through visual communication – even film has a materiality. In the same year of the film release, Schwarzenegger won the title of Mr. Universe, so clearly for the filmmakers he epitomised the visual[56] masculinity required to play Hercules (Arroyo 2000: 28).[57] In both the classical and modern western capitalist visual discourses, the overemphasised musculature of the hypermasculine male is a powerful trope. This especially applies to characters involved with deeds of action and bravery such as Mars and Hercules (and thus arguably, Arnold Schwarzenegger, Sylvester Stallone and other male lead figures in the modern 'action' film genre). Holmlund in her work on gender and film considers why the male action hero continues to appeal and concluded that they represent a masculinity that is removed from reality. As she states, 'today, other bellicose stars might replace Sly [Stallone] or Arnold, but male action figures who move a lot and say little continue to entertain audiences everywhere, *because* they are what we are not' (Holmlund 2002:4). I suggest that this modern example can be useful in the understanding of Greco-Roman visual portrayals of Hercules, as I think that the visual construction of Hercules worked in the same way. His representations offered a superhuman hero victoriously battling a doomed enemy, as civilisation overcomes the unknown. Hercules exemplifies an 'action hero' of the Greco-Roman world and as with Schwarzenegger and Stallone, his treatment and presentation constitute hypermasculine fiction.

53 For more examples of Mercury from Roman Britain see, Phillips 1977 figs 18-28, Lindgren 1980 plates 1-34 and Henig 1993 figs 70, 72-3.

54 For more on the Uley Mercury see, Henig 1993a: 88-94

55 See Chapter 2 – Venus and Mars and Chapter 3 – Diana and Apollo.

56 His voice was not used in the film it was dubbed with an American voice over, his body was the main appeal for the role.

57 For more on Schwarzenegger as 'spectacle' see Arroyo 2000: 27-58.

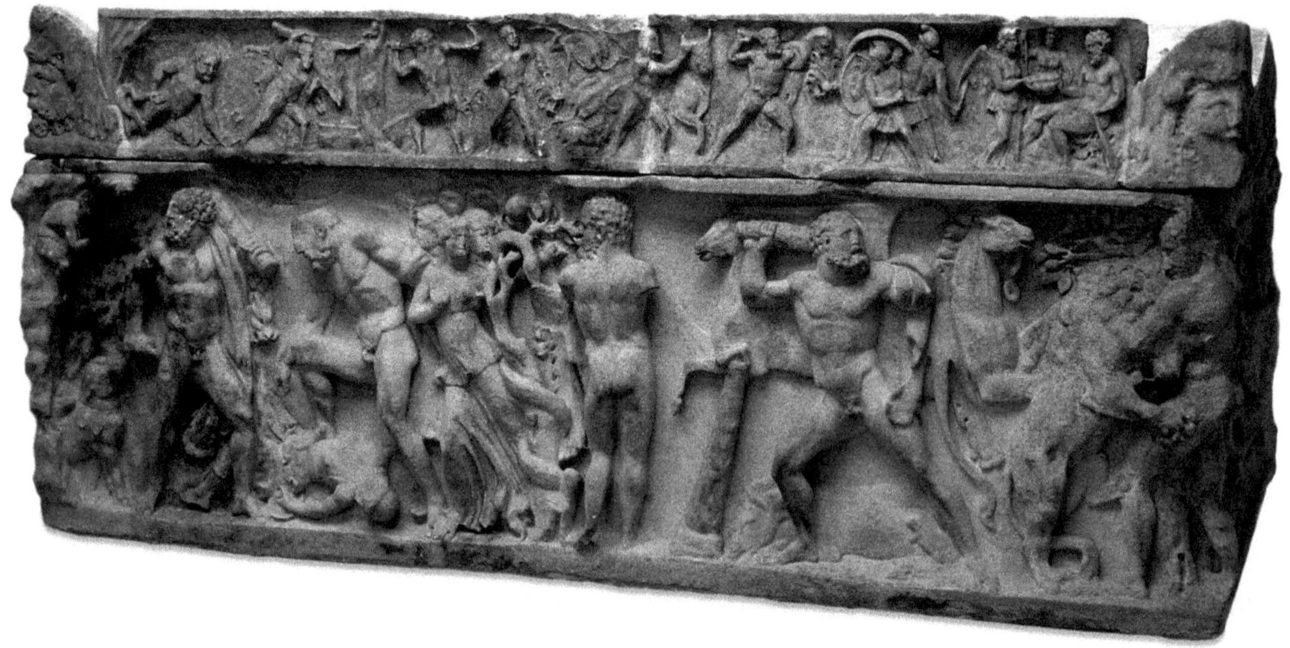

Fig. 14. Labours of Hercules, marble sarcophagus from Genzano on the Via Appia, c. 150-180 AD British Museum, London. © Trustees of the British Museum

Among the most notable of his action packed exploits are the twelve labours set for him by Eurystheus, king of Tiryns, as penance for killing his own wife and children. Hera jealously resented the success of her stepson and decided to bestow insanity upon him. Hercules reacted by murdering his family. On regaining his wits, he went to the Delphic oracle to inquire what he should do. The Pythoness then disclosed his fate, for the next twelve years, he should serve Eurystheus at Tiryns and perform any task required, after which he would earn immortality (Apollodorus 2.4.12; Diodorus of Sicily 4.10-11).

A good example of Hercules as the archetypal 'action' hero is apparent on a sarcophagus from Genzano on the Via Appia, Rome and now in the British Museum (fig. 14).[58] This action packed relief begins with Hercules' first task; the slaying of the Nemean lion is where Hercules acquires his lion skin, an attribute that contributes to his visual recognition. The tasks do not appear to be in any particular order, this is perhaps artistic license making the sculpting more straightforward. For instance, in this depiction of Hercules taking Hyppolyte's girdle (ninth task) and the plucking of the apples of Hesperides (eleventh task), the sculptor utilised the space by carving them from the same piece. The overall sarcophagus composition depicts Hercules performing all twelve labours. Hercules, born a mortal could achieve immortality on completing his tasks; this is probably the reason why the Labours became a popular theme for funerary art (Kleiner 1992:306). In various poses, Hercules is in an active position and this is the fundamental idea; he has an active role performing in some cases violence on another body. The scene mentioned above (the taking of Hyppolyte's girdle) has connotations of sex, rape and violence. In the small scene, Hercules fends off defending Amazons, while he kills Hyppolyte in order to get the girdle (Diodorus of Sicily 4.16; Apollodorus 2.5.9). The scene is graphically violent as Hercules literally steps on the fallen Hyppolyte. By the implication of removing an item form her body he is performing a violation against her fallen body. Fredrick, in his paper on violence in Roman elegy proposes that violence was often a metaphor for sex; the beaten become the penetrable passive sexual partner (Fredrick 1997: 172-193). As he states, 'torn dresses, pulled hair, scratches, and bruises are scattered through elegy, often in association with love making … metaphor apparently becomes penetrable flesh (Fredrick 1997:172). In the case of Hercules and Hyppolyte, the medium is visual rather than textual, but the metaphor is still applicable. The way Hercules steps on Hyppolyte, it could be said that his violence shows sadism, whilst her incapacitated body suggests sexual violation. Furthermore, as an Amazon she represented the epitome of what a women should not be, thus illustrating what happens to women who do not follow state protocols of approved femininity (Tyrrell 1984).

A relief from Corbridge shows a representation of Minerva with Hercules illustrating the second labour of Hercules the slaying of the Lernean Hydra (Corbridge Museum. Toynbee 1962, fig 49). Phillips suggests that this relief was a part of a frieze depicting the Labours of Hercules reminiscent of that from the Temple of Zeus at Olympia (Phillips 1977:3). It is comparable with the illustration of the twelfth Labour of Hercules, the cleansing of the Augeas stables depicted among the east

[58] For a description of the over all scenes see, Walker 1985:34-35, fig. 24.

metopes at Olympia (Olympia Museum, Boardman 1992, fig 23.6).[59] Clearly, the parallel is the inclusion of Minerva as patron guiding Hercules in his task. However, the treatment of illustration is very different, Minerva appears more important in the Olympian example as her status is highlighted by her position in the forefront and her upright height over a crouched Hercules. On the other hand, the Corbridge Minerva is quite the opposite in size. Toynbee suggested that Minerva was smaller in scale than Hercules because of her position in the background (Toynbee 1964:154). However, I would argue that the deliberate size difference relates to the importance of the subjects presented. Minerva is a fraction of the size of Hercules and despite Minerva's higher ranking as a deity, it is clear that Hercules is of more significance in this composition, furthermore he is active as opposed to Minerva's inactivity. Indeed Hercules is literally bursting out of the frame as his club and his foot overlap the borders of the relief. As mentioned above, the work depicts an exploit of Hercules, it shows the actual conflict; Hercules overcoming the Hydra is the core theme. The slab was found in what is thought to be the safe room where the Standards were kept in the Western Headquarters building (site xlv) in 1912 (Phillips, 1977:3.fig.6). If this were the case then Hercules with his colossal strength was an appropriate choice. In the relief, he is about to strike the multiple headed Hydra with his club, Minerva his patroness, beside him, pointing as if showing him the optimal angle from which to attack the Hydra. The Hydra, a twelve-headed monster, represents the non-human 'other' that automatically presents an opposition that was set up to fail. A hypermasculine Hercules encapsulates the masculine brute force required as an inspiration for the viewers to protect the Standards and Rome. There is a contradiction of status creating a three-way polarization amid the subjects depicted. The undersized Minerva, who has the highest status as a deity is the smallest and overshadowed by the overt masculinity of semi-divine Hercules, who in turn overpowers the mortal, non-human Hydra. The emphasis is on hypermasculine Hercules, the hero, perhaps reflecting the tastes of a predominantly male environment from which this relief was a part.

A bronze figurine from Cheapside, London illustrates Hercules in mid action; Henig suggests that this figurine may show Hercules shooting at the Stymphalian Birds (sixth task) (British Museum, Henig 1995:82, fig. 49). Apollodorus and Pausanias mentioned he shot arrows at the Stymphalian birds (Apollodorus *Library* 2.5, Pausanias *Guide to Greece* 8.22.4-6). His overall pose of this figure suggests activity, there was particular attention paid to the animation of hair and beard and his wide, open pose suggests confidence and power aspects associated with promoting correct masculinity (Davies 1997: 102-103).

Conclusively, the embodiment of Hercules as 'action hero' more often than not depends on the composition. His status depends on him having a combatant, a doomed adversary. The general theme, in fact, covers a variety of foes including monsters, giants, unruly women, ferocious animals and chaotic nature all controlled and conquered by 'action hero' Hercules, enforcer of civilization.

Hercules, political propaganda and the Emperors

As mentioned in Chapter 3 (Apollo and Diana), Mark Antony associated himself with Hercules. During and after the civil wars Hercules became part of the visual political propaganda, particularly concerning the myth recounting his dispute with Apollo (with whom Octavian associated himself) and his enslavement to Omphale, queen of the Lydians an analogy of Cleopatra. Although, as far as I am aware there are no examples of Hercules and Omphale for Roman Britain, but as my work focuses on the representation of gender, it is fitting that I should mention illustrations of Hercules and Omphale and the reversed gender roles that feature in the tale. This occurred when Hercules sold himself into slavery as retribution for murdering his guest, Iphitus. Subsequent to the completion of his specified twelve labours, Hercules once again committed murder; this time anger was the catalyst, Iphitus wrongly accused Hercules of theft, so he threw Iphitus to his death from a high tower (Apollodorus 2.6.2; Diodorus of Sicily 4.31). As Mark Antony associated himself with Hercules then Omphale became an easy label for Cleopatra, as she supposedly enslaved Mark Antony (Zanker 1988: 59-60; Kampen 1996a: 235; Montserrat 2000:158-159). Writers of the early imperial period drew attention to their reversed gendered roles, thereby attacking Hercules' (and as a result Mark Antony's) masculinity, as he was not a free citizen, being owned by a woman; at the same time, Omphale's (consequently Cleopatra's) femininity was attacked. Her powerful role and control over Hercules shows aspects normally associated with men; ultimately she represented a non-Roman 'other' analogous with female personas such as Medea and Penthesilea the Amazon (Propertius 3.3.11; Kampen 1996: 235). There was particular emphasis on their lavish and decadent lifestyle and the non-masculine tasks Omphale required of Hercules, particularly such as spinning and dressing up in Omphale's in luxurious eastern clothing whilst she donned his lion skin and club (Propertius 3.11; Ovid *Heroides* 9; Horace, *Epode* 9.15; Plutarch *Antony and Demetrius* 3). An illustration reminiscent of this theme forms the decoration mould for an Arretine clay bowl of Augustan date (c.30 BC, Metropolitan Museum of Art, New York, Zanker 1988: 58-59, fig. 45a-b).[60] The main subjects visually juxtapose each other; they appear in separate, but identical chariots and display a deliberate play on prescribed gender indicators. Hercules is adorned in diaphanous drapery - akin to the female attendants - and lounges as if on a couch, looking over his shoulder to Omphale, who is sitting confidently upright, looking back

[59] For more on the metopes frieze depicting the Labours of Hercules and other sculptural work from the Temple of Zeus at Olympia see Boardman 1992: 33-50, Boardman 1993: 9394.

[60] For an idea of this theme decorating a bowl, see Kampen 1996: 236, fig 97a and 97b.

at him. She is clad in his lion skin and in the crook of her arm she rests his club, as if it was a cornucopia. Kampen suggests that her pose and the position of the club adds to the impression of her dominance, 'Omphale's serious and stable pose [is] made visible by the powerful phallic form of the club and the strong horizontals of the right arm and left thigh' (Kampen 1996a: 236). Omphale's posture offers a contrast against Hercules' relaxed, intoxicated, lounging manner. Zanker draws attention to the attack on Cleopatra's personal conduct, as on the mould, an attendant girl hands Omphale a large drinking vessel. As he states, 'this touch is aimed directly at Cleopatra, who was ridiculed by Octavian and his circle for her bibulousness' (Zanker 1988: 59-60). Attacks on Cleopatra were easier because of her status as a non-Roman woman who had considerable power, a concept that unthinkable for a Roman woman, not only did she have power over her nation but she had power over a member of the Roman elite, Mark Antony. Although both scholars mention the centaurs, they pay no attention to possible reasons why they appear drawing the chariots, or why they are bound. I propose that their inclusion enhances the impression of 'otherness' indicative of a world on the margins of known world where a woman has the authority to rule with the power to make men dress as women and tame the virile centaur and centaurs are themselves ambiguous men/beasts. Their presence indicates a non-civilised 'barbarian' world removed from Roman civilisation where men rule and women comply. Ovid stated that Omphale and Hercules took part in their exchange of clothing, whilst following the rites of Bacchus (Ovid, *Fasti: Lupercalia 25.*). Hercules and Bacchus drinking together became a popular theme particularly for domestic imagery (Kampen 1996:242),[61] for example a later depiction from Roman Britain depicting an intoxicated Hercules on the great dish of the Mildenhall treasure.

Mildenhall Dish: Hercules

A large silver dish, a part of the Mildenhall treasure, from Suffolk depicts a Bacchic scene surrounding a central aquatic theme with Oceanus, sea nymphs and other sea creatures encircled by scallop shells (fourth century AD) (Toynbee 1964:170; Henig 1995: 143). Two male revelers hold up a drunken Hercules, his lion skin and club on the floor beneath him denoting his identity. Bacchus, on the other hand, appears unaffected; in his right hand, he holds up his sacred grapes and in his left holds a thyrsus whilst resting one foot on his panther. This plate is of interest because it demonstrates stereotypical examples of the male nude in the same scene, Bacchus as the passive youth and Hercules as mature and hypermasculine. However, in this example Hercules' intoxicated condition puts him at a disadvantage; he is not in control of his own body and therefore, his masculinity is under attack. As Walters points out, the definition of elite masculinity depended on the protection of the corporeal, 'Roman sexual protocol that defined men as impenetrable penetrators can most usefully be seen in the context of a wider conceptual pattern that characterised those of high social status as being able to defend the boundaries of their own body from invasive assaults of all kinds' (Walters 1997:30). Hercules looks as if he would fall if not held; he could not defend himself from invasive assaults and therefore does not fit the promoted masculine protocol. Drunken, Hercules may then be associated with ridicule, as in the image on the Arretine bowl mould and unusually his muscle-bound body has little effect on the portrayal of his masculinity.

In later Roman history, and presumably when the hostility towards Mark Antony was forgotten, Hercules once again became popular particularly with those who wanted to assert their self-image by associating themselves with him; these include the emperors Commodus (180-192AD) and Caracalla (211-217AD). A good example is the renowned portrait of Commodus in the guise of Hercules from the Esquiline hill, Rome (Museo del Palazzo dei Conservatori, Rome, Kleiner 1992, fig. 243). The quarter length sculpture was originally part of a group where he was flanked by tritons and two Amazon kneel beneath him. His upper body rests on an Amazon peltae above crossing cornucopia the stems of which encircle an orb (Kleiner 1992:276-277; Huskinson 1993: 297,302; D'Ambra 1998: 111-112). Commodus donned the attributes of Hercules and believed himself as a god on earth, Hercules incarnate, calling himself Hercules Romanus (Cassius Dio 73.15) (Coulston and Phillips 1988:77, Kleiner 1992:268). Cassius Dio and Herodian testified that Commodus set up a vast number of statues of himself in the garb of Hercules (Cassius Dio 73.15; Herodian 1.14.8). Furthermore, in the *Historia Augusta*, the author documents that he accepted offerings made to him as the god (*Historia Augusta Commodus Antoninus 9.2*). This is evidenced on the Esquiline sculpture as he holds the apples of Hesperides, suggesting that he portrays Hercules after his labours and thereafter he was made immortal. Or as stated by D'Ambra, 'Commodus may have valued Hercules not only as a superhero of inestimable strength but also as a hero of culture, the tamer of wild things and supporter of the natural order of men and gods' (D'Ambra 1998:111). However, what does this sculpture tell us about the way he (and the sculptor) chose to present his masculinity? The most apparent indicator is his well-formed muscular upper body. His hair and beard fashioned in the same manner as his father, Marcus Aurelius emphasises his dynastic connection (Brilliant 1994:84; Kleiner 1992 fig 237, 238) and therefore his natural authority through his birthright as the son of an emperor. The attributes of Hercules suggest his strength and dominance. Finally and at a basic, level his masculinity literally towers over the miniature feminine Amazons who kneel beneath him (only one remains). Furthermore, their kneeling positions not only make them smaller in comparison, but they display a submissive attitude, particularly since they have one breast revealed, they appear vulnerable. Moreover, it presents an image of the subjugated 'barbarian'. Overall,

[61] For more examples see Kampen 1996:242-243.

the sculpture reflects a combination of political spin doctoring and personal image management.

A gilded copper statuette said to be from Hadrian's Wall near Birdoswald, Cumbria probably illustrates Commodus as Hercules (British Museum). How do we know that this not an outright example of Hercules? The most apparent visual disparity would be the smaller and less muscular body. Furthermore, he has clothing: Hercules generally appears nude, and lastly he has no beard. The latter point is problematic, as both Hercules and Commodus commonly appear bearded. Perhaps this portrays a youthful example of Commodus in the guise of Hercules, perhaps promoting the idea that he had a long history of association with Hercules. According to Coulston and Phillips, he wears a gladiatorial tunic and belt, alluding to his controversial exploits displaying himself as a gladiator in the arena (Cassius Dio 73.17; Herodian 1.15-17) (Coulston and Phillips 1988: 77). He was promoting his own masculinity by exhibiting his power at the amphitheatre in literal displays of strength with fatal assaults on both animals and people (Cassius Dio 73.17). Therefore, in this presentation, the emperor has the attributes of Hercules combined with the concepts of vigorous combatant fighting associated with gladiators. Other than this example, it would be worth postulating the idea that some of the images of Hercules in Britain are present because of the promotion of the deity as a link to Commodus, but unfortunately, without direct evidence there is no way of knowing.

A further emperor, commonly linked with Hercules was the son of Septimus Severus, Caracalla. There are a number of reasons for this: for one Hercules was a sacred deity among the inhabitants of the African city of Lepcis Magna, the birthplace of his father (Marsden and Henig 2002: 421). Secondly, according to Spartianus, Caracalla did not call himself Hercules, but was called this by his friends, because he killed a lion and some other wild beasts (Spartianus, *Life of Antoninus Caracalla* 5). Associations with Hercules apparently started at an early age, as a sculpture from the Museo Capitolino, Rome (c. 190s, Kleiner 1992, fig 285), would seem to demonstrate. The work portrays Caracalla as the infant Hercules about to strangle serpents sent by to kill him by Juno (Apollodorus 2.4.8). Kleiner states that the sculpture can be identified by his physical facial appearance, 'the round face and chubby cheeks, as well as the upturned nose, identify him as Caracalla, whose face was framed with a full cap of drilled and tousled hair (Kleiner 1992:322). However, I think this identification is tenuous and perhaps a little too convenient. How do we know it is a portrait? As mentioned above, Hercules was sacred to the Severans because of their familial background, therefore why can this image not depict Hercules as a child and not a portrait, furthermore why is it Caracalla and not Geta? I think it is later associations that form an easy identification for this work.

According to Marsden and Henig a cornelian intaglio found near Lincoln (c.208-11AD) depicts Victory crowing Caracalla in the guise of Hercules (Marsden and Henig 2002:419-422; Henig 2002: 72, 75). Victory crowns the emperor celebrating his military prowess whilst his adoption of Hercules' lion skin and club associates him with strength. The juxtapositioning of the subjects is an interesting factor, Victory a personification deity is considerably smaller than the figure she is crowning and to reach the subject she stands on a column, and he is still taller. Clearly, the masculine figure was the focal point of the carving. A reduced feminine subject offers a contrast with the muscular, tall and wide masculine type, betraying a hierarchical status. The Victory holds up a laurel wreath to crown the victorious subject. Victory was often depicted crowning the victorious (see Chapter 5), particularly emperors, therefore it is reasonable to note that this may be an emperor in the guise of Hercules. Furthermore, the subject already appears to wear a headdress of some kind, a feature that does not apply to Hercules. Marsden and Henig indicate that this is not a diadem or a laurel wreath, but a radiate crown (Marsden and Henig 2002: 421). Caracalla does appear on coins donned in a radiate crown (Besly 1987:13, fig, 40). However, I would argue that the intaglio carving does not show a spiked ray effect, but when taking a closer look at the image, the effect is rounded and not spiked. Clearly, the artisan had the skill to carry out the type of ray required to carve a radiate crown as evidenced by the pointed palm held by Victory, but this is not depicted. I propose that the headgear shows the engraver's foreshortened interpretation of a laurel wreath indicating an emperor and not Hercules. The wearer of the intaglio associated themselves with the emperor, Hercules and Victory, whilst the image of Caracalla as Hercules travels, increasing the potential propagandist worth of the image.

Conclusion

Minerva exceeds the boundaries of promoted femininity – she has wild, masculine hair that is often concealed by a helmet and not the controlled, managed hairstyles of conventional images of Roman women. Furthermore her voluntary chastity and therefore denial of child bearing was a rejection of her role as a woman. She has a particular masculine-femininity. However, her masculine traits are limited to short hair and the holding of weapons, her long heavy clothing restricts her movement and therefore she appears unable to have that 'masculine' active role. Her masculinity and her femininity are suppressed. Hercules on the other hand, epitomises the all-active hypermasculine 'action hero', with rippling muscles and a full beard.

At the beginning of the chapter I mentioned that it seems probable that artistic representations of Minerva were based on those of Greek Athena goddess of war and wisdom. She was commonly depicted with a winged *Nike* (Victory). The next chapter examines gender construction of Victory and other personifications in Roman art.

Chapter 5

The Use of Personifications in Roman Art with particular reference to Roman Britain

The aim of this chapter is to focus on the personification of abstract themes, ideas and physical places. As an introductory example I examine a seventeenth century engraving depicting personified subjects at the moment Europe discovered America. Other visual examples derive from the Sebasteion, Aphrodisias and Rome, however the majority of examples originated from Roman Britain as this dissertation has a particular reference to this period.

The deification of abstract ideas is thought to date from the fourth century BC and probably earlier still (Beard et al 1998: 2). The themes vary from concepts including particular virtues or the changing seasons to personified places, though in the main they remained non-personalised with no individual personality or mythology. In *The Nature of the Gods*, Cicero offered an explanation of deified personifications as part of an argument that proposed to prove the existence of the gods and their care for humanity (as his estimation was centred explicitly on Stoic philosophy) (Beard et al 1998: 2), through a dialogue between his characters Balbus and Cotta.

> There are also many other aspects of divinity which have been rightly named and recognised in accordance with the great benefits which they confer, by the wisest men of Greece and by our own ancestors. Indeed, whatever brought great benefit to the human race they thought to be the expression of some divine benevolence towards mankind. So they named the various gifts of the gods as though they were gods in their own right ... or a quality which manifests some great power is itself named as a god, such as Faith and Reason ... Wealth, Salvation, Concord, Liberty, Victory – all of these, on account of their great power, which seem to demand a divine origin have been named as gods (Cicero, *The Nature of the Gods* 2.60-2, McGregor 1972:147).

My interest in this chapter is to look at the way personifications were visually constructed and the different ways they were worked within artistic and thematic representation. I consider how personifications were presented in terms of gender representation. This entails an examination of the composition itself with attention paid to the position of the subject within the composition (if applicable), the way in which the subjects were portrayed, the way they were clothed or non-clothed, the types of objects or items depicted with the subjects; all the effects that were attributed to the personification have relevance to the interpretation. I begin by looking at the anthropomorphic forms of places.

Gendered Lands

This begins by examining an engraving (c.1600) by Theodore Galle copied from a drawing by Jan van der Straet customarily known as Stradanus (British Museum, McClintock 1995, fig 1.1). The engraving shows a feminine personification of America and her masculine 'conqueror' Europe. I have chosen this example, as I believe it is an appropriate introduction to post-colonial discourse concerning visual imagery, a theme that is equally applicable and highly visible in Roman art. The composition offers an allegory illustrating the moment America was 'discovered' by Europe, as an eroticised encounter between a man and a woman. Amerigo Vespucci, 'Europe' confronts a naked female 'America'.[62] The juxtaposition of the figures emphasises opposition. Vespucci is standing, fully clothed and armed holding a flag to claim the land; in his other hand he holds scientific paraphernalia, behind him his ship and boat. Before him, he confronts 'America' who is seated, naked with animals and other 'native' nude women behind her; civilisation literally looks down on 'uncivilised' America (Hulme 1984:17; McClintock 1995: 25-28; Webster 1997: 174). This is emphasised further by a scene of cannibalism in the background as indigenous women sit over a fire, spit roasting a human leg.[63] (Before them, on a mound, another severed leg cast away from the fire suggests a sufficient abundance of body parts to discard this particular one). Furthermore, they occupy the edge of the scene acting as a boundary or perhaps the margins of the new world removed from possible civilisation. McClintock appropriately suggests that this image, particularly the elements of cannibalism, reflect an imperialist fear of engulfment, 'the inaugural scene of discovery becomes a scene of ambivalence, suspended between an imperial megalomania, with its fantasy of rapine – and a contradictory fear of engulfment, with its fantasy of dismemberment and emasculation ... is a document of paranoia and megalomania' (McClintock 1995: 26-27). I would propose that these suggestions could be read by the conspicuous way in which Stradanus chose to portray his characters. For example, there is a clear juxtaposition and polarity of the subjects – male: standing, clothed; female: reclining, nude. Moreover the horror of cannibalism is combined with the obvious untamed

---

[62] For more on this image and post-colonial discourse concerning the period from the sixteenth century to the nineteenth century see, Hulme, 1984 and McClintock, 1995.

[63] I would also argue that Stradanus constructed gendered identities to promote patriarchal Christian doctrine as he portrayed femininity as untamed and unyielding sexual promiscuity (Eve as opposed to the Virgin) that is to be tamed and controlled by her masculine conqueror who brandishes the mark of Christianity, the crucifix on his flag.

sexual desire and submission of America the 'virgin' land. This promotes and self justifies colonisation by Europe, the 'honourable' Christian civilisation.

When looking at Roman art of a similar category, for example Claudius slaying Britannia or Nero slaying Armenia (laying aside the overt Christian element of the Stradanus drawing) it is possible to read the same paranoia and megalomania, as the compositions work in the same way, through juxtapositions of constructed gender and concepts of 'civilised' versus 'non-civilised'. Femininity was constructed to appear as an object for voyeurism whilst the corporeal body was represented as vulnerable, a combination that created a fetishised image of femininity. However, the image discussed is not just about femininity; masculinity suffered the same treatment, even though the outcome offered a very different message. Vespucci represented 'Europe' and in doing so his stance, clothing and the objects he holds advertises common perceptions associated with masculinity, which in the artist's view were fitting to portray the continent. 'Europe' was portrayed as a man of religion, education and science, fully equipped with the weapons of war. This was analogous to Roman constructions of masculinity; however, in a number of cases representations were explicitly violent. This is particularly evident on a number of relief sculptures from the Sebasteion of Aphrodisias, Turkey (a temple complex dedicated to the veneration of Aphrodite and the divine Augustus and his Julio-Claudian successors, build around 20-60 AD) (Kleiner 1992: 158).

Appropriately, my first example is Claudius slaying 'Britannia' (Kleiner 1992, fig. 134). The image is unequivocally violent giving the appearance that Claudius is pinning down 'Britannia' (presented as an Amazon) by kneeling on her right thigh whilst yanking back her head in order to strike the fatal blow (the arm is missing). In this fallen position, 'Britannia' is vulnerable physically and sexually. Her body is partially exposed revealing a breast and her short chiton exposes her legs making her vulnerable to sexual assault also. The message here is clear; Rome (masculinity) attacks and overthrows Britannia (femininity). Like Vespucci as 'Europe', Claudius as Rome is fully armed and positioned higher within the compositions. Their encounters, whether sexual or violent, are with representations of women who, unlike Vespucci and Claudius were not based on individual people, which automatically eliminates their importance as a subject. Anonymity reduces their power and they become object-like. This is particularly evident in the relief of Nero slaying Armenia, also from the Sebasteion, Aphrodisias. 'Armenia's' body is particularly lifeless as she literally folds in death. Her closed eyes imply an absence of consciousness, mentality or life itself (McDonald 2001: 56). As she falls, Nero supports her by clutching her upper arms. Nero is literally carrying Armenia, which is in itself suggestive of the conqueror: conquered polarity. Why would a subjugator help the subjugated to the floor? Is this an attempt to show benevolence, the civilised suppressing the 'barbarians' for their own good? Alternatively, is it deliberately ambivalent? Armenia is perhaps supported as part of the empire. Armenia is enemy, and then changes with incorporation into the empire.

'Armenia's' nudity (but for a cloak, foot-wear and a Phrygian hat) enhances her vulnerability. She is exposed and defeated. 'Britannia' portrays a fallen Amazon and 'Armenia', the stereotypical 'barbarian' (this type was also used to illustrate Amazons); both have their vulnerability enhanced by nudity or partially nudity. However one is more exposed than the other, could this present a hierarchy of the 'provinces' Britannia over Armenia or perhaps of the emperors themselves, Claudius over Nero? On the other hand, 'Armenia' appears to have received the fatal blow whilst 'Britannia' is about to be killed, therefore, Nero was presented as a more effective killer than Claudius. It has been suggested by Smith that the Nero and 'Armenia' relief originally represented an Augustan or an unascribed conquest of Armenia and that it was modified during the early part of Nero's reign when he had early triumphs in Armenia (form AD 54): the relief was given a portrait head and his name was inscribed on the base.[64] Furthermore, this exemplifies the Aphrodisians' aptitude for keeping up with topical dynastic conceptions and events in Rome as the building of the Sebasteion continued (Smith. 1987: 90,118). If this were the case then it would be in their interest to have the current emperor look more powerful and indeed more benevolent than the previous one.

At this point, it is appropriate to consider how the identities of the subjects were constructed. As discussed previously (Diana and Apollo, Chapter 3) Amazons were mythical women who lived in a matriarchal society on the margins of civilisation or the known world. They represent the antipathy of acceptable behaviour for the women of the period and were, therefore, commonly depicted being attacked and overthrown. Their femininity was constructed in a way that displayed aspects that generated from representations pertaining to both femininity and masculinity. Their bodies were in part exposed as they were generally adorned in a short chiton, which only covers one breast (occasionally, the chiton is slipped revealing both). The idea for this presumably stems from the concept that Amazons in adulthood cut off one breast to enable them to use the bow more effectively. However, this was never the case in representation where the breast is uncovered drawing your attention to the 'framed' area (Derrida 1987: 45; Nead 1992: 9; McDonald 2001: 58). Although missing from the Claudius and 'Britannia' relief, Amazons were depicted with the weapons of war, usually associated with masculinity. Furthermore, their independence from men was unheard of for the women of the period (Gardner: 1986:5-30) and added to the contrived masculinity of Amazons, independence being a trait associated with men only. If we look at the images of Claudius and Nero, they are both represented nude, with the exception of armour,

[64] For a more detailed examination of the Sebasteion at Aphrodisias see Smith. 1987.

footwear and cloaks. Armour was an obvious assertion of masculinity, however, how do we interpret their so-called 'heroic' nudity? Perhaps the message presumed to make the subjects appear more powerful with no fear of corporeal vulnerability. Ferris, in his work, *Enemies of Rome: Barbarians through Roman Eyes* described his initial reading of the Claudius and 'Britannia' relief as one of a prelude to a violent rape. His reasons for this include the nude juxtapositioning, the violence particularly since her body is exposed, and the way in which Claudius pulls at her hair and pins her down (Ferris 2000:58). Aside from this initial reading, his interpretation of the male nude is attributed to following Greek or Hellenistic models of heroes, in the particular example Achilles overthrowing the Amazon Penthesilea (Ferris 2000: 58; Zanker 1988: 303).

Returning to the image of 'Armenia', as a personification, the subject was fabricated in the same way as Britannia with armour, yet her overt nudity presents a difference. Warner suggests that nude portrayals of women in allegoric form particularly characterise the 'other' (Warner 1985: 324). I would also argue that her nakedness takes the construction of 'Armenia' a step further than that of 'Britannia' as it was used to depict a presumed 'racial' difference. The Phrygian hat was used to signify 'oriental' or 'barbarian'. This stereotype, however artificially constructed, referred real people whereas Amazons were mythic.[65] Therefore this image was and is more affecting and offensive.

A drawing by Nicolas Petit (of a French expedition), carried out in Australia in the early nineteenth century is an example of colonialist art (Collection of Lesueur, Muséum d'Histoire Naturelle du Havre, McDonald 2001, plate 11). The drawing is of a young woman from the tribe of the Cam-Mer-Ray-Gal, 1800-1804. She is nude, her gaze avoids the observer which suggests submission, avoiding confrontation (compare averted gaze with those of 'Britannia' and 'Armenia'). In this particular case there is an inclusion of skin markings, or scars that categorise the onlooker as an authoritative ethnographer, invited to decipher the markings on her body as if it were a conundrum. As stated by McDonald, 'the subjectivity of the particular woman is not as interesting to the ethnographer as is her exotic appearance or the way her body has been literally perforated with meaning by a culture which is, according to European conceptualisation, beyond the boundaries of civilisation' (McDonald 2001: 57). 'Britannia' and 'Armenia' were worked in the same way. Finally, I think it is important to note that once the 'unknown' is illustrated then the fear is removed. Feminised personifications 'framed' in the form of an 'Amazon' and a 'Barbarian' render the 'unknown' as controlled and in the Roman examples discussed above, overthrown.

No all post-colonial, feminine personifications of lands were portrayed victims of violence under attack by their imperial conquerors. These include images on coins, for example Spain, Judea (Breglia 1968: 80, 140) and Dacia (Adby 2002: 34) or busts depicting Africa, Egypt, Asia as on a mosaic from El Djem, (ancient Thysdrus) Tunisia (Ling1998: 84, Huskinson 2000:3, fig 1.1). These can portray lone women embodying imperial provinces contrasting the fallen naked adversary as evidenced from the Sebasteion.

A Sestertius of Galba (68-69 AD) in the Museo Nazionale in Naples depicts the personification of Spain or Spanish region Clunia offering the Palladium (talismanic effigy that protected the city) (Hard 1997:235) (Apollodorus *Library* 3.13.3) to the seated Emperor who reaches out to receive the statuette (Breglia 1968: 80). Breglia states that this composition is uncommon for the period because the Emperor is seated in the presence of a goddess (Breglia 1968:80). Furthermore, she physically serves him (as if an attendant) as she hands him the Palladium. Galba's martial identity is clearly emphasised by his elaborate armour ultimately drawing attention to his military prowess. In opposition the goddess is adorned in diaphanous drapery that clings to her figure allowing the viewer to see her shape. The cornucopia indicates the fertility and opulence associated with her as a personified province. Femininity is represented by an image of a woman with no individual personality or character dressed in sheer drapery creating a voyeuristic subject. In opposition, the Emperor garbed in armour presents a masculinity that highlights his particular role associating him with the military. The Judea coin, also from Naples plainly depicts subservience by the feminine province, as whilst kneeling before her master, she holds up her hand to grasp the protection of her Roman imperial master. The image is free from violence, yet remains highly propagandist, allegedly alluding to Hadrian's crushing of the second Jewish Revolt that broke out 132 AD and was quashed in 135 AD (Breglia 1968: 141). Moreover the infants depicted with her (cupids?) carry peace palms perhaps indicating the return of peace to Judea. Breglia considers the children's presence is 'apparently an allusion to life taking root and flourishing once more where lately there had been nothing but a devastated wilderness' (Breglia 1968: 140).

Further examples of woman as place appear in mosaic such as busts from a house in El Djem, Tunisia (circa second or early third century AD, Museum of El Djem, Huskinson 2000: 3-4). These portray lone female personifications of province framed and contained within hexagonal panels. Each has a distinguishable feature pertaining to their identity. Africa wears an elephant headdress. This perhaps suggests the goddess Africa's potency as the elephant skin and tusks appear as a trophy advertising her ability to control and kill opponents such as a one of the largest of indigenous beasts. Powerful Africa is then controlled by Rome. Egypt holds a rattle utilised during the worship of Egyptian goddess Isis and Asia wears a turreted crown adorned by personifications

[65] For more on Phrygians in Greece and represented in Greek art see, De Vries 2000. 'The Nearly Other: The Attic Vision of the Phrygians and Lydians' 338-364.

of cities in Asia Minor. All are solitary feminine subjects contained and controlled in Roman imperial possession. This is emphasised by the central image depicting the seated representation of Rome/Roma.[66] In her hand she holds the globe representing the world. As stated by Huskinson on discussing the whole composition of the mosaic, 'together these figures are linked in an arrangement which suggests the geographical extent of the Roman empire and its diversity united under the central control of Rome' (Huskinson 2000:4).

As a visual representation, Roma is a complex combination drawing on specific illustrative features of Minerva, Amazons and Venus Genetrix. This makes her a paradoxical visual character. She appears with masculine armour of akin to Minerva and dressed in a short tunic with an exposed breast suggesting a 'barbaric' Amazon, yet the exposed breast could also refer to Venus Genetrix in her role as mother of Rome. An example illustrating Roma, from the Cancelleria relief depicts the goddess with Domitian leaving for the Sarmatian War (92-93 AD, Vatican Museum, Rome, Kleiner 1992, fig 159). According to Kleiner, Roma was a particular favourite of Domitian along with Minerva who is also illustrated facing the emperor creating the impression of eye contact (Kleiner 1992: 192). The way her arm is raised to her helmet offers perhaps a sexual connotation akin to images of Apollo Lykeios or a wounded Amazon (for both see Chapter 3). Domitian's arm is outstretched reaching out to his divine patroness; on his other side Roma makes physical contact with him, her hand under his arm gently urging him on. The emperor is physically linked and flanked by his chosen patronesses. Roma is illustrated in mid-stride actively urging the emperor on to battle. Also depicted are Victory, Mars, Genius of Senators and the Genius of the Roman people. The choice of subjects depicted with the emperor renders this relief as a highly propagandist piece. Kleiner offers an alternative identification, suggesting that, rather than Roma the subject could be Virtus (Virtue, Valour). As the compositions are propagandist both Roma and Virtus are applicable subjects.

A distance slab from Dunbartonshire depicts an image of Virtus accompanied by Victories and Mars (Hunterian Museum, Glasgow, Keppie 1984, fig 150).[67] Her costume appears analogous with that of Roma, short tunic, Amazonian type, with breast exposed. The inscribed *vexillum* held in her left hand confirms identity - '*virtus Aug(ustae)*' the Emperor's Valour (*RIB 2200*). It is notable that the emperor's valour is a feminine subject, perhaps because *virtus* is a feminine noun. Again the composition is ultimately self promoting commemorating the Sixth Legions' construction of 3240 feet of the Antonine Wall. The addition of the Victories perhaps advertises the victorious completion of their task particularly as they hold up the inscription. They partially stand on globes (see below) which combined create a message of Roman supremacy - victory over the world. Additionally this cohort of the Sixth Legion advertised their allegiance with Mars the god of war, with Victory and their loyalty to the emperor. It appears that the creator or patron wanted the cohort's devotion to the emperor to stand out as attention is drawn to the figure's identity by the inscription exhibited on the *vexillum*. As a feminine personification, she occupies an arena normally associated with masculinity. This is stressed further by the objects she holds, the *vexillum*, the sheathed sword resting in the crook of her arm, and her plumed helmet all pieces of military paraphernalia. In accord with images of Diana and Minerva her hair is short or tied back, the Victories also have their hair piled up on their heads, controlled and non-sexual. A cornelian intaglio from Caerleon was identified by Zienkiewicz as probably depicting Roma (second century AD, Roman Legionary Museum, Caerleon, Zienkiewicz 1987). The subject appears to wear a chiton, thus suggesting a feminine persona. Presumably her helmet signifies her identity as Roma, yet this image could easily portray Minerva. Nevertheless, the patron chose this image to represent them affiliating themselves with the goddess and the connotations associated with her.

Victory – Victoria

As numerous examples of Victory survive, it is reasonable to conclude that the personification of Victory was popular in Britain. She was the embodiment of triumph and therefore depicted with objects associated with victory, including a laurel wreath,[68] and a collection of armour belonging to the fallen 'enemy' and displayed as the trophies of war and conquest. She was generally depicted winged but there are a few examples of wingless Victories and she was recurrently positioned standing on a globe (Keppie 1984:12, fig 27). Often she was depicted as a companion to Minerva and can be read as an indicator identifying the goddess of war – victory accompanies successful war. Visual representation of Minerva and Victory followed a formula borrowed from images of Greek Athena and Nike (victory). As the goddess of Athens and war Athena was accompanied by victory, so there was a history of this type of representation that served a propagandist purpose. It has been suggested that Octavian considered Victory as his personal patron goddess (Zanker 1988: 80). Cassius Dio speculated that after his success at Actium and the subjugation of Egypt, Octavian set up a statue of Victory in the Curia to demonstrate that it was from the goddess that he had been awarded the empire (Cassius Dio 51: 22).

[66] See Beard, North and Price 1998: 246-247, 255-256 for more on Roma in Roman religion.

[67] The slab commemorates 3240 feet of the Antonine Wall created by the Sixth Legion and dedicated to the emperor (Keppie 1984: 54-55).

[68] The laurel wreath, a symbol of triumph, was associated with Apollo and the Pythian Games on Delos Pausanias, *Guide to Greece, 2.30.3*, where it was given to the victorious athletes. It is a complex connection concerning various Apolline myths. The laurel is a feature of the Apollo and Daphne myth as she was transformed into a laurel tree by Peneus, to avoid the unwanted and forceful affections of Apollo (Ovid *Metamorphoses* Book 1).

> In the Curia he erected the statue of Victory, which is still in existence; its purpose, it seems likely, was to show that it was from this goddess that he had received the empire. The statue had belonged to the people of Tarentum, and it was now brought from the city to Rome, placed in the Senate chamber, and decorated with spoils from Egypt' (Cassius Dio 51: 22, Scott-Kilvert 1987:82-83).

Placed in the Senate chamber, the statue conveniently acted as a constant reminder of Octavian's success moreover if Dio's statement is fact, then this particular statue of Victory would have been of sufficient importance to transport it rather than commissioning another. According to Zanker representations of Victory were part of a subtle repertoire of simple signs alluding to the victory at Actium including parts of ships, marine creatures and dolphins. This collection of symbols was designed to celebrate a victory without directly referring to the defeated enemy as they were made up mostly of Roman citizens,[69] and Anthony himself had once been an important figure in Rome. As Zanker states, 'since the image of the enemy himself could not be represented, nor could the victory in Egypt alone suffice to convey Octavian's succession to sole power, artists had to employ non-specific and abstract symbols of Victory' (Zanker 1988: 82). Furthermore, he proposes that this marked the beginning of a new compilation of imperial imagery, symbols and signs that were straightforward and easily grasped and could be spread throughout the empire. Zanker also noted that this new imagery was not confined to political monuments but the symbols also turned up as decorative elements in private homes (Zanker 1988: 84). I would argue that if as the symbols were as simple and easy to grasps as he suggests then the use of such emblems could not simply play a decorative role. The symbols were steeped in political meaning, particularly when considering the example he uses, one of which is a gemstone seal (from a finger ring) with a Capricorn, a star and a ship carved into it (Zanker 1988: 84, fig 66).[70]

Returning to the Victory as a symbol, it is possible that symbols change and develop different meanings over time, however, it is reasonable to assume that the employment of Victory images remained constant during the imperial period. Victory has a meaningful history in roman art. As mentioned previously, representations of Victory survive in considerable numbers in Britain. Looking at the Victories depicted there do appear to be a number of different basic Victory 'types' within Romano-British art; formulae were combined depending on the choice of composition, for example winged Victories (with associated attributes including wreath, globe and palm branch), semi-draped Victories and Victories crowning a victor. My first example is the pediment sculpture from the temple of Sulis Minerva at Bath.

The central feature on the Bath pediment is the shield with a gorgonieon-Oceanus mask held by two winged Victories (Roman Baths Museum, Bath, late first century AD, Cunliffe and Fulford 1982:11-12, Toynbee 1964: 162). Each Victory stands on a globe, which became a part of the symbolic language during the reign of Octavian, shortly after the battle of Actium. Furthermore, Octavian, in the early days, probably had a Victory placed on a globe to symbolise his claim for sole power over the Empire (Zanker 1988: 80). According to Henig, the orb signifies the world and the clearly defined bands surrounding it represent the course of the planets around the earth (Henig 1999:422). It may be that not every image of Victory had political or imperial value; they could imply some honorific functions as in funerary art. As stated by Toynbee the addition of Victories 'suggest the vanquishing of death by the souls of those who were buried in the tomb' (Toynbee 1971: 195). However, in the case of the Bath pediment the message appears to be one of Roman supremacy: Rome has won victory over the world and even the surrounding planets. Moreover, to appreciate more clearly the articulation of supremacy, the central aspect of context needs to be recognised: the pediment is in a prime and public position on the temple itself within a large complex.

This same type of 'banded globe' was utilised on two reliefs from Birrens (*Blatobulgium*), Dumfriesshire, south of the Antonine Wall, Scotland (National Museum of Antiquities, Scotland, Edinburgh, Keppie 1984:12-13, fig 27, 27b). The carvings survive as fragments of what were thought to originate from commemorative slabs. One shows how parts of the victory wreath have survived and how these fragments act as a guide indicating the possible function of the relief. Furthermore, the fragment showing drapery, bare legs and one bare foot fixed on a banded globe suggests a representation of Victory. This same characteristic survives on a fragment of the same area (Keppie 1984: 12, fig 26).

---

[69] It was not until the fourth century AD during the reign of Constantine that Romans were depicted fighting other Romans in state art (Ferris 2000: 42).

[70] The gemstone seal ring was a functional piece of jewellery, which represented the owner in two basic ways, firstly, in a personal sense on the body as a ring with a particular choice of theme (of which to be seen wearing) and secondly when the seal was used the image worked as a mobile indicator of the owner. Therefore, the personal identity of the owner was at stake. As reported by Suetonius, Augustus himself had several choices of emblem until he found one that suited him and his family after him.

> The first seal Augustus used for safe-conducts, dispatches, and private letters was a sphinx; next came a head of Alexander the Great; lastly, his own head, cut by Dioscurides, the seal which his successors continued to employ (Suetonius *Augustus*. 50, Graves 1957: 79).

The gemstone chosen by Zanker has highly symbolic images. Capricorn directly signifies Augustus, the zodiac sign he was born under (Suetonius *Augustus* 2.94). The star was a reference to Augustus' connection with his adoptive father 'divine' Caesar whose soul was thought to have shone in the form of a comet over Rome for seven days: 'on the first day of the Games given by his successor Augustus in honour of this apotheosis, a comet appeared about an hour before sunset and shone for seven days running. This was held to be Caesar's soul, elevated to heaven; hence the star, now placed above the forehead of his divine image' (Suetonius *Julius Caesar* 88, Graves 1957: 48).

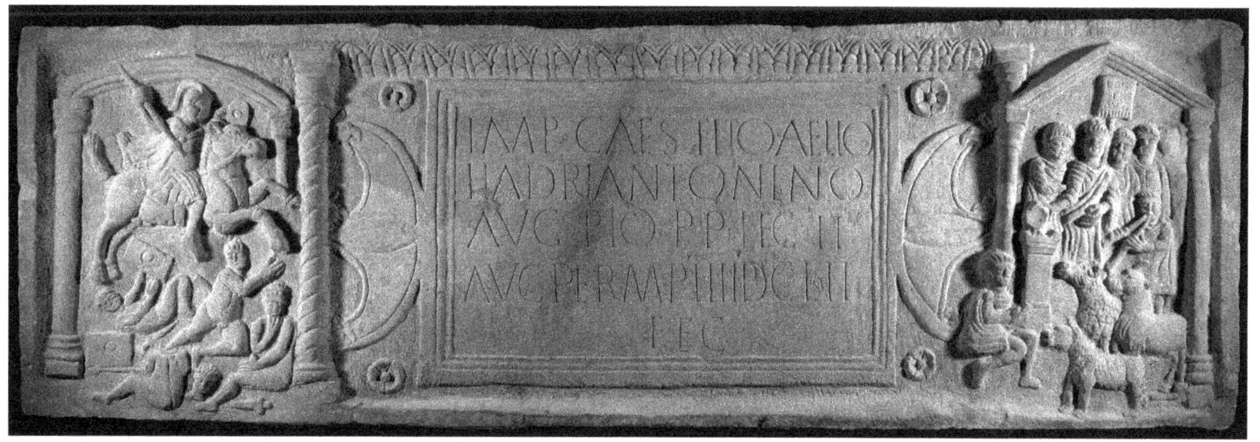

Fig. 15. Bridgeness 'distance slab', Antonine Wall, Antonine date, National Museum of Scotland, Edinburgh. © Trustees of the National Museums of Scotland.

There are several representations of Victory depicted on distance slabs found along the Antonine Wall. These were set up by legions that had played a part in the construction of a particular part of the frontier structure (Keppie 1984: xiii). A distance slab from Lanarkshire (Hunterian Museum, Glasgow. Keppie 1984: 50, fig. 137) celebrates the construction of 3666½ paces of the Wall (between Summerston and Bogton), by a unit from the Second Legion of Augusta dated at approximately 142-3 AD (). The slab is made up of three panels the outer two were carved in relief and the central panel holds the inscription:

Imp(eratori) Caes(ari) Tito Aelio | Hadriano Antonino |
Aug(usto) Pio p(atri) p(atriae) leg(io) II | Aug(usta) Pep m(ilia) p(assuum) III DCLXVI s(emis)

'For the Emperor Caesar Titus Aelius Hadrianus Antoninus
Augustus Pius, father of his counry, the Second Legion of
Augusta (built this) for a distance of 3666 ½ paces.'
RIB 2193

The left relief shows Victory about to crown a cavalryman with a wreath of victory. He is in mid gallop about to attack bound and incapacitated captives beneath him. The arrangement and positioning of subjects is worthy of mentioning as separate areas were allocated for each subject and the areas have hierarchical implications. Presumably, as Victory is a deity she occupies a higher position than humans. She floats in the air above one of the captives; she is a part of the composition, but not a part of the scene, she has a visible invisibility. Her feet almost rest on the head of the captive below her, demonstrating quite literally victory over the enemy. At this point, I think it is important to consider images of the 'enemy' as a personification as it appears that they operate in the same way, particularly those of lands. In most examples (particularly those from the Antonine Wall) the defeated adversaries have no individual or particular characteristics they follow a stereotypical pattern and are usually naked and incapacitated. On the relief discussed above there is illustrated a play of hierarchical masculinity. Roman soldiers as patrons were asserting their masculinity over the 'uncultured barbarian'. As stated by Alston, 'Military service also gave soldiers a self-defining role. Service differentiated them from barbarians. It made them men' (Alston 1998: 218). On his horse the soldier is fully armed and a distance above the captives, he is active as opposed to their incapacity. Furthermore they were depicted showing corporeal vulnerability against the horseman's armoured defence. This scene is particularly violent and illustrates mercilessness on behalf of the assailing soldier, as he is attacking captives who appear to have their hands tied behind their back; they are unable to fight back or even stand, but the horseman still attacks them. The slab may then have acted as a warning to those who were perhaps prepared to threaten the Roman occupation of the area. Furthermore, the horseman could be an analogy of Rome itself showing a ruthless reproach to a faceless potential adversary.

The Bridgeness distance slab, also set up by the Second Legion of Augusta shows a cavalryman about to spear fallen victims of his attack (fig. 15, National Museum of Scotland, Edinburgh, RIB 2139, Toynbee 1962: 166; fig. 97; Keppie 1984: 27. fig. 68; Henig 1995: 43). Again the horseman is fully armed and active towering over his naked and incapacitated adversary. All were depicted in individual positions all suggesting defeat and annihilation, one individual has his severed head beside him. Another victim shows his vulnerability by holding himself, one hand to his chin, the other covering his stomach. This is a pose that was usually associated with that of the Capitoline Venus (see Chapter 2). Davies in her study on gender and body language in Roman art notes the way male and female body language was noted by classical sculptors, particularly that of the Apollo Belvedere and the Capitoline Venus (Davies 1997: 98). She notes that male subjects tend to be depicted in an 'open' pose that is generally upright with gaze directed straight at the viewer, to the left or right but straight, limbs posed to enable genitalia to be displayed (whether covered with clothing or not) thus stressing the subject's masculinity. This is evident for the Apollo Belvedere whose open stride and outstretched arms suggest confidence, or as Davies puts it, 'the pose is that of the assertive dominant male' (Davies 1997: 98). Venus on the other hand has a very different posture; her pose 'closed', she is hunched over slightly; her arms cover her body defensively and her gaze is averted hindering eye contact. As previously mentioned in chapter 2 (Venus and Mars) the positioning of the arms draws attention to the area covered. According to Davies, 'she awaits an invitation, but does not threaten the male observer by seeming over-bold. In other words, her body language is submissive and defensive' (Davies 1997: 99). A personification of Gaul from the Hadrianeum, Rome, (Antonine date Museo del Palazzo dei Conservatori, Kleiner 1992: 284, fig 252) holds herself in this same submissive and defensive manner. Furthermore, she looks away from the viewer generating the impression of passivity and a lack of confidence. The way her arms cross her body draws attention to the folds of her drapery, particularly the area covering the breasts as the fall of the material appears unnatural, stressing the shape and clinging to her thigh, analogous with the 'wet look' diaphanous drapery evidenced on images of Venus Genetrix. Her overall body is fully covered with multiple folds of drapery loosely covering most of her body except the areas mentioned above which, I suggest, seems deliberate.

The representation of 'submissiveness' brings us back to the Bridgeness distance slab and the construction of the fallen 'barbarian' who covers his body (fig. 15). As discussed above this body language was associated with representations of passive femininity. I would argue that this particular subject has been constructed deliberately to attack the masculinity of the so-called 'barbarian' by giving him a pose associated with femininity. Ferris indicates that the four illustrated opponents may in fact be a repeated representation of the same person at different points of the attack commencing with the initial assault and concluding with the execution (Ferris 2000: 115). This is pertinent as the subjects all have the same appearance, they were constructed in the same way apparently they are all nude and their hair appears to have been carved in the same way. However, I would argue that their non-specific appearance might be a deliberate action drawing on a stereotypical example to illustrate the 'non-civilised' by depersonalising the figures. Furthermore one of the 'enemies' directly to the right of the cavalryman's foot, appears to have a stick-like protrusion in his back, perhaps representing a spear handle. This is not repeated on the decapitated figure verifying that this is not the same individual. The right panel enhances the polarity between citizen (Roman) and non-citizen (non-Roman) as a sacrifice scene shows subjects dressed in clothes that indicated Roman identity (fig 5.16a).[71] According to Keppie, the sacrifice was a post-victory ritual cleansing of officers and men in preparation for the duties to come (Keppie 1984: 28).

Another example of the typecast 'barbarian' is evident on a distance slab from Dunbartonshire that was set up by the Twentieth Legion Valeriae Victricix (Hunterian Museum, Glasgow, Hassall 1977: 327; Keppie 1984: 53, fig. 149; Henig 1995: 43; Ferris 2000: 116). According to Ferris, 'these barbarian figures were presumably symbols of a whole group or tribe in defeat rather than of individual captives (Ferris 2000: 116). The relief forms three panels positioned on a low base corresponding to the upper panels which incorporate inscriptions. A central section has a representation of a running wild boar, the emblem of the Twentieth Legion (Hassall 1977: 330). The side sections contain the captives who are both in kneeling positions with hands tied behind their backs; both look towards the central panel where a female figure crowns a bowed figure with a laurel wreath (in her other hand she holds a *patera)*. Behind the subject a column reaches above his head where the imperial eagle looks on. The figures above were compartmentalised within architectural structures, possibly based on triumphal arch design (Hassall 1977: 327; Keppie 1984: 54). It is interesting to note that in this particular slab the captives were depicted separately and framed within a structural design. Furthermore, the captives are placed within the roundels containing in the inscriptions to the left *Antonino* and to the right *Aug(usto) Pio P(atri) P(atriae)* (Augustus Pius father of his country). This enhances the impression of their defeat as not only are they unable to fight or even walk, the architectural frame and the inscription roundels limits their boundaries, therefore they are contained and controlled (Derrida 1987: 45; Nead 1992: 9).

The 'bound and out of action' captive propaganda device was employed on coins under the Severans, again in conjunction with Victory. The bronze coin of AD 210-12 records Severus Septimus' '*Victoria Britannicae*' (Henig 2002a: 73, fig 28). The coin has a representation of a winged Victory adding a shield to a trophy, opposite her presumably is the personification Tyche (associated with fortune and protector of the city, see below) with her turreted crown, and at her feet slumped on the floor a captive has his hands tied behind his back. His lowly position and his inactivity within the composition reiterate the hierarchy of Roman supremacy as noted above, whilst Victory and Tyche loom over him divided by the central feature the trophy of captured arms. The same composition appears on a sestertius of Caracalla of AD 211-212 (Besly 1987: 12, fig 38) restating the message of Severan triumph in Britain, all of who adopted the title 'Brittannicus' (Besly 1987: 12). Furthermore the repeated image and circulation for the coins reiterates the message.

Returning to the Hutcheson Hill distance slab, several scholars have debated the identity of the female subject. As she is crowning a 'victorious' subjugator it has been suggested that this figure may be Victory (Keppie 1984: 54). However, the lack of usual attributes, above all, her wings, obscures her identity. According to Hassall, in all likelihood this could not be Victory, as she was never

[71] Composition interpretation features in Chapter 1, see fig. 1.13.

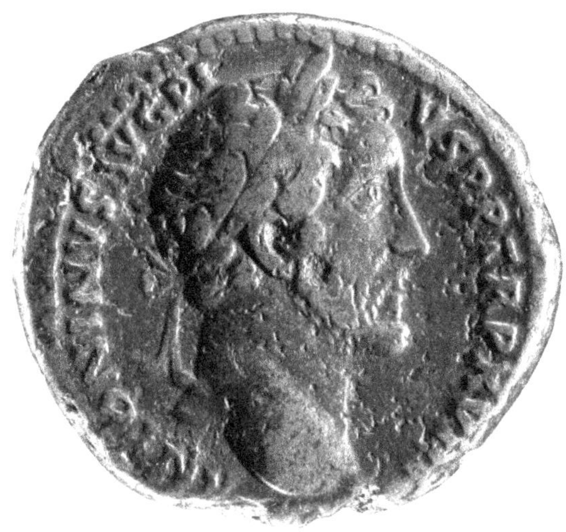

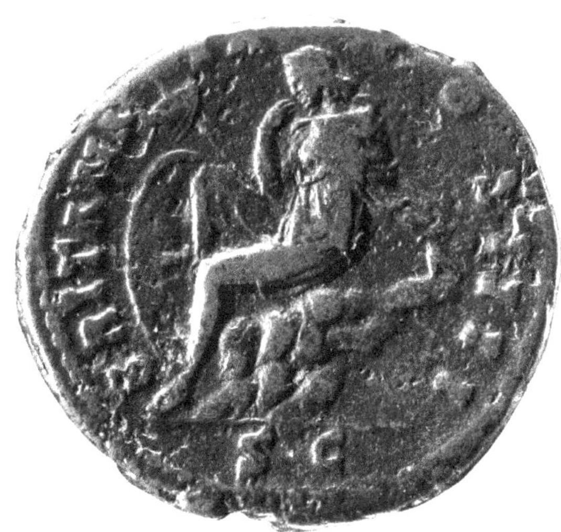

Fig. 16. Bronze coin, As of Antoninus Pius. mid-2nd century AD, British Museum, London. © Trustees of the British Museum.

depicted crowning anyone other than a member of the imperial house or rarely a divinity[72] (Hassall 1977: 336; Henig 2002a: 75; Henig 2002b: 419-420).[73] Henig has suggested Britannia or Roma and Keppie proposed Britannia to represent the newly enlarged province (Keppie 1984: 54; Henig 1995: 43; Henig 2002a: 69). Without an inscription and the obvious attributes to recognize Victory, identification is problematic. However, when examining coins from the Antonine period, images of Britannia differ from those discussed above. The common image on coins was of an armoured goddess seated on an arrangement of rocks, (perhaps celebrating the construction and function of the Antonine wall). According to Besly this first appeared under Hadrian and then under Antoninus Pius (Besly 1987:10). As displayed on an As of Hadrian in the National Museum of Wales, Cardiff (Besly 1987, fig 29) initial visual characteristics chosen for Britannia under Hadrian are close to those of Minerva as the goddess of war (but in a seated position, and as Minerva was rarely depicted in this position, identification becomes obscured) . Later examples under Antoninus Pius presented a somewhat altered representation of Britannia (fig. 16). Casey stated that 'Britannia [is] seated in a dejected pose' (Casey 1999: 34). Presumably, he arrives at this conclusion because she is seated and inactive. But I would take the visual communication of the coin a step further. I would argue that she was presented in the guise of an Amazon with a short tunic and weapons, which therefore carries all the implications and propaganda associated with Amazons, as noted above. These features do not appear on the Hutcheson Hill relief and I propose therefore, that the subject portrayed was not a representation of Britannia or that of Roma (who was presented in a similar way see Zanker 1988: 316, fig 247). As the subject has no direct attributes relating to Victory (apart from an impression of what is thought to be a small victory wreath), I am doubtful that this image should be so identified. While I am not able to place a precise identification on the female figure, I feel that she has more in common with other figures, for example Tyche with her long drapery and particular headdress, or a matronly image of Juno. The identification of this figure is clearly open to debate.

Drawing this particular section to a close it is clear that the use of Victory carried distinct political implications, even more so when Victory was presented in opposition to the stereotypical 'barbarian'. This created a relationship of opposites in which the characters have to be depicted together in order for the composition to work. To be precise the visual hierarchy of conqueror versus the conquered cannot exist unless both characters are depicted. Lastly, it is apparent the feminising of 'Victory' does not constitute a direct portrayal of the feminine as the victorious conqueror, but in actuality the reverse: it presents femininity as objectified and controlled.

Fortuna, Bonus Eventus and Genii

The goddess Fortuna as her name suggests is the personification of good fortune, of chance and luck. Green points out that Fortuna was especially beloved of soldiers, around the Hadrian's Wall area and especially in bath houses where they were nude and vulnerable (Green 1983: 41). Moreover the goddess had various titles including *Fortuna Muliebris* (Fortune of Women), *Fortuna Equestris* (Equestrian Fortune) (Beard et al 1998:297, 322) or *Fortuna Populi Romani* (Fortune of the Roman people) (Coulston and Phillips 1988: 6). Fortuna can be generally identified by the cornucopia symbol of abundance and by a rudder, globe or wheel (Green 1992:102).

[72] For example an intaglio from near Lincoln shows Victory crowning Hercules-Caracalla, see chapter 4 and Henig 2002.
[73] Hassal offers a full discussion on the identity of the female subject on the Hutcheson Hill distance slab (Hassall 1977: 327-340).

An altar from Chesters depicts an illustration of Fortuna in relief (third century AD, Coulston and Phillips 1988: 5, fig 9). Coulston and Phillips state that the altar was found in the extramural bathhouse located between the fort and the North Tyne. The inscription reveals, 'to the goddess Fortune the Preserver Venenus, a German, willingly and deservedly (set this up)' *RIB 1449*. The dedication is to *Fortuna Conservatrix* (Fortune the Preserver). Evidently by commissioning an altar and dedicating it to the goddess, Venenus was bartering for his own preservation. As stated by Coulston and Phillips, 'Inscriptions show that in bathhouses Fortuna was worshipped not only as the giver of good health, but as a protectress who ensured the general well being of her devotees, naked and helpless' (Coulston and Phillips 1988: 5). Furthermore, the patron automatically advertised the ability to afford such a commission in a public place. Fortuna appears in long drapery holding a large cornucopia. Alternative examples of Fortuna depict her seated with cornucopia resting in the crock of her right arm. A sculpture from Cirencester depicts Fortuna in this manner. It was also found in a baths context, discovered within the stoking room of the baths at Cirencester (Beaches Road excavations) (Corinium Museum, Henig 1993:11, fig 24). Her drapery is heavy and according to Henig she is adorned in a *stola* and *palla* (Henig a 1993: 11). These are items of clothing that were worn by Roman women after marriage and are ultimately gender markers signifying societal conventions for women advertising matronly status and sexual inviolability. The cornucopia is also a fertility symbol – is this connected with her presumed matronly status? Moreover, her seated position renders her passive and inactive. A further example is from Lydney Park, Gloucester within the Roman temple site. Henig suggests that this example may be identified as Fortuna or Abundantina (Henig 1993: 11-12) Toynbee suggested the latter (Toynbee 1964:91).

A relief from Caerleon, also found within a bathhouse context depicts Fortuna and her thematic male counterpart Bonus Eventus (late third century AD, Roman Legionary Museum, Caerleon, Brewer 1986, fig 1). The inscription reveals that the patrons were a husband and wife.

> [Fort]une et Bono Eue|nto Corneli(us) Castus et Iul(ia) | Belismicus coniuges | po[s(u)er(unt)]
>
> To Fortune and Bonus Eventus, Cornelius Castus and Julia Belismicus,
> husband and wife, set this up …… *RIB 318*

They advertised both their donor and marital status by exhibiting both their names and mentioning their union. From a purely speculative point of view, it would be interesting to envisage the couple representing themselves in this relief, not as portraits, but symbolically as male and female counterparts - wife and husband, Fortuna and Bonus Eventus, particularly as Bonus Eventus is not depicted in the usual fashion akin to a Genius but is fully clothed as subjects depicted on a tombstone relief (Brewer 1986: 3). According to Brewer, Bonus Eventus is evidenced on only two other monumental inscriptions from Roman Britain one of which is lost and questionable, the other is on an altar from York and linked with Fortuna (*RIB 642*) (Brewer 1986:3). Although the relief is damaged it is still possible to consider a gender marker for Bonus Eventus. Between the couple is an altar and it is he, not Fortuna, who is in the act of offering a sacrifice, holding a *patera* over the altar and confirming his masculine role. The Walbrook statuette depicts a Genius in the same pose about to offer a sacrifice from a *patera* onto an altar (second century AD, from the site of the Walbrook Mithraeum, Museum of London, Toynbee 1962, fig. 25).

A Genius is also a personification, it is the spirit of place or other abstract themes embodied in the form of a semi-nude/nude youth holding a cornucopia and often holding a *patera* over an altar. As confirmed by Toynbee the 'Walbrook statuette belongs to a well-known series of personifications of localities (for example. Genius Loci), classes of society (for example, Genius Populi Romani), and abstract ideas (for example, Bonus Eventus), by means of youthful male figures, either naked or partially draped and distinguished by a variety of attributes and adjuncts' (Toynbee 1962: 139). This statuette is rendered in a way that pays particular attention to the youthful masculine form. The slipped drapery rests on his pelvic area and draped over his right arm, whilst the remaining material clings diaphanously revealing the shape of his legs below, particularly his right thigh as he stands in the *contrapposto* position. This pose highlights the body's shape, specifically the side opposing the raised leg – in this case the left hip and waist. An altar from Cirencester depicts a Genius in the same manner (Corinium Museum, Henig 1993, fig 32). Again the subject is semi-nude holding a *patera* over an altar. He appears to wear a turreted crown, which signifies city walls (Collingwood and Wright 1995: 30; Henig 1993: 13). The inscription further confirms the identity of the subject as Genius *Loci*, 'To the holy Genius of this place' (*RIB 102*). A figure from Carlisle is a sculpture carved in the round depicting a Geniusm (second or third century AD, City Museum, Carlisle, Toynbee 1962, fig 30). The inscription informs us that this is a Genius of a century of soldiers, 'To the Genius of the century the century of Bassilius Crescens gave this as a gift' (*RIB 944*). Toynbee states that this figure personifies a century of a local garrison (Toynbee 1962: 140). The inscription acts as an advertisement highlighting the status of the patron. Bassilius Crescens stressed his hierarchical rank by exhibiting that the century was his and that he could afford to commission such a piece. Visually the formula is the same as the Genii depicted above although the proportions are dissimilar. This does not make the sculpture better or worse – just different. Over all Genii of this type have a masculinity that draws on masculine youth analogous with Apollo, Bacchus and Mercury.

The Seasons

Judging by the personifications discussed above it is perhaps no coincidence that the Seasons were often (but not exclusively) represented feminine. Femininity, as discussed was considered as an indicator of 'nature' over masculine 'civilisation' (Chapter 3 Diana and Apollo). Usually depicted in fours, they can be distinguished by objects related to each particular season, for instance bare branches for Winter or flowers and birds for Spring, they vary according to individual depictions. Surviving representations of the Seasons in Britain are most commonly found on mosaics, dated to a period when they grew in popularity between the second and fourth centuries AD (Scott 2000: 145). I have concentrated mainly on Romano-British mosaics because of the relatively large quantity surviving. Scott has carried out a thorough examination of fourth century mosaics in Roman Britain with a chapter dedicated to the Seasons. The chart below gives a comprehensive overview of Season mosaics in Britain creating a valuable basis for reference including location, form, gender, attributes and other subjects depicted. The majority of representations were within enclosed areas usually located as corner fillers and commonly in bust form. According to Scott, five of the fifteen Seasons are feminised representations; five may possibly be feminine, two reveal their gender to be ambiguous, one is masculine and two are masculine cupids (Scott 2000:147).

Amongst the few scholars who concentrate on mosaics of Roman Britain, Rodgers is distinctive in her focus on representations of gender and the implications associated. In her paper, 'Women Underfoot in Life and Art: Female Representations in Fourth Century Romano-British Mosaics', Rodgers examines representations of women and men including Medusa, Orpheus, the Muses, the Winds, Tyche and the Seasons (Rodgers 1995). Rodgers concludes that the way in which gendered subjects were categorised within particular representational themes may have reaffirmed perceived social roles in a domestic environment. For example, feminine subjects fall within non-specific abstract concepts such as the Seasons, or Tyche (Fortune) with no particular mythology or personality for their own as opposed to specific deities such as Orpheus or Bacchus. Furthermore, feminine subjects were consistently portrayed in relation to nature rather than a presumed universal culture. As she states, 'there was an obvious division in the character of female and male images that often equated female figures with the elements of nature, chaos, disorder; and male images with the elements of a taming civilising culture' (Rodgers 1995: 184). Her first example is that of Medusa as the 'embodiment' of chaos and disorder. According to Rodgers, the fact that in Roman British mosaics, Medusa was always illustrated beheaded and never as a whole being is a significant factor of her interpretation as a subject.

> It is significant that in all of the Romano-British examples, Medusa is depicted as already beheaded … Her power has therefore already been neutralised and destroyed in these representations. She is no longer a potent force of Nature – her destruction by Culture is already complete. As Medusa is never depicted as a whole figure, nature is not shown as intact, and thus is not capable of utilising its strengths – she has been robbed of her power (Rodgers 1995: 179).

I understand and agree with the direction of Rodgers' argument. However she has disregarded the mythology connected with Medusa. Medusa killed more people (and the sea monster, *ketos*) after her death she was beheaded by Perseus (Ovid, *Metamorphoses* iv; Apollodorus ii.4.3). However, I do think that the way representations of Medusa were contained within medallions and roundels limited her potency. She has been controlled and utilised in an apotropaic sense keeping away evil, in the same way that she was controlled and contained in representations on the aegis of Minerva and Athena or on shields (Boardman, 1985:110.) Henig is of the opinion that because Medusa attracts evil and therefore keeps it away from individuals she is a life-giving image (Henig 1984: 179). However, I think that simply reversing the meaning is not appropriate. Just because she attracts evil away from the individual does not mean that she loses her fundamental unique power, which was to turn the onlooker into stone. The gorgoneion worked in the same way as an Amazon or hybrid creature such as the Chimera or Hydra. They were controlled and restrained by their killers who, at the same time, advertised their own power by being able to overthrow the 'other'. Medusa, Amazons, Chimera and Hydra all come under the umbrella term 'other' and therefore all represent wild untamed non-civilised nature. This brings us back to Rodger's original argument that feminine representations were categorised in terms of nature as opposed to masculine representations that embody culture (Rogers 1995:185). This argument is relevant when considering personifications of the Seasons in individual mosaics, for example a mosaic from Thruxton.

The mosaic at Thruxton (as the nineteenth century lithograph after a fourth century AD mosaicshows, Scott 2000: 118, fig 66) originally had a central medallion depicting Bacchus with his leopard (Hutchinson 1986: 392).[74] Visually, Bacchus is associated with the Greek god of wine – Dionysus; this example appears to follow the same Hellenic type.[75] This mosaic was presumably part of the ornamentation of a dining or reception room (Scott 2000: 118). If this was the case then Bacchus was an appropriate choice as the god of wine and altered states reached through intoxication. Visual indicators for Dionysus include grapes, vines, drinking vessels and thyrsus,[76] moreover he was repeatedly depicted with his followers Satyrs and Maenads and his leopard. On the

[74] The names *Quintus Natalius Natalinus et Bodeni…* above the composition may have been those of the patron or that of the mosaicists'.

[75] For an extensive study on Bacchus in Roman Britain see Hutchinson 1986.

[76] The thyrsus was a staff carried by Bacchus and his followers, it consisted of a pole toped with a pine or fur cone with occasionally with vine or ivy leaves entwined around it or enveloping the cone.

outer rim are eight individual representations of heads (or masks) wearing Phrygian hats. Ling suggest that the human masks were employed in a 'purely decorative way' (Ling 1997: 280). However, the Phrygian hats work as a sign indicating 'oriental' perhaps emphasising the concept that Dionysus travelled greatly in the east before he was venerated in Greece (Euripides *Bacchae* 12-69). The Seasons occupy the corner areas outside the medallion to fill the overall rectangular shape of this part of the mosaic. The busts are decorated with leaves and tendrils springing up on either side filling corners fitting around the medallion. Autumn is lost, Winter is adorned in a hood, Spring is encircled by a garland of leaves and flowers and Summer displays a wreath of corn-ears and flowers (Toynbee 1964: 260). The use of feminine Seasons in this example was perhaps considered to complement the Bacchic theme, for example perceptions of women as having untamed sexual desire falls in line with wild Bacchic intoxicated revelling.[77]

A Bacchic theme can be evidenced on the Dyer Street in mosaic in Cirencester (Hutchinson 1986: 400). Bacchus partially survives holding his usual attributes. A Silenus, half draped in a red cloak holding a wine cup rides on a white ass. Other subjects include Actaeon (see chapter 3) Medusa and a nude female carrying a bunch of leaves, presumed to be a nymph or Maenad.[78] All the subjects mentioned have associations with change; for example, changing Seasons, Silenus and Maenads represent Bacchic celebrations and the changing stages between sobriety and intoxication, Actaeon in a state of metamorphosis, Medusa was changed from a woman into a gorgon.

The Seasons at Lullingstone, Kent present an unusual case for analysis (Toynbee 1962, fig 228). As customary, they occupy the four corners (though one has perished) and in the centre, Bellerophon attacks the Chimera whilst four seal-like beasts occupy either side of them. The Seasons show no signs of designated gender. Their gender is ambiguous, whether this was deliberate on the part of the mosaicists or the simply the way the work was carried out, we may never know. However, it would be easy to suggest that the images are feminine and construct an interpretation that categorises the Seasons in the chaotic/nature versus order/culture debate usually associated with images of the Chimera and hybrid beasts. However, this example is not straightforward. Furthermore, as stated previously according to Scott, of the fifteen Season mosaics known of in Britain five may be female, but there is inadequate information and two with uncertain gender (see above, Scott 2000: 147, fig 73). This significant number creates a grey area and thus analysis becomes more complex. The figures in the Lullingstone mosaic were individually constructed characters with attributes associated with their purpose. Winter wears a hooded cloak totally covering the body apart from the face, Spring and Summer have cloaks draped over one shoulder revealing bare skin and Spring is joined by a bird and Summer has wheat arranged in the hair (Scott 2000: 147). The body shape and full cloak gives no sign of the ascribed gender of Winter and neither does the draped cloaks of Spring and Summer (four portrayals of Winter from the above list are hooded obscuring direct identification). In addition, the revealed skin area of both Spring and Summer has no colour change suggesting that there was no deliberate inclusion of breasts, in place there is nothing, not even the suggestion of male breasts. The choice of hair is noteworthy, as the way it was depicted follows similar patterns seen on sculptures of masculine subjects, for example the Mercury from Uley (fig. 17-19).

Therefore, I would propose that these images are masculine. So how does the interpretation change if the Seasons are masculine? It may be that the interpretation reverses, for instance if the Seasons are joined with Bellerophon and the Chimera (as the Lullingston mosaic above) then male Seasons were perhaps associated with the 'hero' rather than the mythical beast. Masculine Seasons contribute to controlling chaos rather than being a part of the chaos. As Scott has shown the Seasons were represented with a number of subjects including Medusa, mythical beasts, Bellerophon attacking the Chimera and predominately Bacchus (Scott 2000: 147). I think it is important to note that the subjects juxtaposed with the Seasons are the contributing factor for interpretation depending upon the designated gender of the Seasons. Finally, I would propose that the uncertainty of gender designation on particular mosaics was due to the way the images were created and not purposely made to be ambiguous.

Conclusion

Drawing to a conclusion, in this chapter I have concentrated on personifications and how they were used as visual communication of predominately political themes within Roman art. The formula works by the juxtapositioning of 'conqueror versus conquered' or 'civilised versus barbarian' through a visual hierarchy within the composition. This effectively creates a dependent relationship of opposed characters. The image of the 'barbarian' was constructed as an oppositional figure set up to be dominated by Roman rule. Political propaganda was not always the case as demonstrated by representations of Fortuna, Bonus Eventus, Genii and the Seasons. The majority of personifications discussed are feminine. It is no coincidence that personifications are mostly feminine; the formative categories of power relations, that is male: female are being articulated here in a hierarchical relation of conqueror: conquered. Dominant relations are understood through hierarchies of power and in terms of that which they can easily objectify. Thus, they will always draw upon the primary essential opposition of male to female (McClintock 1995).

[77] This is best demonstrated in Euripides' *Bacchae*.

[78] However, Maenads are generally depicted clothed see examples from the Mildenhall Treasure see Toynbee 1962: plate 115-116.

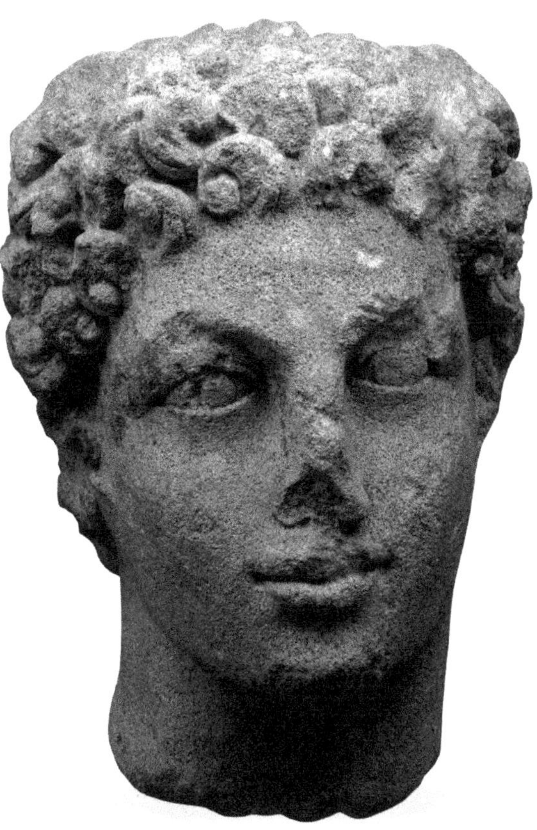

Fig. 17. Head of Mercury, 2nd century AD, from Uley, Gloucestershire, British Museum, London. © Trustees of the British Museum.

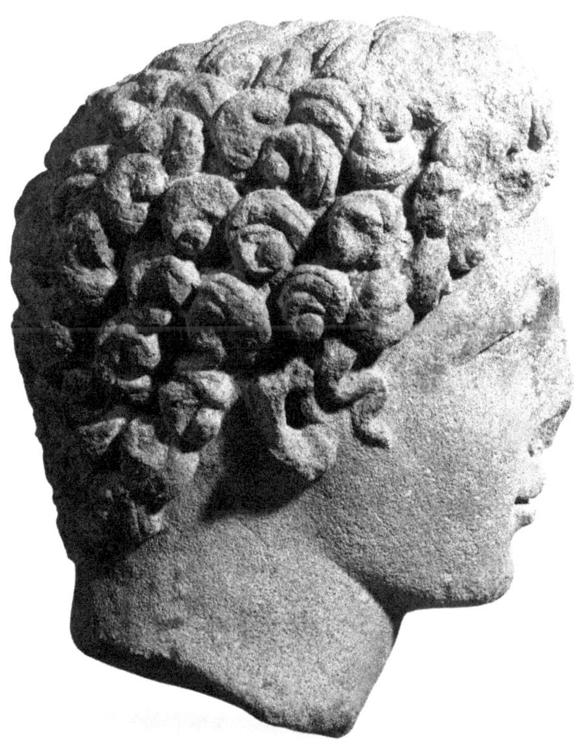

Fig. 18. Side view of the head of Mercury, 2nd century AD, from Uley, Gloucestershire, British Museum, London. © Trustees of the British Museum.

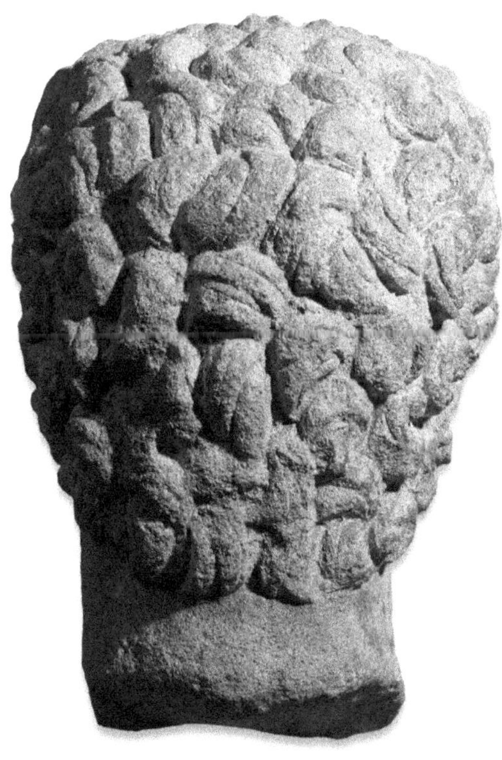

Fig. 19. Back view of head of Mercury, 2nd century AD, from Uley, Gloucestershire, British Museum, London. © Trustees of the British Museum.

Conclusion

Reading and Writing Roman Gender in Roman and Romano-British Art

I have endeavoured to reveal how socially constructed values add to the understandings of gender and Roman art. In the first chapter I demonstrated how clothing acted as gender markers, for example the *toga praetexta* donned by both girls and boys. This garment acted as a visual barrier securing the children's purity from any salaciousness or physical harm. It advertised the child's inviolable state which exemplifies why their gender is different to adults. Boys had the addition of a *bulla*, a pendent containing a phallic amulet, which ultimately acted as a symbol of social status and gender marker as only freeborn boys could sport it. The 'Roman ideal' necessitated that men and women led virtuous lives. Women, particularly matrons, were required to lead selfless lives concentrating on the successful management of the home including wool working, the rearing of children and absolute sexual fidelity within marriage. Clothing and adornments assumed at marriage, namely the *stola*, *palla* and *vittae*, reveal social conventions that in the end constructed the gendered facade of a Roman matron. This is particularly relevant in visual representations as it presented an example to follow, especially if the sculptures portray empresses. Freeborn youths donned the *toga virilis* at the onset of adulthood; this was the gendered mark of manhood and masculinity. Additionally actions were imperative to the 'Roman ideal'; it was essential for men to have control over themselves including physical and sexual restraint. Masculine sexual protocol required that a 'real' man should be the active penetrator - to be a submissive partner denoted a lack of control and ultimately the loss of masculinity, as this was 'the woman's part'. Indeed, precise conventions existed so much so that for women, men, and children to ignore them rendered the offenders open to censure. These conventions apply to the visual construction of deities because it is these socially construed ideals that make representations of gods/goddess products of their environment.

Venus personifies the epitome of 'beauty' and sexual desire; artworks depicting Venus appear to have a dual and conflicting interpretation. Hellenistic copies and retrospectively inspired examples tend to represent nude young women; whilst examples of Venus Genetrix (mother) refer back further into the classical period where the subjects are more respectfully clothed, albeit in clingy drapery, presumably endorsing the sexuality of matrons and mothers. Mars appears to represent a particular construct of masculinity that is associated with maturity and warfare, a factor that was of considerable significance to the stability and expansion of Rome. I suggest that Mars can be described as a hypermasculine character. His masculinity is exaggerated in his physical appearance and enhanced by his role as god of war.

Venus and Mars have distinct roles within the engineered history of Rome. Venus was mother of Aeneas, founder of Rome. The Julian family claimed to descend from the same family line as Aeneas and therefore be directly linked with divinity. Mars fathered Romulus and Remus; their mother Rhea Silvia belonged to the same Trojan family as Aeneas, relating the twins with the Julian dynasty. Consequently Venus and Mars have significant importance in Roman 'history'. Moreover, images of them were employed accordingly particularly in the years of conflict between the end of the Republic into the Principate, for the endorsement of the Julian family. The Algiers relief depicts Venus, Cupid, Mars and possibly deified Caesar. This propagandist piece deliberately collates those accountable for the foundations of Rome. Venus, Mars and their son Cupid present a united family of Rome, whilst their descendent Caesar joins them. The revival of foundation myths was valuable propaganda for the Julian family. As a result, Venus became a promoter of matrons and mothers. The lost Aphrodite of Cnidus by Praxiteles, like many Hellenistic examples, survive in the form of Roman replicas (whether a direct imitation or adapted theme). This work has a legendary status, allegedly as the first sculpture of a nude woman in Greek art and for its notorious reception (Pseudo-Lucian *Affairs of the Heart* 12). This strongly suggests a break with tradition. Therefore, the interpretation becomes more complex specifically with regards to the study of contemporary concepts of femininity associated with sexual identity. The term 'contemporary' however, refers to the Hellenistic period. In the Roman period works such as this reflect the tastes of the patrons and the impression that they wished to present to those viewing the pieces. According to contemporary texts, however sensational, the sculpture became an exhibition revealing the female nude, and subsequently, (for some) it becomes an objectified body and focus of voyeuristic attention. The way Praxiteles chose to depict her, modestly covering herself from onlookers, draws attention to concealed areas, increasing the scopophilic interest. Images of Venus Anadyomene (emerging from the sea) further exemplify retrospective inspiration from Hellenistic art. Other examples include 'crouching' Venus or images of the goddess tying sandals.

On the other hand, Venus Genetrix (mother), because of her title, indicates a sexuality that relates to wives and mothers. These are not nude, but are draped in diaphanous material revealing the female form. Loose, plunging drapery exposes one breast. The sculptures appear to imitate an earlier period of Greek sculpture more classical than Hellenistic and are an area that has to be discussed further.

Mars appears to have two main stylistic types: a mature figure in full military dress and Greek inspired images depicting a nude youth akin to the Ares Borghese, (it is the artistic style that I am comparing and not the characters of Mars and Ares). Hypermasculinity describes an exaggerated masculinity, particularly with regard to physical appearance. I believe it is useful for the interpretation of Mars as it is for other characters such as Hercules and Priapus. Images of Mars are contradictory; on the one hand he was portrayed as the hypermasculine, penetrator and martial war god and on the other hand was represented as the complete opposite, a passive and vulnerable adolescent. The choice of representation presumably depended on what the artist or patron wanted to portray. The cult statue of Mars Ultor, for example, draws on the idea of the god as avenger of the death of Julius Caesar and for this they chose a hypermasculine representation. Alternatively, the Roman copy of Ares in the Borghese Gallery then draws on visual Hellenic inspirations and the connotations this carries with it.

Diana and Apollo as twin deities share a common attribute, their hunting regalia and appropriate animals signifying their role as hunter deities. Yet, as individuals they are as diverse in character as they are in visual illustration. Diana is goddess of the hunt, the moon, a protector of those in childbirth, of small children, young animals and she is guardian of woodlands, harbours and roads. She generally has a guise that bears a resemblance to a specific type of Amazon, with a short tunic allowing for movement, although her upper body is covered unlike Amazons whom were commonly depicted with one breast revealed. Apollo has a number of godheads other than twin hunter god; among them is his prophetic authority, his associations with medicine as the father of Asclepius and his celebrated roles as the god of poetry, music and the sun. Apollo appears as a youthful nude often with long tresses portrayed with various items including his bow, a lyre, fawn and laurel leaves.

Apollo had a particular appeal to Octavian who affiliated himself with the deity during the struggle for control (and eventually sole power) of Rome after the death of Caesar in 44 BC. Apollo embodied converse characteristics that Octavian found valuable. Apollo was a youthful, unassailable god of vengeance, smiting those who strayed further than the proper limits set for mortal ambitions. Yet, he was also regarded as a gentle god of refinement and culture, a solar god and a healer. These character traits were useful to Octavian who amongst other things, promoted himself as one who could heal Rome's aliments. As god of poetry, Apollo became allied with intellectual dexterity and consequently became the favourite of poets and politicians at Rome. Furthermore, Apollo stood for discipline and morality, aspects that suited Octavian in opposition to the excesses of Antony and his divine patrons, among which were, Hercules and Dionysus. Apolline imagery was employed and transmitted through visual images to transmit and remind people of Octavian's endorsed links with Apollo; this includes a snake, a tripod, a lyre and laurel branches.

Visual constructs of Apollo are akin to those of Bacchus/Dionysus. Both appear as nude/partially nude youths often with long hair. These subjects are often referred to as having an ambiguous gender or more stereotypically as 'effeminate'. I do not believe that either are specifically androgynous figures. I suggest that this specific category, in fact, celebrates masculinity and draws on youthful characteristics, which differ, from that of Hercules or Mars. Apollo as a nude appears to represent the epitome of masculine youth and 'beauty' and to embody an object of sexual desire whether homoerotic or heterosexual. I suggest that visual representations of Apollo have a dual explanation. Notwithstanding the religious function of images of the god, underlining there is another role – on view is a youthful, objectified adolescent body. His youth makes him 'other' to adult and Roman conceptions of masculine identity (the dominant penetrator) and therefore sexually desirable.

As previously mentioned Diana resembles images of specific Amazon 'types'. As their patron deity, she shared a special relationship with the Amazons and their all female society. Diana is affiliated with Amazons for a number of reasons: she is chaste rejecting marriage and child bearing (although Amazons welcomed men only for procreation); she inhabits a region removed from the 'civilised' world; both hunt and fight like men and they are self-governing and independent. However, their autonomy was not celebrated. Conversely their very femininity was under attack because they did not conform to the endorsed social norm. This is apparent in the ways that artists and sculptors approached these subjects. The powerful, threatening sexuality of the Amazons were met with violent defeat and humiliation. Nevertheless, for a goddess, this would be inappropriate. Diana's virginity meant that thinking of her, as a sexually active adult woman was impious and forbidden. A potential sexual encounter with her was a transgressive act, as illustrated in the myth of Actaeon. Their independence, coupled with an active existence that features hunting and fighting, are aspects generally associated with masculinity – this contrasts with the specified femininity of personas such as Venus or Minerva.

Apollo and Diana as fraternal twins are an uncommon occurrence, in the literature of the period, as the majority of literature deals principally with identical twins. On starting the chapter I assumed that Diana and Apollo because of their twinship shared gendered aspects, that she was as masculine as he was feminine, but this is not the case. It would be dubious to presuppose that because they are twins their gender ascriptions act on a compensatory basis, for example Diana having masculine weapons because Apollo is supposedly 'feminine'. This is not the case, gender merging does not apply; Diana's contrived gender is definitely feminine and Apollo's masculine. They possess different types of femininity and masculinity. Diana's femininity draws on her aspects as a huntress, virgin, goddess of childbirth, patroness of Amazons and this reflects in her visual appearance. Apollo has a particular masculinity that has little to do with imitating women and more to do with youthful masculine beauty and homoeroticism.

Minerva was an important goddess and part of the Capitoline triad. Her femininity appears to be different from that of Venus or Diana. To determine an interpretation, I endeavoured to examine the components of her visual assemblage, including clothes, physical appearance and attributes together with related mythology. This methodology is applicable in deciphering images of Hercules, whose masculinity is in turn dissimilar from that of Apollo or Bacchus. The study commenced by considering earlier examples from Greece and Rome that may be interrelated with later images of Minerva. In general, Minerva's appearance appears to be based on images of Athena, Greek goddess of war and of patroness of Athens, (particularly those from the classical period onwards). Despite the considerable length of time between classical Greek period and that of imperial Rome, there does appear to be a long history of this figure type. Although it is important not to presume that these personas are one and the same, yet stylistic borrowings do nonetheless come into view. As Athena, Minerva is a goddess of war and bears the equipment as testimony including a Corinthian helmet (a specific retrospective addition?), spear and shield. This is a particular aspect that influences the overall interpretation of Minerva's femininity as she appears with objects generally associated with masculinity, the weapons of war.

The next section focused on images of Minerva from Roman Britain. When examining other examples from Britain, for example, a relief of Minerva and Aesclepius from Hadrian's Wall; a relief of Minerva from the Roman baths site, Bath; a freestanding sculpture of Minerva from Cambridgeshire; and two bronze figurines from London, it becomes apparent that particular attention was paid to the drapery. In the main, her clothing is heavy with an excess of material covering her body and reaching to her ankles, her whole body is covered (although in some illustrations her arms are on view); even a helmet covers her head. As a result, we cannot see her body or her hair, which is short and concealed beneath the helmet. This indicates that we are not permitted to gaze at her body or her hair. Apparent visual signs indicating her sex are concealed beneath clothing and headgear. Her physical form and sexuality are suppressed; we are not to think of her as a sexual being. Her clothing acts as a sign analogous to that of a Roman *matrona* or married women, who on marriage donned the *stola*, which is a long, strapped garment that reached the feet, guarding the lower legs and feet from the gaze of others. Moreover, with such heavy garments movement becomes restricted which ultimately suggests that she is passive and inactive, which contradicts her role as goddess of war. Minerva exceeds the limitations of endorsed femininity – she generally has short and covered hair this diverges from conventional images of Roman women whose hair is controlled and managed. Furthermore, her voluntary chastity hinders the 'natural' role as a child bearer. She has a particular masculine-femininity. However, her masculinity is limited to short hair and the holding of weapons, her long heavy clothing restricts her movement and therefore she appears unable to have a 'masculine' active role. Her masculinity and her femininity are each suppressed.

Hercules epitomises the all-active hypermasculine 'action hero', with rippling muscles and a full beard. His gender is constructed by drawing on his unique super strength that is illustrated by his exaggerated musculature. His status is enhanced by the mythology relating to him as a subject, particularly his Twelve Labours. The general theme of the Labours encompasses a variety of opponents including monsters, giants, an Amazon, ferocious animals and chaotic nature all controlled and conquered by 'action hero' Hercules enforcer of civilization. Hercules was a favourite of Mark Antony who claimed to descend from the same family line as the semi-divine hero. Ultimately, Hercules became an instrument for propaganda against Antony by his enemies who, it is presumed, specifically engaged the sequence of events concerning the exotic Queen of the Lydians, Omphale, to whom Hercules was enslaved as a metaphorical counterpart for Cleopatra and Antony. This is particularly relevant for the tale concerning Omphale ordering Hercules to swap clothing with her. Images of Hercules wearing women's clothes ultimately attack Hercules' (and as a result Anthony's) masculinity, as he was not a free citizen, as a woman owned him. Simultaneously, Omphale's (consequently Cleopatra's) femininity was also attacked because the basic gender roles were reversed. Her powerful role and control over Hercules shows aspects normally associated with men; ultimately she represented a non-Roman 'other' analogous with female personas such as Medea and Penthesilea the Amazon. In later Roman history, Hercules becomes the favourites of emperors Commodus (180 –192AD) and Caracalla (211-217AD), both presumably drawing on affiliations of physical strength. Conclusively, the embodiment of Hercules as 'action hero' more often than not depends on the composition. His status depends on him having a combatant - a doomed adversary.

A personification literally embodies an abstract concept in an anthropomorphic form (chapter 5). This chapter endeavours to interpret the visual language employed to illustrate the personification with particular reference to allocation and application of gender to the individual subject. The majority of these are feminine, although this is not totally exclusive as there are masculine personifications, for example Bonus Eventus (good luck) or Honos (honour). The first part of the chapter concentrated on the personification of places; these tend to be feminine. An introductory image by a sixteenth century artist, Jan van der Straet narrates the moment America was discovered by Europe. In this hierarchical composition, America is a naked, seated women being approached by Europe, a man who is not only fully dressed, but carries items that allude to culture and science. The juxtapositioning of the main characters signify imperial objectives. The women is located amongst animals and behind her a scene of cannibalism. Behind Europe are ships indicating contemporary civilization and progress, their intentions being to 'better' America. This engraving is an unambiguous and valuable introduction for the use of personification in post-colonial representations. It was a method recurrently implemented in Roman art. Claudius about to slay Britannia is perhaps the most appropriate image to the overall research (Sebasteion, Aphrodisias). A relief of Nero slaying Armenia derives from the same setting. In both the conquered territory is represented by a fallen partially clothed woman. On researching the subject further, I became aware that other regions (post- colonial) were depicted in feminine form. However, the way they were portrayed was very different: examples on coins include Spain, Judea (Breglia 1968: 80, 140) and Dacia (Adby 2002: 34). These images depict women embodying imperial provinces that oppose the fallen naked 'barbarian' images witnessed from the Sebasteion. On coins the personifications are in various poses but all are solitary figures that advertise imperial ownership. Perhaps a reason why the embodiments are feminine is that they are controlled. The Sebasteion sculptures present compositions, which heighten the masculine prowess of particular emperors. In these examples, Britannia and Armenia are besieged, they are literally under physical attack, but because of their explicit partial/ nudity the scenes also imply potential sexual assault. This intensifies perceptions of the emperors' masculinity; they are dominant penetrators, which is a prerequisite for approved masculinity. Violence and sexual vulnerability are allied. This is a method employed to depict masculine prisoners of war, adversaries or more precisely the collective stereotype of illustrating the 'barbarian' (see below).

On the other hand, Rome itself was embodied in the form of a woman. As a visual representation, Roma is a complex combination drawing on specific illustrative features of Minerva, Amazons and Venus Genetrix. This makes her a paradoxical character. She has the masculine armour of Minerva and is dressed in a short tunic with a revealed breast suggesting a 'barbaric' Amazon, yet the exposed breast could also refer to Venus Genetrix in her role as mother of Rome.

Numerous examples of Victory survive from Roman Britain, including fragments of Victories from the male gorgon pediment at Bath and several commemoration slabs from Hadrian's and Antonine wall regions. Victories are in essence a means for visual propaganda, communicating imperial supremacy. Victories also appear with clichéd images of the 'barbarian'. This figure 'type' appears to symbolise the universal non-Roman adversary; an impression personified. Their masculinity is one that illustrates vulnerability, as they are generally depicted fallen in combat, and naked, exposing them to corporeal and sexual attack. This portrayal appears to be approached in the same manner as that of Britannia and Armenia discussed above. The 'barbarians' are not in control of their own bodies or of the situation and therefore fall short of what was measured as correct masculinity.

Fortuna embodied good luck, fortune and chance; thematically her male counterpart is Bonus Eventus although images of them together are rare. Dedications to these deities appear commonly in a bathhouse context protecting the patrons in their naked vulnerability. Fortuna is generally depicted as a matronly figure with long drapery totally covering her body. The addition of a cornucopia acts as a recognisable sign for her identification. Images of the Genius – spirit of place or concept - also bear a cornucopia enabling identification. His masculinity draws on youth, as the Genius is generally depicted semi-nude exhibiting the upper body.

The next topic is the personification of Seasons. These are for the most part feminised with several examples deriving from a domestic context as themes depicted in mosaic (including Dyer Street, Cirencester, the Thruxton Bacchus mosaic and Lullingstone showing Bellerophon). Other subjects present contribute to the interpretation, for example Bacchus. As the god of wine he represents the celebration of intoxication and altered states of mind that are uncontrollable and untamed – like the seasons. This may explain the feminisation of the seasons reiterating contemporary perceptions of women as having untamed sexual desire that falls in line with wild Bacchic revelling or the juxtapositioning of Seasons and mythical beasts such as the Chimera as illustrated in Lullingstone.

When I first began exploring this subject the focus was directed at the representation of women only. Through the processes of research I recognised that the study of gender comprises of the investigation of femininity and masculinity. As far as I am aware, apart from my research, this has not been accomplished in the interpretation of Roman British art; therefore more work is needed in this area. This study has attempted to present a theoretical construct of how gender was exhibited, managed and manipulated in Roman and Romano-British art. I hope that my work has provided a model that can be applied not only to Roman Britain but also to other provincial contexts, where gender is recognised as a means of engaging with colonial discourse and the tensions that arise therefore. Finally, it is important to remember that Romano-British art is not worse or bad because it is not hundred percent symmetrical or lifelike – it is just different and as valuable to the history of art as any other period.

Bibliography

Alcock, J. 1996. Life in Roman Britain. *London: B.T.Batsford/English Heritage.*

Aldhouse-Green, M. 2003. *Artefacts and Archaeology: Aspects of the Celtic and Roman world.* Cardiff: University of Wales Press.

Aldhouse-Green, M. 2004. An Archaeology of Images: Iconology and Cosmology in Iron Age and Roman Europe. *London: Routledge.*

Allason-Jones, L. 1989. Women in Roman Britain. *London: British Museum Publications.*

Allason-Jones, L. and Miket, R. 1984. *The Catalogue of Small Finds from South Shields Roman Fort.* Newcastle: The Society of Antiquaries of Newcastle upon Tyne and Wear County Museum Service.

Alston, R. 1998. 'Arms and the man: soldiers, masculinity and power in Republican and Imperial Rome.' In L. Foxhall and J. Salmon J. (eds.). *When Men were Men: Masculinity, Power and Identity in Classical Antiquity.* London: Routledge, pp 205-223.

Apollodorus 1997. *The Library of Greek Mythology.* Translation by R. Hard. Oxford: Oxford University Press.

Archer, L., Fischler, S and Wyke, M. *Women in Ancient Societies an Illusion of the Night.* London: Macmillan.

Argenti, N. 2001. Memory and royal sempiternity in a Grassfields kingdom. In A.Forty and S. Küchler. *The Art of Forgetting.* Oxford: Berg, pp.21-52.

Arroyo J. 2000. *Action/Spectacle Cinema: a Sight and Sound Reader.* London: British Film Institute.

Attfield J. 1996. Barbie and Action Man: adult toys for girls and boys, 1959-1993. In Kirkham P. (ed.) *The Gendered Object.* Manchester: Manchester University Press, pp 80-89.

Augenti, A. (ed.) 2000. *Art and Archaeology of Rome: from Ancient Times to the Baroque.* New York: Riverside Book Company.

Baker A and Vitullo J. 2001. Screening the Italian-American male. In P. Lehman 2001. *Masculinity: Bodies, Movies, Culture.* London: Routledge, pp.213-226.

Barrett, A.A. 1978. Knowledge of the literary classics in Roman Britain. *Britannia* 9: 307-13.

Bartman, E. 1999. *Portraits of Livia: Imaging the Imperial Woman in Augustan Rome.* Cambridge: Cambridge University Press.

Bartman, E. 2001. Hair and the Artifice of Roman Female Adornment. *American Journal of Archaeology* 105 (1): 1-25

Bartman E. 2002. Eros's flame: sexy boys in Roman Ideal Sculpture. In E Gazda (ed.). *The Ancient Art of Emulation: Studies in Artistic Originality and Tradition from the Present to Classical Antiquity.* Michigan: University of Michigan Press, pp 249-272.

Beard, M. and Henderson, J. 2001. *Classical Art: from Greece to Rome.* Oxford: Oxford University Press.

Beard, M. and North, J. and Price, S. 1998. *Religions of Rome. Volume 1: A History* Cambridge: Cambridge University Press.

Beard, M. and North, J. and Price, S. 1998a. *Religions of Rome. Volume 2: A Source Book.* Cambridge: Cambridge University Press.

Becatti, G. 1968 *The Art of Ancient Greece and Rome, From the Rise of Greece to the fall of Rome.* London: Thames and Hudson.

Benwell. B. 2003. *Masculinity and Men's Lifestyle Magazines.* Oxford: Blackwell.

Besly, E. 1987. *Roman Coins Relating to Britain.* Cardiff: National Museum of Wales.

Bieber, M. 1967. *The Sculpture of the Hellenistic Age.* New York: Columbia University Press.

Billington, S. and Green, M. (eds.) 1996. *The Concept of the Goddess.* London: Routledge.

Bird J, Hassall M and Sheldon, H. 1996. *Interpreting Roman London: Papers in Memory of Hugh Chapman.* Oxford: Oxbow Monograph 58.

Black, E.W. 1986. Christian and pagan hopes of salvation in Romano-British mosaics. In M. Henig and A. King (eds.) *Pagan Gods and Shrines in the Roman Empire.* Oxford: Oxford University School of Archaeology, pp. 147–58.

Boardman, J. 1991. *Greek Sculpture: The Archaic Period.* London: Thames and Hudson.

Boardman, J. 1992. *Greek Sculpture: The Classical Period.* London: Thames and Hudson.

Boardman, J. 1993 The classical period. In Boardman, J. (ed.) *The Oxford History of Classical Art.* Oxford: Oxford University Press, pp.83-149.

Boardman, J. 1993. *The Oxford History of Classical Art.* Oxford: Oxford University Press.

Boardman, J. and Griffin, J. and Murray, O. (eds.) 1986. *The Oxford History of the Classical World: The Roman World.* Oxford: Oxford University Press.

Brailsford, J.W. 1958. *Antiquities of Roman Britain.* London: Trustees of the British Museum.

Breglia, L. 1968. *Roman Imperial Coins, Their Art and Technique.* London: Thames and Hudson.

Brendel, O. 1995. *Etruscan Art.* New Haven: Yale University Press.

Brewer, R.J. 1986. *Corpus Signorum Imperii Romani: Great Britain,* Vol.1, Fasc.5: Wales. Oxford: Oxford University Press.

Brisson, L. 2002. *Sexual Ambivalence:Androgyny and Hermaphroditism in Graeco-Roman Antiquity.* California: University of California Press.

Brilliant, R. 1994 *Commentaries on Roman Art: Selected Studies.* London: Pindar Press.

Brown, J.A. 1996. Gender and the action heroine: hardbodies and the Point of No Return. *Cinema Journal* 35: 52-71.

Burnett A. 1977. *The Coins of Roman Britain.* London: British Museum Press.

Burston P. 1995. *What are You Looking at?* London: Cassell.

Butler, J. 1999. *Gender Trouble: Feminism and the Subversion of Identity.* London: Routledge.

Carpenter, T. 1998. *Art and Myth in Ancient Greece.* London: Thames and Hudson.

Cartledge, P. 1993. *The Greeks: A Portrait of Self and Others.* Oxford: Oxford University Press.

Casey, P.J. 1999. *Roman Coinage in Britain.* Buckinghamshire: Shire Archaeology.

Cassius Dio. 1987. *The Roman History: The Reign of Augustus.* Translated by I. Scott-Kilvert, I. London: Penguin Classics.

Caygill, M. 1981. *The Story of the British Museum.* London: British Museum Press.

Champlin, E. 1991. *Final Judgments: Duty and Emotion in Roman Wills, 200 BC-AD 250.* Berkeley-Los Angeles: University of California Press.

Cicero. 1923 *On Old Age. On Friendship. On Divination.* Translation by W.A. Falconer. Cambridge: Loeb Classical Library.

Clark, K. 1956. *The Nude: a Study of Ideal Art.* London: Penguin Books.

Clark, K. 1980. *Feminine beauty.* London: Weidenfeld and Nicolson.

Clarke, J. 1993. The Warren cup and the contexts for representations of male-to-male Lovemaking in Augustan and Early Julio-Claudian Art. *Art Bulletin* 75: 275-294.

Clarke, J. 1998. *Looking at Lovemaking: Constructions of Sexuality in Roman Art 100 BC – AD 250.* London: University of California Press.

Clarke, J. 2002 Look who's laughing at sex, men and women viewers in the *Apodyterium* of the suburban baths at Pompeii. In D. Fredrick, D. *The Roman Gaze, Vision, Power, and the Body.* London: John Hopkins University Press, pp.111-149.

Clarke, J. 2003. *Art in the Lives of Ordinary Romans: Visual Representation and Non-Elite Viewers in Italy 100BC- AD315.* California: University of California Press.

Clarke, J. and Larvey, M. 2003a. *Roman Sex: 100BC to 250 AD.* New York: Harry N. Abrams.

Cohen, B. 1997. Divesting the female breast of clothes in classical sculpture. In A.O. Koloski-Ostrow and C.L. Lyons (eds.) *Naked Truths: Women, Sexuality, and Gender in Classical Art and Archaeology.* London: Routledge, pp. 66-96.

Cohen, B. (ed.) 2000. *Not the Classical Ideal: Athens and the Construction of the Other in Greek Art.* Leiden: Konninklijke Brill.

Cohen, B. 2000a. Man-killers and their victims: inversions of the heroic ideal in classical art. In B. Cohen. *Not the Classical Ideal: Athens and the Construction of the Other in Greek Art.* Leiden: Konninklijke Brill.

Collingwood, R.G and Myers, J. 1937. *Roman Britain and the English Settlements.* Oxford: Clarendon Press.

Collingwood, R.G. and Wright, R.P. 1995. *The Roman Inscriptions of Britain 1: Inscriptions on Stone.* Stroud: Alan Sutton.

Cookson, N. A. 1984. *Romano-British Mosaics: A Reassessment and Critique of some Notable Stylistic Affinities,* Oxford: British Archaeological Reports 135.

Cooper, E. 2002. *Fully Exposed: the Male Nude in Photograph.* London: Routledge.

Corbeill, A. 1997. Dining deviants in Roman political invective. In J.P. Hallett and M.B. Skinner (eds.). *Roman Sexualities.* Princeton: Princeton University Press, pp 99-128.

Cornell, T. and Lomas, K. (eds.) 1997, *Gender and Ethnicity in Ancient Italy: Accordia specialist studies on Italy; Volume. 6.* London: University of London.

Cosh, S. 1989. The Lindinis branch of the Corinian saltire officina. *Mosaic* 16: 7-10.

Cottam, S., Dungworth, D., Scott, S. and Taylor, J. (eds) 1995. *TRAC' 94 Proceedings of the Fourth Theoretical Roman Archaeology Conference.* Oxford: Oxbow Books.

Coulston J.C. and Phillips, E.J. 1988. *Corpus Signorum Imperii Romani:Great Britain, Vol. 1, Fasc. 6: Hadrian's Wall west of the North Tyne and Carlisle.* Oxford: Oxford University Press.

Crawford. M, 1986. Early Rome and Italy. In J Boardman. and J. Griffin and O. Murray (eds.) *The Oxford History of the Classical World: The Roman World.* Oxford: Oxford University Press, pp. 9-38.

Croom, A.T. 2000. Roman clothing and Fashion. *Stroud: Tempus Publishing.*

Crump, T. 1990. The Anthropology of Numbers. *Cambridge: Cambridge University Press.*

Cunliffe, B. 1995. Roman Bath. *London: Batsford/English Heritage.*

Cunliffe, B. 1997. *The Ancient Celts.* Oxford: Oxford University Press.

Cunliffe, B.W. and Fulford, M.G. 1982. *Corpus Signorum Imperii Romani, Great Britain Volume 1, Fascicule 2: Bath and the Rest of Wessex.* Oxford: Oxford University Press.

Cunliffe. B. and Davenport, P. 1985. *The Temple of Sulis Minerva at Bath, Volume 1 (I) the Site I.* Oxford: Oxford University Committee for Archaeology: Monograph No.7.

D'Ambra E. 1993. *Roman Art in Context: An Anthology.* Englewood Cliffs, N.J.: Prentice Hall.

D'Ambra, E. 1993a. *Private Lives, Imperial Virtues: The Frieze of the Forum Transitorium in Rome.* New Jersey: Princeton University Press.

D'Ambra, E. 1996. The calculus of Venus: nude portraits of Roman matrons. In N. B. Kampen. *Sexuality in Ancient Art,* Cambridge: Cambridge University Press.

D'Ambra, E. 1998. *Art and Identity in the Roman World.* London: Orion Publishing Group.

D'Ambra, E. 1998. Representing Roman women. *Journal of Roman Archaeology.* 11: 546-53.

D'Ambra, E. 2000. Nudity and adornment in female portrait sculpture of the second century AD. In D.E.E.Kleiner and S.B.Matheson (eds.) *I Claudia II: Women in Roman Art and Society.* Austin: University of Texas Press.

Daniel, G. E. 1952. *A Hundred Years of Archaeology.* London: Gerald Duckworth and Co. Ltd.

Davies, G. 1997. Gender and body language in Roman art. In T. Cornell and K. Lomas (eds.) *Gender and Ethnicity in Ancient Italy: Accordia specialist studies on Italy; Volume. 6.* London: University of London.

De Angelis M. 2001. *Gay Fandom and Crossover Stardom: James Dean, Mel Gibson and Keanu Reeves*. Durham: Duke University Press.

De Beauvoir, S. 1997 *The Second Sex*. London: Vintage.

De Jersey, P. 1996. *Celtic Coinage in Britain*. Buckinghamshire: Shire Archaeology.

De Vries, K. 2000. The Nearly Other: The Attic Vision of the Phrygians and Lydians. In B. Cohen. *Not the Classical Ideal: Athens and the Construction of Other in Greek Art*. Konninklijke Brill: Leiden, pp. 338-63.

De Rose Evans, J. 1992. *The Art of Persuasion: Political Propaganda from Aeneas to Brutus*. Michigan: University of Michigan Press.

Derrida, J. 1987. *The Truth in Painting*. Chicago: University of Chicago Press.

Dixon, S. 2000. *Reading Roman Women*. London: Duckworth.

Dixon, S. 2001. *Childhood, Class and Kin in the Roman World*. London: Routledge.

Douglas, M. 1966. *Purity and Dander: An Analysis of Conception of Pollution and Taboo*. London: Routledge.

Dover K.J. 1979. *Greek Homosexuality*. London: Duckworth.

Dunbabin, K.M.D. 2001. *Mosaics of the Greek and Roman World*. Cambridge: Cambridge University Press.

Edwards, C. 1997. Unspeakable professions: public performance and prostitution in Ancient Rome. In J.P. Hallett and M.B. Skinner (eds.). *Roman Sexualities*. Princeton: Princeton University .Press, pp.66-95.

Ellis Hanson, A. 2000. Widows too young in their widowhood. In D.E.E. Kleiner and S.B. Matheson. *I Claudia II: Women in Roman Art and Society*. Austin: University of Texas Press, pp. 149-165.

Elsner, J. 1997. *Art and the Roman Viewer: the Transformation of Art from the Pagan world to Christianity*. Cambridge: Cambridge University Press.

Elsner, J. 1996. *Art and Text in Roman Culture*. Cambridge: Cambridge University Press.

Erim, K.T. 1982. A new relief showing Claudius and Britannia from Aphrodisias. *Britannia* 23: 277.

Esmonde Cleary S. 2000. Putting the dead in their place: burial location in Roman Britain. In J. Pearce, M. Millett and M. Struck (eds.). *Burials, Society and Context in the Roman World*. Oxford: Oxbow Books, pp. 127-142.

Euripides. 1972. *The Bacchae*. Translated by P. Vellacott. London: Penguin Books.

Fantham, E. and Peet Foley, H. and Boymel Kampen, N. and Pomeroy, S.B. and Shapiro, H.A. 1995. *Women in the Classical World*. Oxford: Oxford University Press.

Fausto-Sterling, A. 2000. *Sexing the Body: Gender Politics and the Construction of Sexuality*. New York: Basic Books.

Fernie, E. 2001. *Art History and Its Methods*. London: Phaidon.

Ferris, I. 1995. Insignificant Others: Images of Barbarians on Military Art from Roman Britain. S. Cottam, D. Dungworth, S. Scott and J. Taylor (eds.) *TRAC' 94 Proceedings of the Fourth Theoretical Roman Archaeology Conference*. Oxford: Oxbow Books, pp. 24-31.

Ferris, I. 1997. The Enemy Without, the Enemy Within. More Thoughts on Images of Barbarians on Greek and Roman Art. In K. Meadows, C. Lemke and J. Heron (eds.) 1997. *TRAC'97 Proceeding of the Theoretical Archaeology Conference*. Oxford: Oxbow Books, pp. 22-28.

Ferris, I. 2000. *Enemies of Rome: Barbarians through Roman Eyes*. Gloucester: Sutton.

Flemming, R. 2000. *Medicine and the making of Roman Women: Gender, Nature and Authority from Celsus to Galen*. Oxford: Oxford University Press.

Forty, A. and Küchler, S. 2001. *The Art of Forgetting*. Oxford: Berg.

Foucault M. 1985a. *History of Sexuality: An Introduction*. Translated by R.Hurley. New York: Vintage Books.

Foucault M. 1985b. *History of Sexuality: The Care of the Self*. Translated by R Hurley. New York: Vintage Books.

Foucault M. 1985c. *History of Sexuality: The Use of Pleasure*. Translated by R. Hurley. New York: Vintage Books.

Foxhall, L. and Salmon J. 1998. *When Men were Men: Masculinity, Power and Identity in Classical Antiquity*. London: Routledge.

Fraschetti, A. 2001. *Roman Women*. Chicago: University of Chicago Press.

Fredrick, D. 1997. Reading broken skin: violence in Roman elegy. In J.P. Hallett and M.B Skinner. *Roman Sexualities*. Princeton: Princeton University Press, pp. 172-196.

Fredrick, D. 2000 *The Roman Gaze, Vision, Power, and the Body*. London: John Hopkins University Press.

Gabbard K. 2001. "Someone is going to pay," resurgent white masculinity in *Ransom*. In P. Lehman. *Masculinity: Bodies, Movies, Culture*. London: Routledge, pp.7-24.

Gardner J.F. 1986. *Women in Roman Law and Society*. London: Routledge.

Gardner, J.F. 1993. *Roman Myths*. London: British Museum Press.

Gauntlett D. 2002. *Media, Gender and Identity: an Introduction*. London: Routledge.

Gazda, E.K. 1991. *Roman Art and the Private Sphere*. Michigan: University of Michigan Press.

Gazda E.K. 2002. *The Art of Emulation: Studies in Artistic Originality and Tradition from the Present to Classical Antiquity*. Michigan University of Michigan Press.

George, M. 2001. A Roman Funerary Monument with a Mother and Daughter. In S. Dixon. *Childhood, Class and Kin in the Roman World*. London: Routledge, pp. 178-189.

Gero, J.M and Conkey, M.W. 1991. *Engendering Archaeology: Women and Prehistory*. Oxford: Blackwell.

Gero, J.M. 1985. Socio-politics of women-at-home ideology. *American Antiquity*. 50 (2) 342-350.

Gilchrist, R. 1999. *Gender and Archaeology: Contesting the Past*. London: Routledge.

Gill, M. 1989. *Image of the Body: Aspects of the Nude.* London: Bodley Head.

Gleason, M. 1995. *Making Men: Spirits and Self-Presentation in Ancient Rome.* Princeton: Princeton University Press.

Gombrich, E. 1959. *Art and Illusion: A Study in the Psychology of Pictorial Representation.* London: Phaidon.

Gombrich, E. 1967. *The Story of Art.* London: Phaidon.

Green, M.J. 1976. *A Corpus of Religious Material from the Civilian Areas of Roman Britain.* Oxford: British Archaeological Reports 24.

Green, M.J. 1978. *A Corpus of Small Cult-Objects from the Military Area of*

Green, M.J. 1983. *The Gods of Roman Britain.* Buckinghamshire: Shire Archaeology.

Green, M.J. 1986. *The Gods of the Celts.* Gloucestershire: Sutton Publishing.

Green, M.J. 1989. *Symbol and Image in Celtic Religious Art.* London: Routledge.

Green, M.J. 1991 Triplism and plurality: intensity and symbolism in Celtic religious expression. In *Sacred and Profane (Proceedings of a Conference on Archaeology, Ritual and Religion).* In P. Garwood, D. Jennings, R. Skeates and J. Toms. Oxford: Oxbow Books, PP. 100-108.

Green, M.J. 1992. *Dictionary of Celtic Myth and Legend.* London: Thames and Hudson.

Green, M.J. 1993. *Celtic Myths.* London: British Museum Press.

Green, M.J. *1995.* Celtic Goddesses. *London: British Museum Press.*

Green M.J. 2000. *Celtic Wales: a pocket guide.* Cardiff: University of Wales Press.

Green, R and Handley, E. 1995. *Images of the Greek Theatre.* London: British Museum Press.

Gunderson, E. 2000. *Staging Masculinity: the Rhetoric of Performance in the Roman World.* Michigan: University of Michigan Press.

Halberstam, J. 1998. *Female-Masculinity.* Durham N.C.: Duke University Press.

Hallett, J.P. and Skinner M.B. 1997. *Roman Sexualities.* Princeton: Princeton University Press.

Halperin, D.V. 1990. *One Hundred Years of Homosexuality.* London: Routledge.

Harrison, J. 1913. *Ancient Art and Ritual*, Bradford-on-Avon, Wilts: Moonraker Press.

Hassall. M.W.C. 1977. Wingless Victories. In J. Munby and M. Henig. *Roman Life and Art in Britain, Part II.* Oxford: British Archaeological Reports 41 (ii), pp. 327-340.

Havelock, C.H. 1971. *Hellenistic Art: The Art of the Classical World from the Death of Alexander the Great to the Battle of Actium.* London: Phaidon.

Haverfield, F. 1915. *The Romanization of Roman Britain.* Oxford: Oxford University Press.

Haward, A. 1999. *Art and the Roman.* London: Bristol Classical Press.

Hendershot, H. 1996. Dolls: odour, disgust, femininity and toy design. In P. Kirkham. *The Gendered Object.* Manchester: Manchester University Press, pp. 90-102.

Henderson, J. 2002. A doo-dah-doo-dah-dey at the races: Ovid Amores 3.2. and the personal politica of the Circus Maximus. *Classical Antiquity.* 21 41-65.

Henig, M. 1974. *A Corpus of Engraved Gemstones from British Sites Part I: Discussion.* Oxford: British Archaeological Reports 8(I).

Henig, M. 1974a. *A Corpus of Engraved Gemstones from British Sites Part II: Discussion.* Oxford: British Archaeological Reports 8(II).

Henig, M. 1984. *Religion in Roman Britain.* New York: St. Martin's Press.

Henig M. and King, A. (eds.) 1986. *Pagan Gods and Shrines in the Roman Empire.* Oxford: Oxford University School of Archaeology.

Henig, M. 1993. *Corpus Signorium Imperii Romani: Great Britain Volume 1, Fasc. 7, The Cotswolds Region with Devon and Cornwall.* Oxford: Oxford University Press.

Henig, M. 1995. *Art of Roman Britain.* London: B.T. Batsford.

Henig, M. 1997. The Lullingstone Mosaic: Art, Religion and Letters in a Fourth Century Villa. *Mosaic* 24: 4-7.

Henig, M. 1998. A Disappointing Study of Roman Art. *British Archaeology* 33: 17.

Henig M. 1999. A New Star Shining over Bath. *Oxford Journal of Archaeology.* 18 (4): 419-425.

Henig, M. 2000. The Secret of Lullingstone Mosaic. *Kent Archaeological Review.* 139: 196-197.

Henig, M. 2000. A Roman Relief of Mercury and Minerva from Aldsworth, Gloucestershire. *Britannia* 2000: 362-383.

Henig, M. 2002a. *The Heirs of Verica: Culture and Politics in Roman Britain.* Stroud: Tempus.

Henig, M. 2002b. Caracalla as Hercules on an intaglio found near Lincoln. *Oxford Journal of Archaeology.* 21(4): 419-422.

Herodotus. 1972. Histories. *Translation by A. De Sélincourt. London: Penguin Books.*

Hesiod. 1973. *Theogony.* Translated by D Wender. London : Penguin Books.

Hoekstra, A. 1969. *The Sub-Epic Stage of the Formulaic Tradition: Studies in the Homeric Hymns to Apollo, to Aphrodite and to Demeter.* London: North Holland Publishing Company.

Holmlund, C. 2002. *Impossible Bodies: Femininity and Masculinity at the Movies.* London: Routledge.

Hooper, R.W. 1999. translation *The Priapus Poems: Erotic Epigrams from Ancient Rome.* Urbana: University of Illinois Press.

Hope, V. 1997a. Constructing Roman Identity: funerary monuments and social structure in the Roman world. *Mortality* 2: 103-121.

Hope, V.M. 1997b. Words and pictures: the interpretation of Romano-British tombstones. *Britannia.* 28: 245-258.

Hope, V. 2000. Inscription and sculpture: the construction of identity in the military tombstones of Roman Mainz. In G. Oliver (ed.).*The Epigraphy of Death.* Liverpool: Liverpool University .Press, pp. 155-186.

Hope, V. 2003. Trophies and tombstones: commemorating the Roman soldier. *World Archaeology* 35 (1): 79-97.

Hubbard, T.K. 2003. *Homosexuality in Greece and Rome: A Sourcebook of Basic Documents*. California: University of California Press.

Hughes-Hallett, L. 1990. *Cleopatra: Histories, Dreams and Distortions*. London: Pimlico.

Huskinson, J. 1993. The later Roman period. In J. Boardman. *The Oxford History of Classical Art*. Oxford: Oxford University Press, pp. 297-342.

Huskinson, J., 1994. *Corpus Signorum Imperii Romani: Great Britain, Vol. 1, Fasc. 8: East England.* Oxford: Oxford University Press.

Huskinson, J. 2000. *Experiencing Rome: Culture, Identity and Power in the Roman Empire,* London: Routledge in association with the Open University.

Hutchinson, V. J. 1986. *Bacchus in Roman Britain: The Evidence for his Cult*. Oxford: British Archaeological Reports 151.

Irby-Massie, G. L. 1999. *Military Religion in Roman Britain.* Leiden: Mnenosyne, Bibliotheca Classica Batava, Brill.

Irigaray, L. 1993. *Je, Tu, Nous: Toward a Culture of Difference*. Translation by A. Martin. London: Routledge.

Irwin, D. 1972, *Writings on Art.* London: Phaidon.

Isager, J. 1991. *Pliny on art and society: the Elder Pliny's Chapters on the History of Art.* London: Routledge.

Jesnick, I. J. 1997. *The Image of Orpheus in Roman Mosaic*, Oxford: British Archaeology Reports 671.

Johns, C. 1982. *Sex or Symbol: Erotic Images of Greece and Rome.* London: British Museum Publications.

Johns, C. 1996. *Jewellery of Roman Britain.* London: UCL Press.

Johnson, M. 1999. *Archaeological Theory: An Introduction.* Oxford: Blackwell.

Johnson, P. 1982. *Romano-British Mosaics.* Buckinghamshire: Shire Archaeology.

Johnson, S. 1997. Hadrian's Wall. *London: Batsford/English Heritage.*

Johnston, D. 1977. The Central Southern Group of Roman-British Mosaics. J. Munby. and M. Henig. *Roman Life and Art in Britain, Part II.* Oxford: British Archaeological Reports 41 (ii), pp. 195-216.

Joshel, S.R. and Murnaghan, S. (eds.). 2001. *Women and Slaves in Greco-Roman Culture: Differential Equations.* London: Routledge.

Junkelmann, M. 2000. *Familia Gladiatoria:* The Heroes of the Amphitheatre. In E. Kohne & C. Ewigleben (eds.). *The power of spectacle in ancient Rome: Gladiators and Caesars*. Berkeley: University of California Press, pp. 31-74.

Kampen, N.B. 1981. *Working Women in Ostia.* Berlin: Mann Verlag.

Kampen, N.B. 1991. Between public and private: women as historical subjects in Roman art. In S. Pomeroy (ed.) *Women's History and Ancient History.* Chapel Hill: University of North Carolina Press, pp. 218-248.

Kampen, N.B. 1994. *Material Girl: feminist confrontations with Roman Art.* 27 (1): 11-137.

Kampen, N.B. 1996. *Sexuality in Ancient Art.* Cambridge: Cambridge University Press.

Kampen, N.B. 1996a. Omphale and the instability of gender. In N.B Kampen. *Sexuality in Ancient Art.* Cambridge: Cambridge University Press, pp. 233-246.

Kampen, N. B., Marlowe, E.M and Molholt, R.M. (eds.). 2002. *What is a Man? Changing Images of Masculinity in Late Antique Art.* Washington: University of Washington Press.

Kellum B. 1993. Sculptural programs and propaganda in Augustan Rome: the temple of Apollo on the Palatine. In E. D'Ambra 1993. *Roman Art in Context: An Anthology*. Englewood Cliffs, N.J.: Prentice Hall, pp.75.102.

Keppie, L. 1984 *Corpus Signorum Imperii Romani: Great Britain, Vol. 1, Fasc. 4 Scotland.* Oxford: Oxford University Press.

Keppie, L. 1998. *The making of the Roman Army from Republic to Empire*. London: Routledge.

Keuls, E. 1993. *The Reign of the Phallus: Sexual Politics in Ancient Athens*. California: University of California Press.

Kirkham P. 1996. *The Gendered Object.* Manchester: Manchester University Press.

Kirkpatrick, B. 1996. *The Concise Oxford Thesaurus: A Dictionary of Synonyms*. Oxford: Oxford University Press.

Klein, A.M. 1990. Little big man: hustling, gender and narcissism, and bodybuilding subculture. In M.A. Messner and D.F. Sabo (eds.) *Sport, Men and the Gender Order: Critical Feminist Perspectives*. Leeds: Human Kinetics Publishers, pp. 127-139.

Kleiner, D.E.E. 1992. *Roman Sculpture*. New Haven: Yale University Press.

Kleiner D.E.E. 1992a. Politics and Gender in Pictorial Propaganda of Antony and Octavian. In *Echos du Monde Classique/Classical Reviews* 36 (11), pp. 357-67.

Kleiner, D.E.E., and Matheson, S.B. 1996. *I Claudia: Women in Roman Art and Society*. Austin: University of Texas Press.

Kleiner, D.E.E., and Matheson, S.B., 2000, *I Claudia II: Women in Roman Art and Society*, University of Texas Press, Austin.

Knight, L. 1994. *Collins Gem Thesaurus in A-Z Form.* Glasgow: HarperCollins Publishers.

Koloki-Ostrow, A.O. and Lyons, C.L. 1997. *Naked Truths: Women, Sexuality, and Gender in Classical Art and Archaeology.* London: Routledge.

Koortbojian M. 2002. Forms of Attention: Fout Notes on Replication and Variation. In E. Gazda *The Ancient Art of Emulation: Studies in Artistic Originality and Tradition from the Present to Classical Antiquity.* Michigan: University of Michigan Press, pp. 173-204.

Lagerlöf, M. R. 2000. *The Sculptures of the Parthenon: Aesthetics and Interpretation.* London: Yale University Press.

Laing, J. 1997. *Art and Society in Roman Britain.* Gloucester: Sutton.

Larrington, C. (ed.) 1990. *The Feminist Companion to Mythology*. London: Batsford.

Lefkowitz, M.R and Fant, M.B. 1992. *Women's Lives in Greece and Rome: A Source Book in Translation.* Baltimore: Johns Hopkins University Press.

Lehman P. 2001. *Masculinity: Bodies, Movies, Culture.* London: Routledge.

Leipen, N. 1971. *Athena Parthenos: A Reconstruction.* Toronto: Royal Ontario Museum.

Levi-Strauss, C. 1987. *Anthropology and myth : lectures 1951-1982.* Oxford: Blackwell.

Lewis, M.J.T. 1966. *Temples in Roman Britain.* Cambridge: Cambridge University Press.

Lindgren, C. 1980. *Classical Art Forms and Celtic Mutations: Figural Art in Roman.* New Jersey: Noyes Press.

Ling, R. 1998. *Ancient Mosaics.* London: British Museum.

Ling, R. 1997. Mosaics in Roman Britain: discoveries and research since 1945. *Britannia* 28: 259 –297.

Livy 1969 Early History of Rome: Book I-V of the History of Rome from its Foundation. *Translation by A. De Sélincourt. London: Penguin Books.*

Lucretius. 1960. *Nature of the Universe.* Translated by R.E. Latham. London: Penguin Books.

MacDonald, F. 2000. *Women in Ancient Rome.* New York : Peter Bedrick

Mackintosh, M. 1995. *The Divine Rider in the Art of Western Roman Empire.* Oxford British Archaeological Reports 607.

Marsden A. and Henig, M. 2002. Caracalla as Hercules on an intaglio found near Lincoln. *Oxford Journal of Archaeology* 21 (4) 419-422.

Marvin M. 2002. The Ludovisi Barbarians: The Grand Manner. In E. Gazda. *The Ancient Art of Emulation: Studies in Artistic Originality and Tradition from the Present to Classical Antiquity.* Michigan: University of Michigan Press, pp. 205-224.

Mattingly, D.J. 1997. *Dialogues in Roman Imperialism: Power, Discourse, and Experience in the Roman Empire.* Journal of Roman Archaeology Supplementary Series, No.23. Michigan: Cushing-Mallory Inc.

McClintock, A. 1995. *Imperial Leather: Race, Gender and Sexuality in the Colonial Contest.* London: Routledge.

McClure, L. (ed.) 2002. *Sexuality and Gender in the Classical World: Readings and Sources.* Oxford: Blackwell.

McDonald, H. 2001. *Erotic Ambiguities: The Female Nude in Art.* London: Routledge.

Meadows, K. and Lemke, C. and Heron, J. (eds.) 1997. *TRAC'97 Proceeding of the Theoretical Archaeology Conference.* Oxford: Oxbow Books.

Merrifield, R. 1983. *London, City of the Romans.* London: Batsford.

Merrifield, R. 1996. 'The London hunter-god and his significance in the history of Londinium', in Bird J, Hassall M and Sheldon, H. *Interpreting Roman London: Papers in Memory of Hugh Chapman.* Oxford: Oxbow Monograph 58, pp. 105-113.

Messner, M.A. and Sabo, D.F. 1990. *Sport, Men and the Gender Order: Critical Feminist Perspectives.* Leeds: Human Kinetics Publishers.

Miller, J.F. 1994. Virgil, Apollo, and Augustus. In J. Solomon. *Apollo: Origins and Influences.* London: University of Arizona Press, pp. 99-112.

Montserrat, D. 2000. Reading Gender in the Roman World. In J. Huskinson. *Experiencing Rome: Culture, Identity and Power in the Roman Empire.* London: Routledge in association with the Open University.

Moor, J. and Scott, E. 1997. *Invisible People and Processes: Writing Gender and Childhood into European Archaeology*, London: Leicester University Press.

Morgan, T. 1886. *Romano-British Mosaic Pavements.* London.

Morwood J. 1994. *The Pocket Oxford Latin Dictionary.* Oxford: Oxford University Press.

Munby, J. and Henig, M. 1977. *Roman Life and Art in Britain, Part II.* Oxford: British Archaeological Reports 41 (ii).

Nead, L. 1992 *The Female Nude: Art, Obscenity and Sexuality*, London: Routledge.

Neal, D. 1981 *Roman Mosaics in Britain.* London: London Society for the Promotion of Roman Studies.

Neimark, J. 1994. The Beefcaking of America. *Psychology Today* 27(6): 34–35.

Nochlin, L. 1973. Why have there been no Great Women Artists? T. Hess and E. Barker (eds.) *Art and Sexual Politics.* New York: Basic Books, pp.145-178.

Nochlin, L. 1989. *Women, Art and Power.* London: Thames and Hudson.

Nochlin, L. 1999. *Representing Women.* London: Thames and Hudson.

Oppliger P. 2004. *Wrestling and Hyper-Masculinity.* London: McFarland and Company.

Osborne, R. 1997. Men without clothes: heroic nakedness and Greek art. *Gender and History* 9 (3): 504-528.

Ovid. 1982 *The Erotic Poems.* Translation by P. Green. London: Penguin Books.

Parker, R. and Pollock, P. 1981. *Old Mistresses: Women, Art and Ideology.* London: Routledge.

Pausanias. 1979. *Guide to Greece, Volume 1: Central Greece.* Translation by P. Levi. London: Penguin Books.

Pearce, J. and Millett M. and Struck M. 2000. *Burials, Society and Context in the Roman World.* Oxford: Oxbow Books.

Phillips, E. J. 1977. *Corpus Signorum Imperii Romani: Great Britain*, Vol.1, Fasc.1: Corbridge, Hadrian's Wall east of the North Tyne. Oxford: Oxford University Press.

Platt V. 2002. Viewing, desiring, believing: confronting the divine in a Pompeian house. *Art History* 25(1): 87-112.

Pliny the Elder. 1991. *Natural History: A Selection.* Translation by J.F. Healy. London: Penguin Books.

Plutarch. 1936. *Moralia: Volume* 5. Translation by R.F.C. Babbit. Loeb, London: Harvard University Press.

Pointon M. 1997. *History of Art: A Student's Handbook.* London: Routledge.

Pollitt. J.J. 1966, The art of Rome,c753 BC-337AD: Sources and documents. Englewood Cliffs, NJ: Prentice-Hall

Pollitt, J. 1990. *The Art of Ancient Greece: Sources and Documents*. Cambridge: Cambridge University Press.

Pollitt, J. 1993.Rome: the Republic and early Empire. In J. Boardman (ed.). *The Oxford History of Classical Art*. Oxford: Oxford University Press, pp. 217-295.

Pollock, G. 1999. *Differencing the Cannon: Feminist Desire and the Writing of Art's Histories*. London: Routledge.

Pollock, G. 1988. *Vision and Difference: Femininity, Feminism and the Histories of Art*. London: Routledge.

Pollock, G. 1996. *Generations and Geographies in the Visual Arts: Feminist Readings*. London: Routledge.

Pomeroy, S. 1975. *Goddesses, Whores, Wives and Slaves: Women in Classical Antiquity*. London: Pimlico.

Pomeroy, S. 1976. The Relationship of married women to her blood relatives at Rome. *Ancient Society* 7: 215-227.

Pomeroy. S. 1991. *Women's History and Ancient History*. London: University of North Carolina Press.

Potts, A. 1994. *Flesh and the Ideal: Winckelmann and the Origins of Art History*. London: Yale University Press.

Pseudo-Lucian. 1967. *Lucian*. Translated by M.D. Macleod. vol. 8. London: Loeb Classical Library.

Rainey, A. 1973. *Mosaics in Roman Britain*. Newton Abbot: David and Charles.

Ramakers, M. 2000 *Dirty pictures: Tom of Finland, Masculinity, and Homosexuality*. New York: St. Martin's Press.

Richlin, A. 1993. Not before homosexuality: the materiality of the cinaedus and the Roman law against love between men. *Journal of the History of Sexuality* 3 (4): 523-573.

Ridgway, B.S. 1974. A story of five Amazons. *American Journal of Archaeology*. 78: 1-17.

Ridgway, B.S. 1984. *Roman Copies of Greek Sculpture: the Problem of the Originals*. Michigan: University of Michigan Press.

Robertson, M. 1991. *A Shorter History of Greek Art*. Cambridge: Cambridge University Press.

Robinson, J. 1991. *Wayward Women: A Guide to Women Travellers*. Oxford: Oxford University Press.

Roccos, L.J. 2002. The Citharode Apollo in villa contexts: a Roman theme with variations. In E. K. Gazda (ed.) *The Ancient Art of Emulation: Studies in Artistic Originality and Tradition from the Present to Classical Antiquity*. Michigan: University of Michigan Press, pp. 273-300.

Rodgers, R. 1995. Women Underfoot in Life and Art: Female Representations in Fourth-Century Romano-British Mosaics. *Journal of European Archaeology*. 3 (15): 178-187.

Rodgers, R. 1998. *Imagery and Ideology: Aspects of Female Representation in Roman Art, with Special Reference to Britain and Gaul*. PhD Thesis: University of Durham.

Rodwell, W. 1980. *Temples, Churches and Religion: Recent Research in Roman Britain*. Oxford: British Archaeology Reports 52.

Ross, A. 1967a. A Celtic three-faced head from Wiltshire. *Antiquity* 161: 53-55.

Ross, A. 1967b. *Pagan Celtic Britain*. London: Routledge.

Salomon, N. 1997. Making a world of difference: gender, asymmetry, and the Greek nude. In A.O. Koloski-Ostrow and C.L. Lyons. *Naked Truths: Women, Sexuality, and Gender in Classical Art and Archaeology*. London: Routledge, pp. 197-219.

Schefold, K. 1966. *Myth and Legend in Early Greek Art*. London: Thames and Hudson.

Scheid, J. and Svenbro, J. 1996. *The Craft of Zeus: Myths of Weaving and Fabric*. London: Harvard University Press.

Schwartz H. 1996. *The Culture of the Copy: Striking Likenesses, Unreasonable Facsimiles*. New York: Zone Books.

Schwarz, C. (ed.) 1994. *The Chambers Dictionary*. Chambers Harrap.

Scott Anderson, A. 1984. *Roman Military Tombstones*. Buckinghamshire: Shire Archaeology.

Scott, S. 2000 *Art and Society in Fourth-Century Britain: Villa Mosaics in Context,* Oxford: Oxford University School of Archaeology Monograph 53.

Scott, S. and Webster J (eds.) 2003. *Roman Imperialism and Provincial Art*. New York: Cambridge University Press.

Sebseta, J.L. and Bonfante L. 1994. *The World of Roman Costume*. Wisconsin: University of Wisconsin Press.

Sebesta, J.L. 1997. Women's Costume and Feminine Civic Morality in Augustan Rome. *Gender and History*. .9 (3): 529-541.

Shelton, J. 1998. *As the Romans Did: A Sourcebook in Roman Social History*. Oxford: Oxford University Press.

Smith, D.J. 1965. Three Fourth-Century Schools of Mosaic in Roman Britain. H. Stern, H. and D Picard (eds.). *La Mosaïque Gréco-Romaine*. Paris, pp. 95-116.

Smith, D.J. 1969. The Mosaic Pavements. In A.L.F. Rivet (ed,) *The Roman Villa in Britain*, London, pp.75-125

Smith, D.J. 1977. Mythological figures and scenes in Romano-British mosaics. In J. Munby and M. Henig. *Roman Life and Art in Britain, Part II,* Oxford: British Archaeological Reports 41 (ii), 105-194.

Smith, R.R.R. 1987. The Imperial reliefs from the Sebasteion at Aphrodisias. *Journal of Roman Studies* 77: 88-138.

Smith, R.R.R. 1995. *Hellenistic Sculpture*. London: Thames and Hudson.

Solomon, J. 1994. *Apollo: Origins and Influences*. London: University of Arizona Press.

Sorking Rabinowitz, N and Richlin, A. (eds.)1993. *Feminist Theory and the Classics*. London: Routledge.

Spivey, N. 1997. *Etruscan Art*. London: Thames and Hudson.

Spivey, N. 1997a. *Greek Art*. London: Phaidon.

Stewart, P. 2003. *Statues in Roman Society: Representation and Response*. Oxford: Oxford University Press.

Strong, D. 1976. Roman Art. London: Penguin Books.

Suetonius. 1957. *The Twelve Caesars.* Translated by R Graves. London: Penguin Books.

Thesander, M. 1997. *The Feminine Ideal.* London: Reaktion Books

Toynbee, J.M.C. 1962. *Art in Roman Britain.* London: Phaidon.

Toynbee, J.M.C. 1964. *Art in Britain under the Romans.* London: Clarendon Press.

Toynbee, J. M. C. 1971. *Death and Burial in the Roman World.* London: Thames and Hudson.

Toynbee, J. M. C. 1973. *Animals in Roman Life and Art.* London: Thames and Hudson.

Treggiari, S. 1991. *Iusti Coniuges from the Time of Cicero to the time of Ulpian.* Oxford: Oxford University Place.

Tsiafakis, D. 2000. 'The Allure and Repulsion of Thracians in the Art of Classical Athens' in Cohen, B. 2000. *Not the Classical Ideal: Athens and the Construction of the Other in Greek Art.* Leiden: Konninklijke Brill, pp. 364-389.

Tufi, S. R. 1983. *Corpus Signorum Imperii Romani: Great Britain, Vol.1, Fasc. 3: Yorkshire.* Oxford: Oxford University Press.

Tyrrell, W.B. 1984. *Amazons: a Study in Athenian Mythmaking.* London: Johns Hopkins University.

Virgil. 1986. *The Aeneid.* Translated by C. Day Lewis. Oxford: World's Classcis.

Vitruvius Pollio. 1999. *Ten Books on Architecture.* Translated by I.D. Rowland.

Von Heintze, H. 1990. *The Herbert History of Art and Architecture: Roman Art.* London: The Herbert Press.

Walker, S. 1985. *Memorials to the Roman Dead.* London: British Museum Press.

Walters, J. 1997. Invading the Roman Body: Manliness and the Impenetrability in Roman Thought. In J.P. Hallett and M.B. Skinner M.B. *Roman Sexualities.* Princeton: Princeton University Press.

Walters, J. 1998. Making a spectacle: deviant men, invective, and pleasure. *Arethusa* 31 (3): 355-367.

Warner, M. 1985. *Monuments and Maidens: The Allegory of the Female Form.* London: Weidenfeld and Nicolson.

Waywell, G. B. 1986. *The Lever and Hope Sculptures: Ancient Sculptures in the Lady Lever Art Gallery, Port Sunlight and A Catalogue of the Ancient Sculptures formerly in the Hope Collection, London and Deepden.* Berlin: Gebr. Mann Verlag.

Webster, G. 1970. *A Short Guide to the Roman Inscriptions and Sculptured Stones in the Grosvenor Museum, Chester.* Chester: G. R. Griffith/Grosvenor Museum.

Webster, G. 1993. Military Equestrian tombstones. In M. Henig. *Corpus Signorium Imperii Romani: Great Britain Volume 1, Fasc. 7, The Cotswolds Region with Devon and Cornwall.* Oxford: Oxford University Press pp.45-48.

Webster, J. 1997. A negotiated syncretism: readings on the development of Romano-Celtic religion. In Mattingly, D.J. *Dialogues in Roman Imperialism: Power, Discourse, and Experience in the Roman Empire.* Journal of Roman Archaeology Supplementary Series, No.23. Michigan: Cushing-Mallory Inc, pp. 164-184.

Webster, T.B.L. 1967. *Hellenistic Art.* London: Methuen.

Wheeler, M. 1964. *Roman Art and Architecture.* London: Thames and Hudson.

White S. 2001. T(he)-Men's Room: Masculinity and Space in Anthony Mann's *T-Men.* In Lehman P. *Masculinity: Bodies, Movies, Culture.* London: Routledge, pp. 95-114.

Wiegman, R 1995. Feminism, 'The Boyz,' and other matters regarding the Male. In S. Cohan and I. Rae Hark. *Screening the Male: Exploring Masculinities in Hollywood Cinema.* London: Routledge, pp173-193.

Williams, C.A. 1995. Greek Love at Rome. *Classical Quarterly.* 45: 517-539.

Williams, C.A. 1999. *Roman Homosexuality: Ideologies of Masculinity in Classical Antiquity.* Oxford: Oxford University Press.

Winckelmann, J. J. (1764) 1968 *History of Ancient Art.* New York: Ungar.

Winkler J.J. 1990. *Constraints of Desire: The Anthropology of Sea and Gender in Ancient Greece.* London: Routledge.

Witts, P. 1994. Interpreting the Brading 'Abraxas' Mosaic. *Britannia.* 25: 111-117.

Woodward A. and Leach P. (eds.) *The Uley Shrine: Excavation of a Ritual Complex on West Hill, Uley, Gloucestershire: 19779.* London: British Museum Press.

Wright RP and Richmond IA. 1955. *Catalogue of the Roman inscribed and sculptured stones in the Grosvenor Museum, Chester.* Chester: Chester and N Wales Archaeol Socociety.

Wyke, M. (ed.) 1998. *Gender and the Body in the Ancient Mediterranean.* Gender and History Special Issues 9 (3). Oxford: Blackwell.

Wyke, M. *The Roman Mistress: Ancient and Modern Representations.* Oxford: Oxford University Press.

Zanker, P, 1988. *The Power of Images in the Age of Augustus.* Translated by A.Shapiro. Michigan: University of Michigan Press.

Zanker, P. 1995. *The Mask of Socrates: the Image of the Intellectual in Antiquity.* Translated by A.Shapiro. California: University of California Press.

Zienkiewicz, J.D. 1987. *Roman Gems from Caerleon.* Cardiff: National Museum of Wales.

Zienkiewicz, D. 1994: *Roman Legion.* Cardiff: National Museum of Wales.

www.ingramcontent.com/pod-product-compliance
Lightning Source LLC
La Vergne TN
LVHW070534110826
845147LV00017BA/985

* 9 7 8 1 4 0 7 3 0 4 2 7 4 *